The Best of Lord Krishna's Cuisine
is a selection of favorite recipes from
Lord Krishna's Cuisine: The Art of Indian Vegetarian Cooking
(E.P. Dutton/Bala Books, 1987),
recipient of the
International Association of Culinary Professionals'
"Best Cookbook of the Year" Award

Of this 1987 work, reviewers said:

"This is a splendid work...one of the most important cookbooks published in years."
— *Kirkus Reviews*

"*Lord Krishna's Cuisine* must stand as definitive."
— Leo Lerman, *Gourmet*

"The vegetarian bible...interesting and fun to read."
— *Philadelphia Inquirer*

"Encyclopedic...a work of scholarship."
— *Washington Post*

"A prodigious 800-page labor of love."
— *Publishers Weekly*

"The Taj Mahal of cookbooks...an invaluable volume for serious cooks and/or vegetarians."
— *Chicago Tribune*

"Wide ranging, detailed...the product of a spiritual and culinary journey."
— *New York Times*

"So much good food...that any serious cook should find it gratifying...
...monumental."
— Barbara Kafka, *Vogue*

"Big and Beautiful."

— Julia Child, *Good Morning America*

ABOUT THE AUTHOR

YAMUNA DEVI has been both a devout vegetarian and an eloquent advocate of India's vegetarian ideal for the past 25 years. Her studies included many years touring the Indian subcontinent, tracing the culinary tradition at its roots and learning the art from India's master chefs. She lives in Washington, D.C., where she lectures, writes a food column, and has finished work on her second book.

THE BEST OF
LORD KRISHNA'S
CUISINE

Favorite Recipes from
The Art of Indian Vegetarian Cooking

YAMUNA DEVI

A PLUME BOOK

PLUME
Published by the Penguin Group
Penguin Books USA Inc., 375 Hudson Street,
New York, New York 10014, U.S.A.
Penguin Books Ltd, 27 Wrights Lane,
London W8 5TZ, England
Penguin Books Australia Ltd, Ringwood,
Victoria, Australia
Penguin Books Canada Ltd, 2801 John Street,
Markham, Ontario, Canada L3R 1B4
Penguin Books (N.Z.) Ltd, 182-190 Wairau Road,
Auckland 10, New Zealand

Penguin Books Ltd, Registered Offices:
Harmondsworth, Middlesex, England

Published by Plume, an imprint of New American
Library, a division of Penguin Books USA Inc. Previously published in a
Dutton edition in different form.

First Plume Printing, October, 1991
10 9 8 7 6 5 4 3 2 1

 REGISTERED TRADEMARK — MARCA REGISTRADA

LIBRARY OF CONGRESS CATALOGING-IN-PUBLICATION DATA:

Yamuna Devi, 1942-
    [Art of Indian vegetarian cooking, Selections]
    The best of Lord Krishna's cuisine: favorite recipes from The art
of Indian vegetarian cooking / Yamuna Devi : illustrations by David
Baird.
            p.   cm.
        Includes index.
        ISBN 0-452-26683-1
        1. Vegetarian cookery.   2. Cookery, India.   I. Title.   II. Title:
Lord Krishna's cuisine.
TX837.Y3525 1991
641.5'636—dc20   91-16491
                                                 CIP
Printed in the United States of America
Original hardcover edition edited by: Joshua M. Greene and Philip Gallelli
Original hardcover edition designed by: Marino Gallo and Barbara Berasi
Illustrations by David Baird

BOOKS ARE AVAILABLE AT QUANTITY DISCOUNTS WHEN USED TO PROMOTE PRODUCTS OR SERVICES. FOR
INFORMATION PLEASE WRITE TO PREMIUM MARKETING DIVISION, PENGUIN BOOKS USA INC., 375 HUDSON
STREET, NEW YORK, NEW YORK 10014.

ACKNOWLEDGMENTS

This paperback edition has been brought to life by a handful of people who deserve special mention.

Bala Books publisher Joshua M. Greene years ago shared my vision of seeing this cuisine in America's kitchens. His intelligent structuring of the manuscripts has greatly enhanced the contents of this volume, generating enthusiasm for future projects.

Philip Gallelli, Bala Books production manager, has painstakingly overseen several aspects of this publication—from editing to book design. His expertise and dedication are reflected on every page.

Kelly Thompson's graphic artistry and technical skill is evidenced on every spread. Dina Sugg excercised sensitivity and skill in her final copy editing. Indexer Bill Feik has made the book easy to reference and use.

Photographer Vishakha Dasi shot more than 300 photos as a reference for the illustrations, but also spent months collecting props and testing recipes. Illustrator David Baird painstakingly turned the photographs into works of art. Melanie Parks has captured the freshness and simplicity of the cuisine in her cover artwork.

A special thanks to Toni Rachiele, my editor at Nal/Dutton, and to Judith Weber, my agent. A heartfelt thanks goes to Jonathan Rice for having made the entire effort possible.

CONTENTS

INTRODUCTION TO
THE HARDCOVER EDITION

Every cookbook author must feel that there is something unique in his or her work that justifies the effort of producing it. I'm no exception. My feeling is that in this book you will find the richly varied foods from India's regional cuisines presented in a unique way, a way that explains India's culinary heritage in a spiritual light.

My involvement with both an Indian and vegetarian lifestyle began in 1966 when my sister invited me to attend her wedding in New York. She informed me that she and her fiancé had met an Indian Swami, called Srila Prabhupada, and were taking Sanskrit classes and studying *Bhagavad Gita* with him.

I arrived the day before the wedding and was unexpectedly whisked to lunch at the Swami's apartment. Everything about the experience was exotic, even though I was told it was an everyday meal: nutrition from grains, protein from beans, and vitamins from fresh vegetables. There were two hot vegetable dishes, *dal* soup, rice and buttered wheat flat breads. A yogurt salad and chutney served as accompaniments. They were ordinary vegetables, but cooked extraordinarily well. This meal bore little resemblance to the Indian restaurant food I had experienced—it was light, vibrant and subtly seasoned. As a cook, I was fascinated.

At the close of the meal, Prabhupada explained to me that it was the custom for the family members of the bride to prepare the wedding feast and, although he would be doing the cooking, he invited me to assist him in the task. The irony of the situation was almost comical to me. Here I was, with my inexorable apathy toward anything "spiritual," having come to New York expecting a traditional wedding, and finding instead an Indian "swami" performing a "hindu" marriage ceremony with me helping to cook the wedding feast! Yet my curiosity was roused and his sincerity was infectious, so I gladly accepted.

The day of the wedding, I arrived at Srila Prabhupada's apartment and was met with genuine hospitality. Prabhupada escorted me in and immediately served refreshments. More new tastes: flaky lemon-flavored crackers laced with crushed peppercorns and a frothy chilled yogurt drink sprinkled with sugar and rose water. As we spoke, I relished the sensational new flavors. He was a gentleman, a patient listener and an interesting speaker. He did not try to overwhelm me with emotional charisma, nor did he drone on with dry philosophy. He was quite unlike any religious man I had ever met.

Within an hour of my arrival at his apartment, I was introduced to numerous new spices and seasonings, unfamiliar ingredients and foreign cooking techniques. Given the stationary task of shaping potato-stuffed pastries, called *aloo kachoris*, I observed him from the adjoining room. Working in a narrow galley kitchen, he was organized and impeccably clean, simultaneously preparing up to four dishes at a time. His flow of activity was efficient and graceful, and, save for his instructions to me, his attention focused solely on his craft. He performed a number of tasks by hand, without the help or likely hinderance of tools. Each spice was measured in his left palm before use. Dough was hand-kneaded, *bada* dumplings hand-shaped, and fresh cheese hand-brayed until smooth—and, despite his advanced age, all with lightning speed. I was intrigued by the obvious satisfaction he experienced in every task he undertook. After having cooked all day, he performed the wedding ceremony that evening—the event culminating with the lavish eighteen-course feast he had prepared.

My planned two week stay in New York lengthened to nearly three months. When I returned to the West Coast with my sister and brother-in-law, we enlisted our friends to help bring Srila Prabhupada to San Francisco. In January, 1967, he left New York's Lower East Side and moved into San Francisco's Parnassus Hill District. During the following months, prompted largely by my inquiries on morning walks, cooking classes or informal visits, Srila Prabhupada explained the workings of a Vaishnava kitchen in India. He explained that cooking was a spiritual experience for a Vaishnava, much like meditation—a means of expressing love and devotion to the Supreme Lord, Krishna. He touched on more than external standards, relating the subtle effects a Vedic lifestyle creates in the kitchen.

No matter what its size, the Vaishnava kitchen is divided into two areas: one for preparation and cooking and another for storage of staples, cookware, implements, and cleanup. The first area could take up only a few square feet—often a bare space devoid of anything except a stove. A cook bathes and puts on clean clothes before entering the kitchen, then sits comfortably on a low stool and uses the floor as countertop space. Only kitchen shoes or no shoes are allowed in this area, as it is kept spotlessly clean. Cooks develop a sixth sense for their ingredients, and, without assistance from recipes or measuring tools, they prepare sumptuous meals, never tasting the foods while cooking. While I resided in India, I learned to apply these principles in my kitchen, and, though much of what I learned is impractical in my American kitchen, the basic lessons in cleanliness and purity in the ingredients, cooking procedures and hygiene have become an integral part of my life.

In March of 1967, I asked Prabhupada to take me as his disciple, and that is how Joan Campanella became Yamuna Devi. Off and on over the next eight years, I was fortunate enough to serve as his personal cook. During some of this time, we traveled the length and breadth of India, giving me the invaluable opportunity to study in depth the country's varied regional cuisines. For two years I was part of a group that accompanied Srila Prabhupada on extensive tours of the subcontinent. This gave me the opportunity of learning from scores of famous temple *brahmana* cooks. In some cases, I was privileged to be the first Westerner allowed in previously restricted temple kitchens. Lavish royal kitchens sometimes engage as many as fifty such cooks and 100 servers for festival events—and though thousands of dialects are spoken in India, kitchen language is universal.

Of the 760 million residents in India today, more than eighty percent, or 600 million people, are vegetarian. Hundreds of thousands of these vegetarians are Vaishnavas or devotees of Lord Krishna, and their homes all have small temples in them. Further, there are thousands of established public Krishna temples in cities and villages across the country. Traveling with Srila Prabhupada afforded me the opportunity of visiting these Vaishnava devotees in their homes.

Sometimes I was able to attend fairs or *melas* devoted to reading sacred texts and the chanting of sacred songs. Such festivals around the pastimes of Lord Krishna are attended by millions of pilgrims and provide yet more opportunity to learn about the dietary habits and the roots of Lord Krishna's cuisine at its source.

Looking back, I can only say that when I first climbed the stairs to Prabhupada's apartment, I could never have imagined the treasure of transcendental philosophy, music, art and cuisine that awaited me.

INTRODUCTION TO
THE BEST OF LORD KRISHNA'S CUISINE

This book is offered in thanks to the many people who wrote letters of appreciation for *Lord Krishna's Cuisine: The Art of Indian Vegetarian Cooking*. They span the globe, from a Parisian yoga teacher who uses it as a textbook for cooking classes to an Atlantic City chef who reads it nightly to ward off insomnia. My heartfelt thanks to these and all my other new friends for their praise and enthusiasm for this new style of cooking traditional Indian cuisine.

The recipes selected for inclusion in *The Best of Lord Krishna's Cuisine* are personal favorites. They focus on ease of preparation and lightness. They offer vibrant flavor and are fresher than the counterparts one finds in Indian restaurants. To prepare an easy work day dinner, try any of the rice, *dal*, salad or vegetable dishes as the basis of the meal. For entertaining, you might add a selection from among the *Savories* and *Dessert* sections.

Try adding flavor-infused *ghee*, fresh chutney or dry roasted spices to enhance your favorite ingredients. For example, to steamed julienne carrots add a drizzle of *Ginger Ghee*. To diced green beans, fold in a spoon of *Creamy Cashew Chutney*.

I hope that this selection of favorite recipes increases for you even more the pleasure offered by the art of Indian vegetarian cooking.

Yamuna Devi
Washington, D.C.

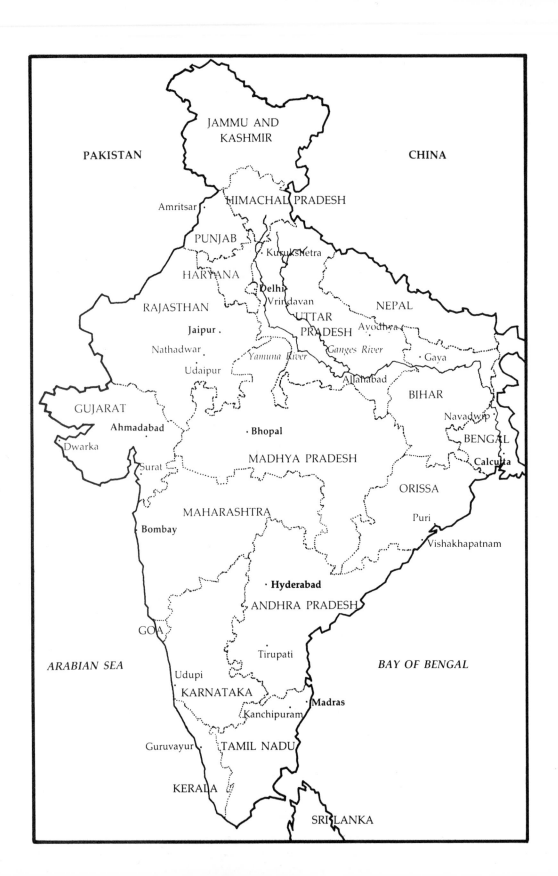

HOW TO MEASURE AND USE THE RECIPES

India, like most of the world, uses the metric system for measurement today. Most Indian cooks do not rely on cookbooks or volume measurements for accuracy; rather, they choose to measure by weight ratios. A dozen or so memorized formulas enable a cook to demonstrate versatility in thousands of ways. For instance, the formula for a moderately sweet Bengali *sandesh* is: for each given weight of *chenna* cheese, add one-quarter of that weight in sugar.

If you use recipes, accurate measuring techniques and equipment are essential to prevent culinary disasters and avoid guesswork. America is the only country that has not converted to the metric system, though there is little justification for the holdout. The metric system is easy and accurate. Americans use the customary volume measurements with graduated spoons and cups; British cooks use both the Imperial and metric systems, while Australians and Canadians exclusively use metric weights and measurements.

Both American and metric measurements are given in this book, and both systems use graduated spoons to measure small quantities of liquids or solids. A basic set of measuring spoons includes four spoons: the American set measures from ¼ teaspoon to 1 tablespoon; the metric set measures from 1 ml to 15 ml. All measurements are level unless otherwise specified.

Liquid measuring containers, made of clear glass or strong plastic, usually contain both cup and liter markings. The best metric liquid container I have come across is the Metric Wonder Cup by Wecolite, available at better cookware stores. With 10 ml gradations from 10 ml to 500 ml (½ liter), it meets all metric requirements. For accuracy, read the container at eye level.

Measuring dry ingredients by weight is far more accurate than measuring by volume, especially for main ingredients like flour and sugar. Accurate spring balance scales are available in better cookware stores, and many have dual American ounce/pound and metric gram/kilogram markings.

If you are using American cups for measuring dry goods, it is important to know how ingredients are handled in this book. Cereals, legumes and whole grains can be scooped out of containers and leveled off with your fingers. Before measuring, whole wheat and *chapati* flours are sieved to remove bran, and chickpea flour, icing or other lumpy sugars are sifted to lighten them and remove lumps. These ingredients, along with all other flours, are then spooned into an appropriate cup and then leveled with a spatula or knife. If you shake a cup to level an ingredient, the measurement will be inaccurate.

To get the most out of the recipes, try the following suggestions:

1. Read through the entire recipe—from the initial description of the dish through its final stages—to make sure you understand it. When trying out a complicated recipe, allow a little extra time for preparation, organization and cleaning up.

2. Estimated preparation time does not include the time needed to assemble the ingredients. Therefore, soak, chill, cut or cook ingredients in advance when indicated. Next, arrange the ingredients near your cooking area to assure a smooth, uninterrupted work flow. Many cooks find it helpful to measure all the spices and ingredients beforehand and set them where they can be easily reached.

3. Pan size is specified whenever important. When too little food is cooked in a large pan, the ingredients spread out, liquids evaporate faster than desired and foods easily scorch on high heat.

4. The recipes were tested on varied heat sources: electric stoves, household and restaurant gas stoves, electric glass cooktops and even cast-iron wood stoves. The cooking times are based on the average cumulative times and serve only as guidelines. Whatever your heat source, take its capabilities and liabilities into consideration and adjust cooking times accordingly. Keep in mind that, compared to gas, electric burners are slow to warm up and cool down.

A certain amount of repetition has been necessary in the forwards and recipes in order to prevent referrals from one chapter to another.

Rice

You are what you eat. Many people have come to agree with George Bernard Shaw that our bodies and minds are greatly affected by the things we eat. If this is true, then few foods have influenced the development and character of humankind more than rice. Throughout history it has been a staple food for three-fourths of the world's population, remaining so even today—and with good reason. Rice is easy to grow, inexpensive and almost always available. Nutritionally, rice complements the proteins in other foods, and when eaten together with dried beans, nuts or dairy products, rice increases their combined food value by up to forty-five percent. Rice is a versatile grain that can be almost habit-forming, especially when accompanied by the salad, vegetable or *dal* dishes in this book.

Rice is selected and graded with careful attention to shape, color, fragrance, age, taste and cooked texture. Although there are a purported 10,000 varieties of rice cultivated worldwide, from a cook's point of view all rice is classified according to length and width: short-, medium- or long-grain, and then coarse, fine or extra-fine. Like their ancestors, Vedic cooks almost exclusively use polished, or white, rice, *arwa chaval*. It has a significantly longer storage life than *ukad chaval*, unpolished, or brown, rice. Indian brown rice has a strong flavor which even seems to overpower seasonings. So great is the preference for white rice that only the poorest eat brown rice and, more often than not, the brown rice available at bazaar grain shops is an inferior strain, with a large percentage of broken or cracked grains and a considerable amount of roughage.

Polished short-grain rice, fat or oval, white and somewhat chalky in appearance, is glutinous when cooked, and used primarily in southern and eastern cuisines. Medium-grain rice, about three times as long as it is wide, holds its shape when cooked, but is soft-textured. Over half of India's short- and medium-grain rice is parboiled and called *sela chaval*. Long-grain rice, four to five times as long as it is wide, when properly cooked is transformed into fluffy, well-separated grains. *Basmati* long-grain rice was used in all recipe testing, and all the recipes are written exclusively for long-grain varieties. Easy-to-cook, instant rices are completely shunned in the Vedic tradition for reasons of both taste and nutrition.

Three recommended long-grain rice varieties are widely available: North Indian *patna*, American Carolina and—the one rice rated par excellence—Indian or Pakistani *basmati*. *Patna* and Carolina rices are similar in flavor, and both cook into dry, fluffy long grains. Less readily available but worth searching for is brown *basmati*, or Calmati, a cross between brown rice and Indian *basmati* grown in the cool climate of California's Sacramento Valley. Texmati—a flavorful long-grain grown in Texas—and wild pecan from Louisiana are also delicious. Cooking times differ depending on processing. The slightly amber-colored Carolina, Texmati and wild pecan varieties do not require washing or soaking before cooking, and experience will teach you the exact amount of liquid that each variety absorbs. *Patna* rice has a soft white color and is noted for its mild bouquet and long, thin grains. I recommend that you give *patna* a good washing to remove surface starch and small bits of husk. It does not, however, require soaking before cooking.

For authentic, delectable Vedic rice cooking, *basmati* is the highly recommended choice. It is a relative newcomer to most Americans but is widely available in Indian and Middle Eastern grocery stores, specialty or gourmet stores and some health food shops and co-ops. This rice is prized for its good-looking kernels, pale yellow to creamy white color, fragrant bouquet and faintly nutlike flavor. For centuries, *basmati* rice has been harvested, husked and winnowed by hand, with minimal processing, in an efficient collective village ritual. Extended processing is avoided. Bleaching, pearling, oiling and powder-coating may produce more appealing commercial products, but such refinements diminish both flavor and nutritional value. Most imported *basmati* rice has been aged from six months to a year to enhance and intensify its flavor, bouquet and cooking characteristics. For this reason, and because of limited cultivation, *basmati* rice will usually cost a little more than Carolina or *patna*.

The imported *basmati* rice available in America comes from three places. The best, hard-to-find Dehradhun *basmati*, comes from Dehradhun in North India. The others are *patna basmati* from Bihar State in North India and Pakistani *basmati* from Pakistan. Each of these rices is graded according to its percentage of unbroken, long, pointed grains; translucent milk-white color; delicate perfume; and buttery, nutlike flavor. To ensure fluffy and tender *basmati* rice, it is necessary to follow the time-honored ritual of cleaning, washing and soaking the rice before use. Brown *basmati* has a coarser grain, with typical brown-rice flavor and nutrition, and takes approximately 45 minutes to cook.

CLEANING INDIAN *BASMATI* RICE: Spread the rice out on a clean table, countertop or large metal tray so that all of the grains are visible. Working on a small portion at a time, pick out all foreign matter such as pieces of dirt, bits of stone, stems and unhulled rice grains. Push the finished portion to one side and continue until the rice is free of impurities.

WASHING *PATNA* AND INDIAN *BASMATI* RICE: Place the rice in a large bowl and fill it with cold water. Swish the rice around to release starches clinging to the grains and to encourage any husk and bran flakes to float to the surface. Pour off the milky residue and repeat the process several times until the washing water remains clear. Drain in a strainer.

SOAKING INDIAN AND BROWN *BASMATI* RICE: Soak the washed and drained *basmati* rice in warm water for 10 minutes to allow the long, pointed grains to absorb water and "relax" before cooking. This warm water is drained off and used as the cooking water after the rice has been soaked. Valuable nutrients and flavors are preserved by this process. Drain the rice in a strainer, collecting the premeasured water for cooking. Air-dry the rice for 15–20 minutes before cooking.

COOKING RICE: Rice is not hard to cook, and there are several methods. Some cooks prefer to cook rice like pasta, boiling it in large quantities of salted water until it is just over half done. It is then drained and cooked until tender in the oven. Rice can also be partially steamed on top of the stove and then finished off in the oven, using the exact amount of water needed for absorption. There are also different ways to steam rice completely on top of the stove. You'll find several methods of rice in this chapter.

Since there are thousands of varieties of rice, is there one foolproof method for steaming long-grain rice on top of the stove? Is it safer to follow package instructions or rely on the proverbial ratio of two parts water to one part rice? The answer depends on three variables: the strain of rice you use, the type of pan you select and your heat source. As a general rule, I find that the two parts water is more than required for the rices I have mentioned. In most of the recipes I have suggested 1⅔–1¾ cups (400–420 ml) of water to 1 cup (95 g) of rice, no matter what type. This is only a general guideline, since only you can determine whether you prefer a softer or firmer consistency. I find that *basmati* requires slightly less water than Carolina, *patna* or Texmati, while all brown rice requires more, especially medium-grain.

Use a heavy pot for good heat distribution and make sure the lid fits tightly. Since rice is cooked in the minimum amount of water, it is important that the precious steam inside the pot not escape. Three types of pots are excellent for cooking rice: Silverstone on heavy aluminum, Cuisinart or Revere Ware stainless steel and Le Creuset enameled cast-iron pots. The rice should steam over very low, evenly distributed heat. If you cannot reduce your heat to a very low setting on gas, improvise by raising your pot above the heat source. Place a pair of tongs or a Chinese wok ring over the burner and place the pot on it. On electric stoves use heat diffusers.

Here are a few reminders for cooking the rice dishes in this chapter:

1. Always use long-grain rice.

2. A sprinkle of lemon or lime juice or a dab of *ghee*, butter or oil added during cooking helps the grains to remain separate and light.

3. Generally, 1 cup (95 g) of uncooked rice yields 2¾–3 cups (650–710 ml) of cooked rice. The ratio of water to rice varies not only with the type of rice used but also according to the degree of firmness desired. Brown rice absorbs more water than white rice.

4. Thick walls on your pot will help distribute the heat evenly throughout the rice, bringing all the grains to the same degree of tenderness. If your rice is cooking unevenly (perhaps the top layer is not cooked enough while the rest of the rice is tender), it is likely that your lid does not fit tightly enough. Try covering the pot with a tight sheet of aluminum foil, then replace the lid. Good-quality nonstick cookware is excellent for preventing rice from burning or scorching once the liquid is absorbed. A golden crust will form, but the rice will not burn if kept over low heat.

5. Once the lid has been placed on the rice, the heat must remain very low, just high enough to maintain a very gentle simmer. If you cannot achieve a sufficiently low setting from your burner, try cooking the rice in a well-covered, ovenproof dish in a preheated 325°F (160°C) oven for 25 minutes.

6. Never stir or otherwise disturb the rice while it is covered and steaming. Keep the rice well covered with a tight-fitting lid and let it cook undisturbed until all the water is absorbed and the rice is tender and fluffy. Removing the lid will allow precious steam to escape and make the rice cook unevenly.

7. Rice is at its best when prepared just before serving. Try to time your rice so that it has cooked and rested before fluffing. A rice pilaf or simple rice dish will remain piping hot for up to 20 minutes, provided you've used a heavy pot with a tight-fitting lid. If there is an unavoidable delay and the rice must sit before serving, transfer the entire dish into a wire-mesh strainer and set it over barely simmering water. Place a folded kitchen towel over the saucepan and replace the lid.

Sautéed Rice
KHARA CHAVAL

This simple way of steaming rice works equally well with either washed and drained *basmati* or unwashed American long-grain. By frying the rice in butter or *ghee* for a few minutes, you can keep the grains distinct, unsplit and fluffy. You may, of course, omit the frying step if you prefer: simply put all the ingredients except butter or *ghee* in a saucepan or electric rice cooker and cook as directed. Depending on the type of electric rice cooker, the rice will firm up 5–10 minutes after the red light goes off.

Preparation time (after assembling ingredients): 5 minutes
Cooking time: 25–35 minutes
Serves: 3 or 4

1 cup (95 g) *basmati* or other long-grain white rice
1½ tablespoons (22 ml) unsalted butter or *ghee*
1⅔–2 cups (400–480 ml) water
1 teaspoon (5 ml) fresh lemon or lime juice
¾ teaspoon (3.5 ml) salt

1. If *basmati* rice is used, clean, wash, soak and drain as explained on page 4.
2. Heat the butter or *ghee* in a heavy 1½-quart/liter nonstick saucepan over moderate heat until the butter froths or the *ghee* is hot. Pour in the rice and gently stir-fry for about 2 minutes.
3. Add the water, lemon juice and salt, increase the heat to high and quickly bring the water to a full boil.
4. Immediately reduce the heat to very low, cover with a tight-fitting lid and gently simmer without stirring for 20–25 minutes or until the rice is tender and the water is fully absorbed. Turn the heat off and let the rice sit, covered, for 5 minutes to allow the fragile grains to firm up.
5. Just before serving, uncover and fluff the piping-hot rice with a fork.

Simple Boiled Rice

OBLA CHAVAL

Indian rice pots are very heavy, giving excellent heat distribution. They are usually made of tinned brass or bell metal and have round bottoms, narrow necks and saucerlike lids. When rice is cooked in these pots, it is boiled until about half done. Then muslin cloth is tied over the neck and the water is drained off. Next, the lid is put in place, live coal embers are put in the lid and the pot is set on dying coal embers. The rice slowly dries off and cooks until tender. In the villages, the cooking water is often reserved and used to starch cotton garments or fed to the calves and cows as extra nourishment.

Whether the quantity of rice is small or large, it is easy to control the degree of tenderness by first boiling the rice and then finishing it in the oven. When done, the long, slender grains should be separate, fluffy and soft. Test by pressing a grain between the thumb and finger: it should have no hard core. It can be either firm, *al dente*, or very soft.

Preparation time (after assembling ingredients): 5 minutes
Cooking time: 25–35 minutes
Serves: 4 or 5

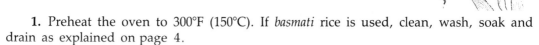

1½ cups (130 g) *basmati* or other long-grain white rice
8–10 cups (2–2.5 liters) water
½ teaspoon (2 ml) fresh lemon or lime juice
1 teaspoon (5 ml) salt (optional)
2 tablespoons (30 ml) butter or *ghee* (optional)

1. Preheat the oven to 300°F (150°C). If *basmati* rice is used, clean, wash, soak and drain as explained on page 4.

2. Bring the water, lemon juice and salt to a full boil in a 5-quart/liter pan. Stirring constantly, slowly pour in the rice and return the water to a full boil. Boil rapidly, without stirring, for 10–12 minutes or until the rice is no longer brittle though still firm.

3. Pour the cooked rice into a strainer and drain. Quickly transfer the rice to a flat ovenproof dish and spread it out evenly. Put half of the butter or *ghee* over the hot rice and cover tightly. Place in a preheated 300°F (150°C) oven for 15–20 minutes or until the rice has dried out and is tender. Add the remaining butter, gently toss with a fork and serve piping hot.

Savory Rice and Green Pea Pilaf
MASALA HARI MATAR PULAU

A savory, eye-catching centerpiece, this rice pilaf is perfect for the buffet table or as an adaptable main dish for a light luncheon or dinner. It is rich with color, texture and flavor.

Preparation time (after assembling ingredients): 5 minutes
Cooking time: 30–40 minutes
Serves: 4

1 cup (95 g) *basmati* or other long-grain white rice
3 tablespoons (45 ml) *ghee* or vegetable oil
¼ cup (35 g) raw cashew, almond or peanut bits or halves
1 teaspoon (5 ml) cumin seeds
1–2 teaspoons (5–10 ml) minced seeded hot green chilies
½ tablespoon (7 ml) scraped, finely shredded
    or minced fresh ginger root
1⅔–1¾ cups (400–420 ml) water
¾ cup (180 ml) shelled fresh green peas
    or frozen baby peas, defrosted
1 teaspoon (5 ml) turmeric
½ teaspoon (2 ml) *garam masala*
¼ cup (35 g) raisins or currants
½–1 teaspoon (2–5 ml) salt
3 tablespoons (45 ml) mixed fresh herbs (basil, oregano, thyme, etc.) or
    1½ tablespoons (22 ml) mixed dried herbs

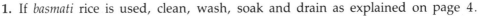

1. If *basmati* rice is used, clean, wash, soak and drain as explained on page 4.

2. Heat the *ghee* or oil in a heavy 1½-quart/liter nonstick saucepan over moderately low heat. Add the cashew, almond or peanut bits or halves. Fry, stirring constantly, until the nuts are golden brown. Remove the nuts with a slotted spoon.

3. Raise the heat to moderate and toss in the cumin seeds, green chilies and ginger root. Fry until the cumin seeds turn brown. Pour in the rice and stir-fry for about 2 minutes.

4. Pour in the water, fresh peas (if you are using them), turmeric, *garam masala*, raisins, salt and herbs. Raise the heat to high and bring to a full boil.

5. Immediately reduce the heat to very low, cover with a tight-fitting lid and gently simmer without stirring for about 20–25 minutes, depending on the type of rice, or until all the water is absorbed and the rice is tender and fluffy. If you are using frozen peas, defrost them in a strainer under hot running water. After the rice has cooked for 15 minutes, remove the lid and quickly sprinkle the peas on top. Replace the cover and continue cooking for 5–10 minutes, until all the water is absorbed and the rice is tender and fluffy.

6. Turn the heat off and let the rice sit, covered, for 5 minutes to allow the fragile grains to firm up. Just before serving, remove the cover, pour in the fried nuts and fluff the piping-hot rice with a fork.

Rice with Shredded Carrots and Coconut
GAJAR PULAU

This is a pale golden rice marbled with shredded carrots and toasted shredded coconut. A touch of raisins adds a little sweetness. You may want to remove the whole cloves, peppercorns and cinnamon stick before serving, as they are not meant to be eaten. This is a good choice for luncheon or evening menus along with any *dal* soup or tossed salad. This dish is quick, colorful, aromatic and, most important, delicious.

Preparation time (after assembling ingredients): 5 minutes
Cooking time: 25–35 minutes
Serves: 3 or 4

1 cup (95 g) *basmati* or other long-grain white rice
2 tablespoons (30 ml) *ghee* or vegetable oil
1½ tablespoons (22 ml) sesame seeds
6 whole cloves
6 black peppercorns
1½-inch (4 cm) piece of cinnamon stick
3 tablespoons (45 ml) fresh or dried shredded coconut
1⅔–2 cups (400–480 ml) water
1½ cups (360 ml) scraped and shredded carrots
    (about 8 ounces/230 g)
1¼ teaspoons (6 ml) salt
2 tablespoons (30 ml) raisins or currants

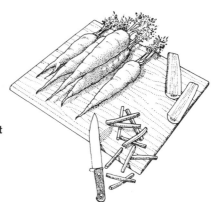

1. If *basmati* rice is used, clean, wash, soak and drain as explained on page 4.
2. Heat the *ghee* or oil in a heavy 1½-quart/liter nonstick saucepan over moderate heat until it is hot but not smoking. Add the sesame seeds, cloves, peppercorns, cinnamon stick and coconut. Stir-fry until the coconut turns light brown. Stir the rice into the mixture and fry for a few minutes until the rice grains are slightly translucent.
3. Add the water and the remaining ingredients, raise the heat to high and bring to a full boil.
4. Reduce the heat to low, cover with a tight-fitting lid and gently simmer without stirring for 20–25 minutes or until the rice is fluffy and the vegetables are tender-crisp and all of the liquid has been absorbed.
5. Turn the heat off and let the rice sit, covered, for 5 minutes to allow the fragile grains to firm up. Just before serving, remove the cover and fluff the piping-hot rice with a fork.

Piquant Lemon Rice
NIMBU BHAT

This light, mildly piquant lemon-flavored rice dish is enlivened with crunchy bits of cashew nuts. The final burst of flavor comes from a fried seasoning called *chaunk*, made of mustard seeds and split *urad dal* fried in *ghee* or sesame oil until the aromatic oils in the seeds are released and the *dal* turns golden brown. This South Indian delight is simple to make and can be served at any time and at any occasion, from a simple noonday lunch to an elaborate banquet.

Preparation time (after assembling ingredients): 5 minutes
Cooking time: 25–35 minutes
Serves: 4

1 cup (95 g) *basmati* or other long-grain white rice
1⅔–2 cups (400–480 ml) water
1 teaspoon (5 ml) salt
3 tablespoons (45 ml) *ghee* or sesame oil
½ cup (75 g) raw cashew bits or halves
½ tablespoon (7 ml) split *urad dal*, if available
1 teaspoon (5 ml) black mustard seeds
⅓ teaspoon (1.5 ml) turmeric
⅓ cup (80 ml) fresh lemon or lime juice
3 tablespoons (45 ml) minced fresh parsley or
    coarsely chopped coriander
¼ cup (25 g) fresh or dried shredded coconut for garnishing

    1. If *basmati* rice is used, clean, wash, soak and drain as explained on page 4.
    2. Bring the water to a boil in a heavy 1½-quart/liter nonstick saucepan. Stir in the rice, salt and ½ tablespoon (7 ml) of the *ghee* or oil. Cover with a tight-fitting lid. Reduce the heat to very low and gently simmer without stirring for 20–25 minutes or until the rice is fluffy and tender and the water is fully absorbed. Set aside, still covered.
    3. Heat the remaining 2½ tablespoons (37 ml) of *ghee* or oil in a small saucepan over moderately low heat until it is hot. Drop in the cashew nuts and stir-fry until golden brown. Remove with a slotted spoon and pour them over the cooked rice. Cover the rice again.
    4. Raise the heat under the saucepan slightly, toss in the *urad dal* and the mustard seeds and fry until the mustard seeds turn gray and sputter and the *dal* turns reddish-brown.
    5. Pour the fried spices into the cooked rice and sprinkle with the turmeric, lemon or lime juice and parsley or coriander. Gently fold until well mixed.
    6. Remove from the heat and garnish each serving with a sprinkle of coconut.

Rice with Ginger-Seasoned Yogurt
DAHI BHAT

This dish is centuries old and is mentioned in the ancient Vedic texts. It is nutritious and easy to digest. It is served at room temperature or slightly chilled and is a good selection on a light summer luncheon menu with any vegetable or salad. It is also good on a dinner menu, because the rice can be cooked and cooled or chilled beforehand and finally assembled at the last moment.

Preparation time (after assembling ingredients): 5 minutes
Cooking time: 25–35 minutes
Serves: 4

1 cup (95 g) *basmati* or other long-grain white rice
1⅔–2 cups (400–480 ml) water
2 tablespoons (30 ml) butter or *ghee*
1 teaspoon (5 ml) salt
1¼ cups (300 ml) plain yogurt, buttermilk or sour cream,
    at room temperature or chilled
¼ teaspoon (1 ml) ground ginger or 1 teaspoon (5 ml) scraped,
    finely shredded or minced fresh ginger root

1. If *basmati* rice is used, clean, wash, soak and drain as explained on page 4.

2. Bring the water to a boil in a 1½-quart/liter nonstick saucepan. Add the rice, stir, reduce the heat to very low and cover with a tight-fitting lid. Simmer gently without stirring for 20–25 minutes or until the rice is soft and fluffy and the water is fully absorbed. Remove from the heat and let the rice sit, covered, for 5 minutes to allow the fragile grains to firm up.

3. Spoon the cooked rice into a flat dish. Add the butter or *ghee* and the salt. Mix gently.

4. When the rice has cooled to room temperature or been chilled, and you are ready to serve it, gently fold in the yogurt, buttermilk or sour cream and ginger.

Chilled Yogurt Rice with Shredded Mango
DADHYODHANA

This moist, pleasantly seasoned rice and yogurt dish in the South Indian tradition takes only a short time to prepare. Whenever rice is combined with yogurt, the result is refreshing, nutritious and easy to digest. The combination may be served either chilled or at room temperature, so it fits into many different menus. This particular rice dish is a welcome favorite, especially in the summer season, when a light rice is preferred.

Preparation time (after assembling ingredients): 5 minutes
Cooking time: 20–30 minutes
Serves: 5 or 6

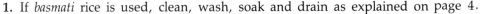

1 cup (95 g) *basmati* or other long-grain white rice
1⅔–2 cups (400–480 ml) water
1½ cups (360 ml) plain yogurt or mixture of sour cream and yogurt
1 teaspoon (5 ml) salt
1¼ teaspoons (6 ml) ground ginger
¼ teaspoon (1 ml) freshly ground black pepper
⅔ cup (160 ml) peeled, shredded green raw mango, firm but underripe
    (cucumber or carrot can be substituted for the mango)
1½ tablespoons (22 ml) *ghee* or sesame oil
½ tablespoon (7 ml) split *urad dal*, if available
1 teaspoon (5 ml) black mustard seeds
6–8 curry leaves, preferably fresh
a few sprigs of fresh parsley or coriander for garnishing

1. If *basmati* rice is used, clean, wash, soak and drain as explained on page 4.
2. Bring the water to a boil in a heavy 1½-quart/liter nonstick saucepan. Stir in the rice and reduce the heat to very low. Cover and gently simmer without stirring for 20–25 minutes or until the rice is tender and fluffy and all of the water is absorbed. Remove from the heat and let the rice sit, covered, for 5 minutes to allow the fragile grains to firm up.
3. Spoon the cooked rice into a flat dish. Let cool to room temperature. Gently fold in the yogurt, salt, ginger, pepper and mango until evenly mixed.
4. Heat the *ghee* or oil in a small saucepan over moderate heat until it is hot but not smoking. Toss in the *urad dal* and mustard seeds. Fry until the *dal* is richly browned and the mustard seeds turn gray and sputter and pop. For the last 3–5 seconds of frying the spices, toss in the curry leaves. Pour the fried spices into the rice and mix gently. Chill if desired.
5. Garnish each serving with parsley or coriander.

Toasted Coconut Rice
NARIYAL-KI CHAVAL

If you have a piece of fresh coconut in your refrigerator, try this recipe. It is quick, easy and delightful. The rice is cooked with whole sweet spices, and golden-fried coconut strips are folded in along with the *chaunk* (spices cooked in *ghee* or coconut oil), which adds to the flavor. Finally, the dish is garnished with more coconut strips. This is a most attractive rice dish, with a slightly crunchy texture and faintly sweet, toasty flavor. It can be served on any menu in any season.

Preparation time (after assembling ingredients): 5 minutes
Cooking time: 25–30 minutes
Serves: 4 or 5

1 cup (95 g) *basmati* or other long-grain white rice
1⅔–2 cups (400–480 ml) water
¾ teaspoon (3.5 ml) salt
1½-inch (4 cm) piece of cinnamon stick
6 whole cloves
3 tablespoons (45 ml) *ghee* or coconut oil
¼ fresh coconut, peeled and cut into slices ⅛ inch
　　(3 mm) thick and ½ inch (1.5 cm) long
1 teaspoon (5 ml) cumin seeds
½ teaspoon (2 ml) black mustard seeds

   1. If *basmati* rice is used, clean, wash, soak and drain as explained on page 4.

   2. Bring the water to a boil in a heavy 1½-quart/liter nonstick saucepan over high heat. Stir in the rice, salt, cinnamon stick and cloves. When the boiling resumes, reduce the heat to very low, cover with a tight-fitting lid and gently simmer without stirring for 20–25 minutes or until the rice is tender and fluffy and the water is absorbed.

   3. Remove from the heat and let the rice sit, covered, for 5 minutes to allow the fragile grains to firm up. In the meantime, heat the *ghee* or oil in a small frying pan over moderate heat. Stir-fry the coconut strips until golden brown. Remove with a slotted spoon. Toss in the cumin seeds and black mustard seeds and fry until the mustard seeds turn gray and sputter and pop. Pour this seasoning into the rice, add two-thirds of the fried coconut, gently mix and remove the whole cloves and cinnamon stick.

   4. Spoon the rice onto a serving platter and garnish with the remaining fried coconut.

Sweet Saffron Rice with Currants and Pistachios
MEETHA KESARI BHAT

This relatively simple sweet rice is made regal by the color and flavor of saffron. The success of the dish depends on the delicate balance of flavors contributed by the rice, saffron and sweetener. *Jaggery*, light brown sugar, or maple sugar is the best sweetener for this dish. If you use maple syrup or honey, omit 2 tablespoons (30 ml) of water. *Basmati* rice is highly recommended.

Preparation time (after assembling ingredients): 5 minutes
Cooking time: 25–30 minutes
Serves: 4 or 5

1 cup (95 g) *basmati* or other long-grain white rice
1¾–2 cups (420–480 ml) water
⅓ teaspoon (1.5 ml) high-quality saffron threads
1½-inch (4 cm) piece of cinnamon stick
6 whole cloves
¼ teaspoon (1 ml) salt
½ cup (75 g) crumbled *jaggery*, maple sugar
　　or equivalent raw sugar, lightly packed
1 teaspoon (5 ml) cardamom seeds, coarsely crushed
2 tablespoons (30 ml) *ghee* or vegetable oil
3 tablespoons (45 ml) slivered or sliced raw pistachios or almonds
3 tablespoons (45 ml) raisins or currants
2 tablespoons (30 ml) blanched raw pistachios, sliced into thin curls for garnishing

1. If *basmati* rice is used, clean, wash, soak and drain as explained on page 4.
2. Bring the water to a boil in a heavy 1½-quart/liter nonstick saucepan. Place the saffron threads in a small bowl and add 2½ tablespoons (37 ml) of the boiling water. Allow the threads to soak for 10–15 minutes while cooking the rice.
3. Stir the rice into the boiling water and add the cinnamon stick, cloves and salt. When the water resumes boiling, reduce the heat to very low, cover with a tight-fitting lid and gently simmer without stirring for 20–25 minutes or until the rice is tender and fluffy and all of the water is absorbed. Remove from the heat and let the rice sit, covered, for 5 minutes to allow the fragile grains to firm up.
4. In the meantime, combine the saffron water, sweetener and cardamom seeds in a small saucepan. Place over moderate heat and stir until the sweetener is dissolved. Lower the heat slightly and simmer for about 1 minute. Pour the syrup into the rice and quickly re-cover.
5. Heat the *ghee* or oil in a small pan over moderately low heat until it is hot but not smoking. Fry the nuts and raisins until the nuts turn golden brown and the raisins swell. Pour the nuts, raisins and *ghee* or oil into the piping-hot rice and gently fluff with a fork to mix. Spoon onto a serving platter and sprinkle with the sliced pistachio nuts.

Buttered Steamed Rice
SADA CHAVAL

Though rice is generally steamed in a tightly closed pan over direct heat, in this recipe I recommend a "double-steamed" procedure. Measured rice and water rest in a closed pan which rests in a larger steamer pan. Steam surrounds the entire closed rice pan, producing very soft, evenly cooked rice with well-separated, unsplit grains.

My spiritual master, Srila Prabhupada, was expert in all kitchen matters and very particular about his daily steamed rice. One cooking utensil which always accompanied him in his world travels was a three-tiered brass steamer, known simply as "Prabhupada's cooker" by his resident cooks. At each port of entry, the cooker was unpacked and polished until it shone like gold. An entire lunch for four people—dal or shukta in the bottom chamber, assorted vegetables in the middle and double-steamed rice in the top—cooked in about 45 minutes. The tempered heat in the top of the steamer yielded the butter-soft grains he preferred.

More and more, cooks' catalogs and better cookware stores are offering two- and three-tiered steamers. Italian stainless steel steamers are available in various sizes and, though costly, will prove invaluable. Calphalon and enamel steamers are also excellent. Those who don't foresee using steamers on a regular basis can improvise by making a rice steamer with available pots and pans. I've used a covered Pyrex dish resting on a cake rack in an electric frying pan filled with water ½ inch (1.5 cm) deep. Or try putting any 4-cup (1 liter) ovenware dish with a tight-fitting lid on a vegetable steaming rack or steaming trivet inside a 5–6-quart/liter pot filled with water 1 inch (2.5 cm) deep. This will suffice for steaming up to 2 cups (180 g) of raw rice.

Preparation time (after assembling ingredients): 5 minutes
Cooking time: 35–45 minutes
Serves: 3 or 4, depending on accompanying dishes

1 cup (95 g) *basmati* or other long-grain white rice
1½–1¾ cups (360–420 ml) water
1 teaspoon (5 ml) salt
1–2 tablespoons (15–30 ml) *ghee* or butter (optional)

1. If *basmati* rice is used, clean, wash, soak, and drain as explained on page 4.

2. Combine the water (or reserved soaking water if you are using *basmati* rice), salt, half of the *ghee* or butter and the rice in a pan or dish capable of being steamed. Cover tightly with heavy-weight aluminum foil or a secure lid.

3. Set up your steaming equipment in any pan that can easily hold the rice dish. Bring the water to a boil. Add your steaming tier to the steamer, or place a trivet in the large pan which clears the water by at least ½ inch (1.5 cm). Reduce the heat to low once the water boils. Place the covered rice in the steamer or on the trivet and cover the steaming pan. Cook the rice very slowly over simmering water for 35–45 minutes, depending on the texture desired. Remove the rice from the heat, uncover, add the remaining *ghee* or a butter pat and gently fluff with a fork.

Cracked Black Pepper Rice
MOLA HORA

This zesty side dish is particularly pleasing in a large, full-course meal with two or more varieties of rice. It is served at room temperature, sometimes chilled, but it always retains a pungent warmth from its substantial quantity of cracked black pepper. The rice is best cooked *al dente*, so that the grains are not soft but remain just firm to the bite.

Preparation time (after assembling ingredients): 5 minutes
Cooking time: 15 minutes
Serves: 5 or 6

1 cup (95 g) *basmati* or other long-grain white rice
8 cups (2 liters) water
1 tablespoon (15 ml) fresh lemon or lime juice
3 tablespoons (45 ml) butter or *ghee*
1 small cassia or bay leaf
½–1 teaspoon (2–5 ml) salt
1–1½ teaspoons (5–7 ml) cracked black pepper
5 or 6 lemon or lime wedges or twists for garnishing

    1. If *basmati* rice is used, clean, wash, soak and drain as explained on page 4.

    2. Bring the water, lemon or lime juice, ½ teaspoon (2 ml) of the butter or *ghee* and the cassia or bay leaf to a full boil in a large pan or stockpot over high heat. Stirring constantly, pour in the rice in a slow stream. Cook uncovered in briskly boiling water for 12–15 minutes or until the rice is just tender and fluffy.

    3. Pour the rice into a strainer or colander and drain. Let cool for 1–2 minutes, pick out the cassia or bay leaf and spoon the rice onto a serving platter. Stir in the remaining butter or *ghee*, salt and black pepper. Toss gently to mix.

    4. Chill or let cool to room temperature. Garnish with citrus wedges or twists.

Dals

For centuries, dried peas and beans—now recognized as protein-rich staple foods—have been a part of the Vedic culinary tradition. In India, the generic name for all members of the dried pea and bean family, and the dishes made from them, is *dal*. The repertoire of *dal* dishes is so vast that you can make a different one every day, without repetition, for months. *Dals* can be made into liquid soups, thick purées, sauces, stews, fried savories, moist raw chutneys, crispy pancakes, sprouted salads and sweets. The thoughtful cook can select a *dal* dish to suit any meal, from breakfast to late dinner. You can also vary your *dal* dishes according to season: warm and hearty in winter, light and refreshing in summer. The *dal* dish you choose for any meal should complement the flavors, appearances and textures of the other dishes.

Nutritionists say that all dried beans are rich in iron, vitamin B and substantial amounts of incomplete proteins that yield their total nutritional value only when combined with other proteins. The Vedic tradition suggests that to obtain the maximum nutritional value from dried *dals* you should combine them with other protein-rich foods, such as grains, nuts, yogurt or milk. The harmonious blending of these simple ingredients will not only produce delicious meals but will also round out the full potential nourishment dormant in the *dal*. Although the world's agriculturists have produced numerous strains of dried beans, it was the Vedic vegetarians who cultivated the best ones—easily digested, highly nutritious and quickly prepared.

The fried seasoning called *chaunk* is especially important with *dals* because it stimulates the digestive processes and enhances the flavor, aroma and appearance of the dish. Fresh ginger root, long recognized as a digestive calmant, is invariably present. The *chaunk* is added sometimes at the beginning of cooking, sometimes at the end. The later it is added, the more it retains its own character. Its flavor depends on the ingredients and how long they are fried. How long the *chaunk* should brown and when it should be added depend largely on personal preference. Cooking the spices in *ghee* or oil until they are just lightly roasted produces a mild *chaunk*; slightly charring or blackening the spice seeds produces a pungent one.

There are two approaches to cooking *dal* in the Vedic tradition, which divides food into two classes: raw (*kacha*) and cooked (*pakka*). Raw foods include not only raw vegetables, fruits and grains, but also any foods cooked in water, whether boiled, steamed, stewed or soaked. The *dal* recipes in this chapter are the everyday *kacha* selections prepared in any wet cooking method. Only baked and fried foods are considered cooked or *pakka*.

CLASSIFICATION OF *DALS*

Dals are available whole, split with skins, split without skins and ground into flour. Here is a short alphabetical list of the principal varieties of *dals* used in Vedic cooking and where to find them.

ADUKI BEANS: Also known as adzuki, adsuki and feijao beans. These are small, oblong, reddish-brown beans native to Japan and China. Called the "king of beans" in Japan, adukis were little known or used in the West until recently. They have an unusually sweet, quite strong flavor, and make excellent sprouts that are used raw in salads or briskly-sautéed in other dishes. The aduki bean is noted for its medicinal properties and is available at health food, specialty or gourmet stores and Chinese or Japanese grocery stores.

BLACK-EYED PEAS: Known as cowpeas in America. In India, when split and husked they are known as *chowla dal*. Whole, they are called *lobya*. Widely available in the southern United States and at health food stores.

CHANA DAL: A variety of small chickpea, sold split and without the skin. They are pale buff to bright yellow and about ¼ inch (6 mm) in diameter. *Chana dal* is classically used in thick-textured *dal* purées. It is also soaked, drained and deep-fried as a munchy snack, or ground into wet pastes to be seasoned and fried into savories. *Chana dal* is used raw in fresh chutney and ground into flour for extensive use in sweets and savories. It is available at Indian grocery stores.

CHICKPEAS (*KABLI CHANA*): Also known as garbanzo beans. A cousin to the smaller *chana dal*, chickpeas are pale buff to light brown and are used whole, without skins. They look like wrinkled peas and are about ⅓ inch (1 cm) in diameter. Chickpeas are popularly used as whole dried beans with potatoes, savory sauces, yogurt sauces or tomatoes. They can also be roasted and ground into flour for sweets and savories. Chickpeas are available at supermarkets and health food stores, Indian grocery stores and Latin American stores.

KALA CHANA: A cousin to the chickpea. *Kala chanas* are somewhat smaller and darker brown than chickpeas, but have the same shape. Despite their apparent similarities, these two beans are not interchangeable, as they have different flavors and cooking requirements. *Kala chanas* are popular in whole bean dishes and, like chickpeas, are exceptionally nutritious, providing more vitamin C than most other legumes and nearly twice as much iron. They are also very high in protein. *Kala Chanas* are available at Indian and Middle Eastern grocery stores.

KIDNEY BEANS (*RAJMA DAL*): Red-brown, oval beans. They are used in a spicy North Indian vegetarian chili and other whole bean dishes. They are available at Indian and Middle Eastern grocery stores as well as at health, specialty or gourmet food stores.

MUNG *DAL*: Also known as mung beans and green grams. Mung *dal* is popular in three forms:

1. Whole mung beans, with skins (*sabat moong*). These are BB-sized, pale yellow oval beans with moss-green skins, easy to digest and relatively quick to cook. They are used primarily for sprouts and dry bean dishes. You can get whole mung beans at Indian and Middle Eastern grocery stores, health food stores and specialty or gourmet food stores.

2. Split mung *dal* without skins (*moong dal*). These are used extensively in soups, stews and sauces. They become slightly glutinous when cooked into thick purées and make excellent *dal* soup. They can be soaked, drained and fried into crispy snacks. Mung *dal* is available at Indian grocery stores.

3. Split mung *dal* with skins (*chilke moong dal*). These are recommended whenever soaked beans are required for savories and chutneys. They too are available at Indian grocery stores.

MUTH **BEANS:** Known as dew bean. The beans are used fresh as a vegetable; dried in whole bean dishes; and soaked, drained and fried as crunchy snacks. The greenish-brown beans are available at Indian grocery stores.

SPLIT PEAS (*MATAR DAL***):** There are two popular varieties—green and yellow. Both are about ¼ inch (6 mm) in diameter. The yellow can be used as a substitute for *chana dal* or *toovar dal*. The green is ideal for thin to medium soups or purées. Split peas are readily available at all supermarkets and health food stores and Indian grocery stores.

TOOVAR DAL: Also known as *arhar dal, tuar dal* and pigeon peas. The pale yellow to gold lentils, about ¼ inch (6 mm) in diameter, are sold split, without skins. Slightly sweet, they are popular in *dal* soups and purées and the South Indian daily staple known as *sambar*. They are available at some supermarkets and Latin American stores and all Indian grocery stores.

URAD DAL: Also known as black gram. These beans are popular in three forms, all available at Indian grocery stores:

1. Whole *urad* beans, with skins (*sabat urad*). These BB-sized, oval ivory beans have gray-black skins. They are used whole in dried bean dishes.

2. Split, without skins (*urad dal*). Used in purées and soups and ground into flour for savories and sweets.

3. Split, with skins (*chilke urad dal*). Used just like *urad dal*; many cooks prefer the lighter texture of fried savories made from soaked *chilke urad*.

HOW TO CLEAN AND WASH *DALS*

Imported *dals* arrive minimally processed and should be picked through for kernels that have become too hard and for foreign matter such as dried leaves, stems and stones. You can observe the time-honored ritual of cleaning *dal* by following these two steps:

1. Pour the *dal* onto one end of a large cookie sheet or metal tray. Working on a small amount, pick out the unwanted matter and move the clean *dal* to one side. Clean the rest of the *dal* the same way.

2. Put the *dal* in a sieve and lower it into a large bowl filled two-thirds with water. Rub the *dal* between your hands for about 30 seconds. Lift out the sieve, discard the water and refill the bowl. Repeat the process three or four times or until the rinse water is practically clear. Drain or soak as directed in the recipe.

GUIDE FOR PRESSURE COOKING *DALS*

TYPE OF *DAL*	SOAKING TIME	DAL-TO-WATER RATIO (*dal* measured before soaking)	COOKING TIME (under pressure)
Whole: chickpeas, kidney beans, black-eyed peas, *kala chana dal*	8 hours or overnight	1 to 3½	30–40 minutes
Whole: aduki beans, mung beans, *urad* beans, *muth* beans	5 hours or overnight	1 to 3	20–25 minutes
Split: mung *dal*, urad dal	no soaking required	1 to 6 for soup	20–25 minutes
Split: toovar dal / chana dal / split peas	3 hours / 5 hours / 5 hours	1 to 6½ for soup	25–30 minutes

The hardness or softness of the water will affect the cooking time. Because hard water increases cooking time, salt—a mineral—is never added during cooking.

COOKING *DALS*

The simplest way to cook split *dal* is to put it in a heavy saucepan with the suggested amount of water, a dab of butter or *ghee*, fresh ginger root and a dash of turmeric. Stirring occasionally, bring to a boil over high heat. Reduce the heat to moderately low, cover with a tight-fitting lid, and gently boil until the *dal* is thoroughly softened, anywhere from 45 minutes to 1½ hours. Cooking time varies with the type of *dal*, the hardness or softness of the water, and the age of the *dal*; old *dal* may take twice as long as new *dal*. The consistency of the *dal*—liquid or dry—is determined by the amount of water. Small whole beans—mung, aduki, *muth* and *urad*—take up to 45 minutes more.

Thin split *dal* soups and whole beans cook rapidly in a pressure cooker: a small amount of *dal* soup cooks to perfection in 20–25 minutes, and whole chickpeas become butter-soft in 30–40 minutes. For medium to thick *dal* purées and sauces, use the saucepan method described above, as they tend to stick to the bottom of the pressure cooker and clog the vent on the lid.

Some manufacturers caution against cooking dried peas and beans in a pressure cooker, because legumes cooked without enough water or insufficiently washed tend to froth up and clog the vent. To prevent this, fill the pressure cooker no more than half full; use at least 6 parts water to 1 part split *dal* or 3 parts water to 1 part whole beans; and keep the heat moderately low. The first few times you pressure cook *dals*, watch for signs of clogging, such as a suddenly still vent weight. If this happens, take the pan off the heat, put it in the sink and run lukewarm water over it, gradually changing to cold. After several minutes, tilt the weight and slowly reduce the pressure, aiming the release away from you. Finish cooking the *dal*, covered but not under pressure.

Bean Sprouts

Another way to prepare dried beans is to sprout them. The food value of beans skyrockets as they sprout, making them among the most vital and nutrition-packed of foods. Sprouting beans greatly multiplies their levels of vitamins C, E, and all of the B group. Their proteins become extremely digestible, and their starches turn to sugar, making them pleasantly sweet. Minerals, enzymes, and fiber combine to make bean sprouts a superfood, yet they are low-calorie. Moreover, sprouted beans are a very economical addition to the diet.

Eat sprouted beans as soon as they reach the desired size in order to enjoy the full nutritional benefits. They can be served raw in salads, sautéed with spices or briefly steamed to make a healthy and delicious breakfast, especially during winter. You can also add sprouts to stir-fried dishes, broths and *dal* soups just before serving, or use them as a garnish for many dishes.

To sprout ½ cup (100 g) whole beans, such as chickpeas, mung, aduki, *muth* or *urad* beans, you will need a medium-sized mixing bowl, a 1-quart/liter wide-mouthed jar, a doubled square of cheesecloth (4½ inches/11.5 cm square) and a strong rubber band. If you become fond of sprouts, you can buy a sprouter in a health food store.

1. Buy only those beans that are sold specifically for sprouting. They are available at health food stores and through mail order sources. Select clean, whole beans. Pick through them to remove broken beans, dead kernels, chaff, stones and other unwanted matter.

2. Thoroughly wash the beans. Soak for 8–12 hours, or overnight, in a bowl of lukewarm water. After soaking, drain the swollen beans and rinse them in clean water three or four times or until the rinse water is clear. Do not throw away the soaking water. It will be yellow, musky and none too fragrant, but just what your houseplants have been waiting for.

3. Put the beans in the jar, stretch the cheesecloth over the mouth of the jar, and secure it with the rubber band. Turn the jar upside down and set it at a 45° angle in the mixing bowl to give the excess water a place to drain into. Keep the jar this way in a cool, dark cupboard, and rinse the beans with fresh water three or four times a day. Depending on their size, the beans should sprout in three to five days.

4. Generally, sprouted beans are ready when the tails are ¼–½ inch (6 mm-1.5 cm) long. Serve at once or refrigerate, loosely covered, for up to 2 days.

DAL SOUPS

Simple Mung *Dal* Soup
SADA MOONG DAL

This smooth, liquid mung *dal* soup is seasoned with a simple *chaunk*. It is easy to prepare and easy to digest, and its light consistency makes it appealing in any season. Serve it accompanied by a wheat bread or rice and a vegetable. To complete the meal, serve yogurt or green salad.

Preparation time (after assembling ingredients): 10 minutes
Cooking time: 1¼ hours or 25 minutes in a pressure cooker
Serves: 4 to 6

⅔ cup (145 g) split *moong dal*, without skins
6½ cups (1.5 liters) water (5½ cups/1.3 liters if pressure-cooked)
1 teaspoon (5 ml) turmeric
2 teaspoons (10 ml) ground coriander
1½ teaspoons (7 ml) scraped, finely shredded or minced fresh ginger root
1 teaspoon (5 ml) minced seeded hot green chili (or as desired)
1¼ teaspoons (6 ml) salt
2 tablespoons (30 ml) *ghee* or vegetable oil
1 teaspoon (5 ml) cumin seeds
2 tablespoons (30 ml) coarsely chopped fresh coriander or minced fresh parsley

   1. Sort, wash and drain the split mung beans as explained on page 21.
   2. Combine the mung beans, water, turmeric, coriander, ginger root and green chili in a heavy 3-quart/liter nonstick saucepan. Stirring occasionally, bring to a full boil over high heat. Reduce the heat to moderately low, cover with a tight-fitting lid and boil gently for 1 hour or until the *dal* is soft and fully cooked. For pressure cooking, combine the ingredients in a 6-quart/liter pressure cooker, cover and cook for 25 minutes under pressure. Remove from the heat and let the pressure drop by itself.
   3. Off the heat, uncover, add the salt and beat with a wire whisk or rotary beater until the *dal* soup is creamy smooth.
   4. Heat the *ghee* or oil in a small saucepan over moderate to moderately high heat. When it is hot, toss in the cumin seeds. Fry until the seeds turn brown. Pour into the *dal* soup, immediately cover and allow the seasonings to soak into the hot *dal* for 1–2 minutes. Add the minced herb, stir and serve.

Golden Mung *Dal* Soup

KHARA MOONG DAL

This is a variation of the simple *dal* soup, using the same ingredients as the previous recipe, but a different seasoning procedure changes the flavor considerably. The contrast between these recipes shows the possibilities of using different procedures to produce varieties of flavors. This dish will go well in any lunch menu, such as a rice, salad and vegetable of your choice.

Preparation time (after assembling ingredients): 10 minutes
Cooking time: 1¼ hours or 25 minutes in a pressure cooker
Serves: 4

⅔ cup (145 g) split *moong dal*, without skins
6 cups (1.5 liters) water
   (5½ cups/1.3 liters if pressure-cooked)
½ teaspoon (2 ml) turmeric
2 tablespoons (30 ml) *ghee* or vegetable oil
½ tablespoon (7 ml) coriander seeds
½ tablespoon (7 ml) cumin seeds
1 teaspoon (5 ml) salt
2 teaspoons (10 ml) scraped, finely shredded or minced fresh ginger root
1 teaspoon (5 ml) minced seeded hot green chili (or as desired)
2 tablespoons (30 ml) minced fresh parsley or coarsely chopped coriander

1. Sort, wash and drain the split mung beans as explained on page 21.
2. Place the mung beans, water, turmeric and a dab of the *ghee* or oil in a heavy 3-quart/liter nonstick saucepan and, stirring occasionally, bring to a full boil over high heat. Reduce the heat to moderately low, cover with a tight-fitting lid and boil gently for 1 hour or until the *dal* is soft and fully cooked. For pressure cooking, combine the ingredients in a 6-quart/liter pressure cooker, cover and cook for 25 minutes under pressure. Remove from the heat and let the pressure drop by itself.
3. Meanwhile, slowly dry-roast the coriander and cumin seeds in a heavy iron frying pan for about 8 minutes. Remove and coarsely crush with a mortar and pestle, kitchen mallet or rolling pin.
4. Off the heat, uncover the *dal* and add the salt and roasted spices. Beat with a wire whisk or rotary beater until the *dal* soup is creamy smooth.
5. Heat the *ghee* or oil in a small saucepan over moderately high heat. When it is hot, toss in the ginger root and green chili. Fry until golden brown, then pour into the soup. Cover immediately and let the seasonings soak into the hot *dal* for 1–2 minutes. Sprinkle in the minced herb, stir and serve.

Creamy Mung *Dal* with Chopped Spinach
PALAK MOONG DAL

Moong, North India's most popular *dal*, was a great favorite of my spiritual master, Srila Prabhupada. It is easy to digest and has a good flavor and high vitamin content. The spinach, preferably fresh, enhances the texture and marbled color of this power-packed *dal* soup, and the fried spices poured in at the end of the cooking add lashings of flavor.

Preparation time (after assembling ingredients): 10 minutes
Cooking time: 1¼ hours or 25 minutes in a pressure cooker
Serves: 5 or 6

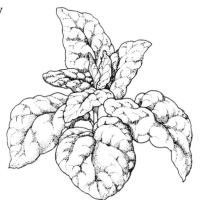

⅔ cup (145 g) split *moong dal*, without skins
8 ounces (230 g) fresh spinach, washed, trimmed, patted dry
    and coarsely chopped, or ½ of a 10-ounce package
    of chopped frozen spinach, defrosted (140 g)
6½ cups (1.5 liters) water
    (5½ cups/1.3 liters if pressure-cooked)
1 teaspoon (5 ml) turmeric
½ tablespoon (7 ml) ground coriander
½ tablespoon (7 ml) scraped, finely shredded
    or minced fresh ginger root
2 tablespoons (30 ml) *ghee* or vegetable oil
1¼ teaspoons (6 ml) salt
1 teaspoon (5 ml) cumin seeds
¼ teaspoon (1 ml) yellow asafetida powder (*hing*)*
¼–½ teaspoon (1–2 ml) cayenne pepper or paprika
½ tablespoon (7 ml) lemon juice

*This amount applies only to yellow Cobra brand. Reduce any other asafetida by three-fourths.

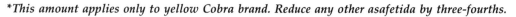

    1. Sort, wash and drain the split mung beans as explained on page 21. If you are using frozen spinach, defrost it at room temperature, place it in a strainer and press out all excess water.

    2. Place the mung beans, water, turmeric, coriander, ginger root and a dab of *ghee* or oil in a heavy 3-quart/liter nonstick saucepan. Stirring occasionally, bring to a full boil over high heat. Reduce the heat to moderately low, cover with a tight-fitting lid and gently boil for 1 hour or until the *dal* is soft and fully cooked. For pressure cooking, combine the ingredients in a 6-quart/liter pressure cooker, cover and cook for 25 minutes under pressure. Remove from the heat and let the pressure drop by itself.

    3. Off the heat, uncover and add the salt. Beat with a wire whisk or rotary beater until the *dal* soup is creamy smooth. Add the fresh spinach, cover and boil gently for 5–8 minutes more; or cook frozen spinach for 2–3 minutes.

    4. Heat the *ghee* or oil in a small saucepan over moderate to moderately high heat. When it is hot, pour in the cumin seeds and fry until they are brown. Add the asafetida and cayenne or paprika and fry for just 1–2 seconds more. Then quickly pour the fried seasonings into the soup. Cover immediately. Let the seasonings soak into the hot *dal* for 1–2 minutes. Add the lemon juice, stir and serve.

Double-*Dal* Soup
MOONG TOOVAR DAL

Toovar dal is also known as *arhar* or *tuar dal* and pigeon peas. The mildly seasoned combination of *moong* and *toovar dals* in this recipe is popular in cool-weather months.

Dal soaking time: 3 hours for *toovar dal*, 5 hours for yellow split peas
Preparation time (after assembling ingredients): 10 minutes
Cooking time: 1½ hours
Serves: 4 to 6

⅓ cup (75 g) split *moong dal*, without skins
⅓ cup (70 g) split *toovar dal* or yellow split peas
5¾ cups (1.5 liters) water
½ teaspoon (2 ml) turmeric
1 teaspoon (5 ml) scraped, finely shredded or minced fresh ginger root
1 teaspoon (5 ml) minced seeded hot green chili (or as desired)
3 tablespoons (45 ml) *ghee* or vegetable oil
2 tablespoons (30 ml) minced fresh parsley or coarsely chopped coriander
1 tablespoon (15 ml) fresh lemon or lime juice
1 teaspoon (5 ml) salt
1 teaspoon (5 ml) black mustard seeds
4–6 small curry leaves, preferably fresh

1. Sort, wash, and drain the split mung beans and *toovar dal* or split peas as explained on page 21. If using *toovar dal*, soak in 2 cups (480 ml) of hot water for 3 hours; if using yellow split peas, soak in 2 cups (480 ml) of hot water for 5 hours. Drain well.

2. Place the water, turmeric, ginger root, green chili and 1 tablespoon (15 ml) of the *ghee* or oil in a heavy 3-quart/liter nonstick saucepan. Bring to a boil over high heat. Stir in the *dals*, cover with a tight-fitting lid and reduce the heat to moderately low. Simmer for 1½ hours or until the *dals* are soft and fully cooked. Remove from the heat and beat with a wire whisk or rotary beater until the *dal* soup is creamy smooth. Stir in the fresh herb, lemon juice and salt.

3. Heat the remaining *ghee* or oil in a small saucepan over moderate to moderately high heat. When it is hot, add the black mustard seeds. Fry until they turn gray and sputter and pop. Remove from the heat and add the curry leaves. Fry for 1–2 seconds. Pour this hot seasoning into the cooked *dal* and cover immediately. Allow the seasonings to soak into the hot *dal* for 1–2 minutes, then stir and serve.

Mung *Dal* Soup with Tomatoes
TAMATAR MOONG DAL

Dals are perhaps the most popular and the most economical foods in Vedic cuisine. They are relished by everyone, rich and poor, and are part of almost every Vedic lunch. A bouquet of delicate flavors in this creamy *dal* soup comes from the spices, seasonings, tomatoes and sweetener added in the final stages of cooking. The recipe comes from the skilled hands of a great devotee of Krishna from West Bengal, Srila Prabhupada's younger sister, Bhavatarini, lovingly known to his disciples as Pishima (Aunt).

Preparation time (after assembling ingredients): 10 minutes
Cooking time: 1¼ hours
Serves: 4 to 6

¾ cup (170 g) split *moong dal*, without skins
7¼ cups (1.75 liters) water
¾ teaspoon (3.5 ml) turmeric
2-inch (5 cm) piece cinnamon stick
3 tablespoons (45 ml) *ghee* or vegetable oil
2 teaspoons (10 ml) coriander seeds
1 teaspoon (5 ml) cumin seeds
½ teaspoon (2 ml) fennel seeds
½ tablespoon (7 ml) sesame seeds
3 whole cloves
4 green cardamom pods
5 black peppercorns
1½ teaspoons (7 ml) salt
1–2 seeded hot green chilies, cut into large pieces
1 tablespoon (15 ml) sugar or equivalent sweetener
2 medium-sized firm ripe tomatoes, coarsely chopped
3 tablespoons (45 ml) minced fresh parsley or coarsely chopped coriander

1. Sort, wash and drain the split mung beans as explained on page 21.
2. Combine the mung beans, water, turmeric, cinnamon stick and a dab of the *ghee* or oil in a heavy 3-quart/liter nonstick saucepan over high heat. Reduce the heat to moderately low, cover with a tight-fitting lid and boil gently for 1 hour or until the *dal* is soft and fully cooked.
3. While the *dal* is cooking, warm a heavy iron frying pan over low heat. Add the coriander seeds, cumin seeds, fennel seeds, sesame seeds, cloves, cardamom pods and peppercorns. Dry-roast, stirring occasionally, for 8–10 minutes or until the sesame seeds are golden brown. Remove and set aside.
4. Take out the cardamom pods. Remove the black seeds and put them with the other roasted spices. Discard the pods. With an electric coffee mill or a stone mortar and pestle, reduce the spices to a powder. Add enough water to make a moist paste.
5. When the *dal* is cooked, remove from the heat and take out the cinnamon stick. Add the salt and beat with a wire whisk or rotary beater until the *dal* is smooth.
6. Heat the *ghee* or oil in a small frying pan over moderate to moderately high heat. When it is hot, add the chilies and the moist spice paste. Stir-fry for about 30 seconds.

Vishakha's Cream of Vegetable *Dal* Soup
SABJI DAL SHORBA

Here is a quick pressure-cooker soup. The rice and legumes complement each other nutritionally and—with the vegetables, seasonings and powdered spices—make a full-bodied creamy soup. Practically a meal in itself, this dish needs only a fresh flatbread and salad to make an excellent light lunch. If the vegetables listed are not available, you can substitute peeled Jerusalem artichokes, winter squash, summer squash or fresh peas in equivalent amounts.

Dal soaking time: 1 hour
Preparation time (after assembling ingredients): 10 minutes
Cooking time: 25 minutes
Serves: 4 or 5

3 tablespoons (45 ml) yellow or green split peas
3 tablespoons (45 ml) split *moong dal* or *toovar dal*,
    or 3 more tablespoons (45 ml) of split peas
3 tablespoons (45 ml) *basmati* or other long-grain white rice
2 tablespoons (30 ml) butter or *ghee*
½ teaspoon (2 ml) turmeric
¼ teaspoon (1 ml) yellow asafetida powder (*hing*)*
½ seeded small hot green chili (or as desired)
½-inch (1.5 cm) piece of fresh ginger root, peeled
2 medium-sized carrots, peeled and cut into 1-inch (2.5 cm) pieces
½ small cauliflower, stemmed and cut into flowerets
6 whole red radishes
5¼ cups (1.25 liters) water
1 tablespoon (15 ml) ground cumin
1 tablespoon (15 ml) ground coriander
1 teaspoon (5 ml) *garam masala*
½ teaspoon (2 ml) freshly ground black pepper
1½ teaspoons (7 ml) salt
2 tablespoons (30 ml) fresh minced parsley or coriander

*This amount applies only to yellow Cobra brand. Reduce any other asafetida by three-fourths.

   1. Soak the split peas in hot water for 1 hour, then drain. Sort, wash and drain the split *moong* or *toovar dal* as explained on page 21.
   2. Combine the rice, legumes, butter or *ghee*, turmeric, asafetida, green chili, ginger root, vegetables and water in a 6-quart/liter pressure cooker. Cook under pressure for a little more than 20 minutes. Remove from the heat and allow the pressure to drop.
   3. Blend half of the cooked vegetables and 2½ cups (600 ml) of broth from the pressure cooker in a blender. Blend at high speed to make a creamy smooth soup. Transfer to a heavy 2-quart/liter nonstick saucepan. Blend the other half of the cooked vegetables with the remaining broth plus enough water to make 2½ cups (600 ml) of liquid and add to the soup.
   4. Sprinkle in the ground coriander, cumin and *garam masala*. Bring the soup to a gentle boil, stirring occasionally to prevent sticking, and boil for 1–2 minutes. Remove from the heat.
   5. Add the black pepper, salt and minced herb. Stir and serve.

Quick Cream of Split Pea Soup with Sliced Carrots
GAJAR MATAR DAL

Here is an elegant, mildly seasoned *dal* soup that is good the whole year round. The ingredients are easily obtained, and the texture is light and pleasant. Yellow or green split peas are transformed into a smooth, creamy soup, and sliced carrots lend color and nutrition.

Dal soaking time: 5 hours
Preparation time (after assembling ingredients): 10 minutes
Cooking time: 1½ hours or 30 minutes in a pressure cooker
Serves: 6 to 8

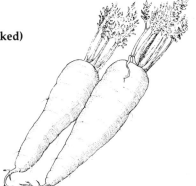

1 cup (210 g) yellow or green split peas
7½ cups (1.75 liters) water (6¾ cups/1.5 liters if pressure cooked)
1 teaspoon (5 ml) scraped, minced fresh ginger root
1–2 hot green chilies
½ teaspoon (2 ml) turmeric
1 tablespoon (15 ml) ground coriander
4 tablespoons (60 ml) *ghee* or a mixture of
vegetable oil and unsalted butter
4 medium-sized scraped carrots, sliced
1¼ teaspoons (6 ml) salt
2 tablespoons (30 ml) minced fresh parsley
or coarsely chopped coriander
1¼ teaspoons (6 ml) cumin seeds
¼–½ teaspoon (1–2 ml) yellow asafetida powder (*h∶ng*)*

*This amount applies only to yellow Cobra brand. Reduce any other asafetida by three-fourths.

1. Soak the split peas in 3 cups (710 ml) of hot water for 5 hours, then drain.

2. Combine the split peas, water, ginger root, green chilies, turmeric, ground coriander and a dab of the *ghee* or oil-butter mixture in a heavy 3-quart/liter nonstick saucepan. Bring to a boil over high heat.

3. Reduce the heat to moderately low, cover with a tight-fitting lid and boil gently for 1 hour. Add the carrots, cover and continue to cook for 30 minutes or until the split peas are soft and fully cooked. For pressure cooking, combine the ingredients in a 6-quart/liter pressure cooker, cover and cook for 30 minutes under pressure. Remove from the heat and let the pressure drop by itself.

4. Off the heat, uncover and stir in the salt and herb.

5. Heat the remaining *ghee* or oil-butter mixture in a small saucepan over moderate to moderately high heat. When it is hot, toss in the cumin seeds and fry until they turn brown. Sprinkle in the asafetida and fry for just 1–2 more seconds, then quickly pour the fried seasonings into the *dal*. Cover immediately and allow the *chaunk* to soak into the *dal* for 1–2 minutes. Stir and serve.

Nutritious Whole Grain, Split Pea and Vegetable Soup
SABJI MATAR DAL

This is a quick pressure-cooker soup that is warming, nutritious and very welcome on cold winter days. You can vary this recipe by substituting parsnips, green beans, zucchini or corn for any of the suggested vegetables. A nice stew can be obtained by adding large, even-sized pieces of potato or winter squash. (You will need to increase the amount of water a bit when cooking these starchy vegetables.) Try your own favorite combinations according to the season and time of day. You can get whole grains and split peas at most health food stores and co-ops, so the next time you are out shopping pick up a pound (455 g) each of whole barley, wheat, rye, brown rice, millet and split peas. At the rate of only 1–2 tablespoons (15–30 ml) per pot of soup, you will be able to stretch these wholesome ingredients over many meals. This soup is a meal in itself, and it also goes especially well with *Buttered Steamed Rice*, a bowl of *Homemade Yogurt* and a tossed green salad.

Grain and *dal* soaking time: 2 hours
Preparation time (after assembling ingredients): 5 minutes
Cooking time: 25 minutes in a pressure cooker
Serves: 6 to 8

2 tablespoons (30 ml) each barley, wheat, rye, brown rice,
    wild rice, millet and split peas
7 cups (1.75 liters) water
1 medium-sized carrot, scraped and cut into ¼-inch
    (6 mm) rounds
1 medium-sized celery stalk and leaves, sliced
1 large firm ripe tomato, cut into 8 pieces
a generous handful of spinach (about 1 ounce/30 g),
    washed, dried, stemmed and coarsely chopped
½ tablespoon (7 ml) scraped, finely shredded or minced fresh ginger root
1 teaspoon (5 ml) minced seeded hot green chili (or as desired)
1 teaspoon (5 ml) turmeric
½ tablespoon (7 ml) ground coriander
1½ teaspoons (7 ml) salt
2 tablespoons (30 ml) minced fresh parsley or coarsely chopped coriander
4 tablespoons (60 ml) *ghee* or vegetable oil
1 teaspoon (5 ml) cumin seeds

    1. Mix together the grains and split peas and soak in hot water for 2 hours. Drain.
    2. Combine them with the remaining ingredients except the salt, parsley or coriander, 2 tablespoons (30 ml) of the *ghee* or vegetable oil and the cumin seeds in a 6-quart/liter pressure cooker. Cover and cook under pressure for 20 minutes. Remove the pan from the heat and allow the pressure to drop. Uncover and stir in the salt and herb.
    3. Heat the remaining 2 tablespoons (30 ml) of *ghee* or vegetable oil over moderate heat in a small saucepan. When it is hot, add the cumin seeds and fry until they are brown. Pour them into the soup and cover immediately. Allow the seasonings to soak into the hot *dal* for 1–2 minutes. Stir and serve.

WHOLE BEAN DISHES

Sautéed Sprouted Mung Beans with Julienne Ginger Root
SABAT MOONG USAL

Ginger marinating time: 30 minutes
Preparation time (after assembling ingredients): 5 minutes
Cooking time: 5 minutes
Serves: 4 or 5

1½-inch (4 cm) piece of scraped fresh ginger root
1¼ teaspoons (6 ml) salt
3 tablespoons (45 ml) fresh lemon juice
¼ teaspoon (1 ml) yellow asafetida powder (*hing*)*
1 tablespoon (15 ml) ground coriander
¼ teaspoon (1 ml) cayenne pepper or paprika
½ teaspoon (2 ml) turmeric
3 tablespoons (45 ml) *ghee* or vegetable oil
1½ teaspoons (7 ml) cumin seeds
1½ teaspoons (7 ml) black mustard seeds
1½ cups (305 g) whole mung beans, sorted, washed and sprouted
    until the tails are ¼ inch (6 mm) long (page 23)
    (about 3½ cups/830 ml sprouted beans)
1–2 tablespoons (15–30 ml) water
2 teaspoons (10 ml) raw sugar or equivalent sweetener
3 tablespoons (45 ml) minced fresh mint
1 tablespoon (15 ml) butter or *ghee*
4 or 5 radish roses and celery curls for garnishing (optional)

*This amount applies only to yellow Cobra brand. Reduce any other asafetida by three-fourths.

1. Cut the ginger root into paper-thin slices, stack and cut again into paper-thin julienne strips. Place all of the strips in a small bowl, sprinkle with ¼ teaspoon (1 ml) of the salt and ½ teaspoon (2 ml) of lemon juice and set aside for 30 minutes.

2. Mix the asafetida powder, ground coriander, cayenne or paprika and turmeric in a small bowl. Heat the *ghee* or oil in a heavy 3–4-quart/liter casserole over moderate to moderately high heat. When it is hot, stir in the cumin seeds and black mustard seeds. Fry until the cumin seeds turn brown. Toss in the powdered spices, and 2 or 3 seconds later stir in the sprouts.

3. Add the 1–2 tablespoons (15–30 ml) of water and cover. Cook for a few minutes if you want your sprouts crunchy, or up to 10 minutes if you want them tender-crisp. Then stir in the sweetener and the rest of the lemon juice and salt.

4. Pour onto a warmed platter or individual plates. Sprinkle with the marinated ginger strips, mint and a drizzle of melted butter or *ghee* and serve immediately. If you like, garnish each serving with a crisp radish rose and celery curl.

Tender-Crisp Sprouted *Urad* Beans in Sesame-Yogurt Sauce
SABAT URAD USAL

Whole *urad* or *muth* beans are the traditional favorites, but you can also use sprouted chickpeas, aduki or mung beans in this dish. Sprouted beans are bursting with nutrition because they are a living, growing food. When left raw, their flavor may be unpalatable to the newcomer. In this dish, however, flavor is obtained without sacrificing the nutritive value of the sprouts.

Preparation time (after assembling ingredients): 10 minutes
Cooking time: 5–10 minutes
Serves: 5 or 6

1½ teaspoons (7 ml) cumin seeds
2 teaspoons (10 ml) coriander seeds
6 black peppercorns
½ teaspoon (2 ml) fennel seeds
2 teaspoons (10 ml) sesame seeds
8 whole cloves
¼ cup (25 g) unsweetened shredded coconut, lightly packed
⅔ cup (160 ml) plain yogurt or sour cream
3–4 tablespoons (45–60 ml) *ghee* or vegetable oil
1½ teaspoons (7 ml) scraped, finely shredded
    or minced fresh ginger root
1½ teaspoons (7 ml) minced hot green chili (or as desired)
1 teaspoon (5 ml) black mustard seeds
12 small fresh or dried curry leaves, if available
1 cup (195 g) whole *urad* beans, *muth* beans, mung beans, or chickpeas, sorted, washed and
    sprouted until (page 23) ⅓ inch (1 cm) long (about 2½–3 cups/600–710 ml sprouted)
1 teaspoon (5 ml) salt
1 teaspoon (5 ml) sugar or equivalent sweetener
1 tablespoon (15 ml) fresh lemon juice
2 tablespoons (30 ml) coarsely chopped fresh coriander or minced parsley

1. Place the cumin seeds, coriander seeds, black peppercorns, fennel seeds, sesame seeds and cloves in a heavy frying pan over moderately low heat. Dry-roast for about 5 minutes. Add the coconut and, stirring frequently, dry-roast it until golden brown. Transfer the roasted ingredients to a blender and blend on high speed until reduced to a powder. Add the yogurt or sour cream and blend on moderately high speed for about 1 minute. Transfer the mixture to a small bowl.

2. Heat the *ghee* or oil in a large frying pan over moderate to moderately high heat. When it is hot, drop in the ginger root, green chili and black mustard seeds. Fry until the mustard seeds turn gray and sputter and pop. Add the curry leaves and immediately pour in the yogurt seasoning. Fry, uncovered, until half of the liquid has cooked away.

3. Stir in the sprouts, salt and sweetener. Cover and reduce the heat to moderately low and cook until the sprouted beans are warmed through and slightly softened. How long you cook them is up to you, anywhere from 3 minutes (crunchy) to 10 minutes (tender-crisp).

4. Pour onto a small serving platter or individual plates and sprinkle with lemon juice and chopped herb.

Savory Chickpeas in Tangy Tomato Glaze
TAMATAR KABLI CHANA USAL

Soaking time: 8 hours or overnight
Preparation time (after assembling ingredients): 10 minutes
Cooking time: 2–3 hours or 30–40 minutes in a pressure cooker
Serves: 6

1¼ cups (235 g) dried chickpeas
5½ cups (1.3 liters) water (4 cups/1 liter if pressure-cooked)
5 tablespoons (75 ml) *ghee* or peanut oil
1½ teaspoons (7 ml) scraped, minced fresh ginger root
1½ teaspoons (7 ml) minced hot green chili (or as desired)
1½ teaspoons (7 ml) cumin seeds
½ teaspoon (2 ml) black mustard seeds
8–12 small curry leaves, preferably fresh
5 medium-sized tomatoes, peeled, seeded and diced
1 teaspoon (5 ml) turmeric
1 teaspoon (5 ml) *chat masala* or 2 teaspoons (10 ml)
    fresh lemon juice
1 teaspoon (5 ml) *garam masala*
¼ cup (60 ml) minced fresh parsley or coarsely chopped coriander leaves
1¼ teaspoons (6 ml) salt
6 lemon or lime twists for garnishing

1. Place the chickpeas in a bowl, add 5½ cups (1.3 liters) of water and soak for at least 8 hours or overnight at room temperature.

2. Place the chickpeas and their soaking liquid in a heavy 3–4-quart/liter saucepan, add a dab of *ghee* or oil and bring to a full boil over high heat. Reduce the heat to moderately low, cover with a tight-fitting lid and gently boil for 2–3 hours or until the chickpeas are butter-soft but not broken down. For pressure cooking, combine the ingredients in a 6-quart/liter pressure cooker, cover and cook under pressure for 30 minutes. Remove the pan from the heat and allow the pressure to drop by itself before removing the lid. Drain the chickpeas, saving the cooking liquid.

3. Heat 3 tablespoons (45 ml) of *ghee* or oil in a heavy 3-quart/liter nonstick saucepan over moderate to moderately high heat. When it is hot, stir in the ginger root, green chili, cumin seeds and black mustard seeds. Fry until the cumin seeds turn brown.

4. Drop in the curry leaves, and just 1–2 seconds later stir in the tomatoes. Add the turmeric, *chat masala*, *garam masala*, and half of the minced herb. Stir-fry over moderate heat, adding sprinkles of water when necessary, for 3–5 minutes or until the *ghee* or oil separates from the sauce and the texture is smooth and even.

5. Add the chickpeas and ¼ cup (60 ml) of the saved cooking liquid. Reduce the heat to low, cover and gently simmer for about 10 minutes, stirring occasionally. If necessary, add small quantities of the cooking water to keep the mixture from sticking to the saucepan.

6. Remove from the heat and add the salt, the remaining *ghee* or oil and the remaining minced herb. Garnish each portion with a twist of lemon or lime.

Vegetables

The diversity of vegetables available to American cooks today is exhilarating. All across the country, a growing number of farms sell fresh produce, often organic, at roadside stands and farmers' markets. Even big-city shoppers can ferret out good local produce, though they may have to look around a bit; in New York City, outdoor greenmarkets offer variety and unusual specialties. More and more corner greengroceries and supermarkets offer European, Middle Eastern and Asian produce, while ethnic outlets tempt us with the exotic—bottle gourds and bitter melons, Italian and Japanese eggplants, water chestnuts and colocasia, Indian *mooli* and lotus root. This vegetarian cornucopia, along with other influences—travel abroad, interest in health and nutrition, and the inspiration provided by some outstanding restaurants—has sent cooks leafing through international cookbooks for new ideas. But although the French, Middle Easterners, Chinese and Japanese have an undeniable talent for vegetable cookery, the cradle of the art is India, the land of Lord Krishna's cuisine.

In a country housing over 500 million vegetarians—over 80 percent of the population—it is no wonder that India produces one of the largest assortments of vegetables, fruits and legumes in the world. Its *sabji* bazaars, or vegetable markets, are filled with freshly picked vegetables. Before dawn, workers unload bullock carts and arrange dew-covered squash, earth-speckled potatoes and washed spinach leaves in neat mounds for inspection. As in the open-air markets of Europe, early shoppers wander about, compare, poke here and there, and haggle for a good buy. The *subjiwalla* (greengrocer), sitting cross-legged behind a scale, calls out his wares. The prices vary according to quality and availability.

By and large, India's vegetarians embrace a diet similar to their ancient ancestors, and especially in the villages, cooks reflect regional standards and tradition. City vegetarians are far more creative, influenced by new trends, ingredients, and the current worldwide fascination for "light" and "healthy" cuisine. But it must be brought out that the major distinction between India's vegetarian cooks and others of fine stature is a reverence for God and His creation. A devotional attitude in the kitchen is as essential as organization. In particular, Vaishnavas—worshippers of Lord Krishna—take ultimate care in their cooking. Whether shopping, gardening or planning a menu, whether designing a clay stove or a sleek marble kitchen, Vaishnavas are veritable conductors of a culinary symphony. Because they cook as an offering to the Lord, their standard of cleanliness is not limited to the external: it includes speech, thought and action. It is not surprising to find out that this approach in the kitchen is not limited to cooking, but extends to all aspects of Vaishnava life.

While some of the recipes in this chapter are centuries old, others are contemporary variations of classic dishes. Hopefully it will put to rest the lingering myth that Indian vegetarian cuisine means overcooked, tongue-blistering concoctions from a poverty-stricken land. Although some of the ingredients may be unfamiliar to you, the recipes have been composed to preserve authenticity—a *shukta* must be bitter; a *charchari*, charred; fried plantain wafers, crispy—and they do not shock the palate. The recipes are arranged according to technique or texture. Aside from exploring numerous wet and dry cooking methods, they include diverse flavors—sweet, bitter, pungent, sour, and astringent. You can use them to add variety to a Western menu, or cook a surprisingly diversified three-course Vedic vegetable dinner, perhaps combining a purée, a stuffed vegetable and a sautéed vegetable.

Vedic purists do not believe in reheating vegetables, feeling that, like flat breads, they should be cooked to perfection and served immediately. This is especially true for stir-fried dishes cooked over moderately high heat. Some vegetable stews hold well over gentle heat, while others are served at room temperature or slightly chilled. Keep in mind that reheating breaks down vegetable fiber and increases nutrient loss—likewise for vegetables prepared for cooking long before use, or kept under prolonged refrigeration or light. If you must cook vegetables in advance, cool to room temperature, seal well and immediately refrigerate. Moist vegetables reheat with minimal changes in a double boiler or a steamer.

Heat and timing are important in vegetable cooking, but personal panache assuredly depends on spices, herbs and seasonings, over 50 of which are mentioned in this chapter. You will quickly notice the absence of onions, garlic, leeks, shallots and mushrooms, both as foods and as seasonings. Vedic vegetarians avoid them because they are considered *rajasic*, causing the same bodily distress as excessively salty or pungent dishes. Instead, you will find exotic flavor from ingredients such as fresh ginger root, coriander leaves, coconut milk, palm sugar, lime juice and hot chilies. From New Orleans cajun to Bombay Marawadi, heat belt cuisines invariably include chilies, not only for flavor, but to induce perspiration and relief from tropic temperatures. There is a considerable flavor and heat range in fresh green chilies, from smoky and sweet to mild or searing. I have used easy-to-seed jalapeños in recipe testing because they keep well, are medium-hot and are widely available. If you use smaller, lighter-green serranos, unseeded, expect the hotness to increase considerably, and use much less.

Look for young ginger root, also known as green ginger; it should have a thin, glossy, gossamer skin that can easily be scraped off. The roots are virtually fiberless and can be puréed or finely shredded. Old ginger is more pungent, with tough fibers, and the thick skin must be peeled off with a knife. Fresh coriander, also known as cilantro or Chinese parsley, is one of the world's most used herbs. Its indescribable flavor will grow on you. It is rich in vitamin C and worth the effort to locate. Though it can be used interchangeably with fresh parsley, it has a taste of its own and lends authenticity especially to Gujarati and Maharastrian dishes.

Far from stamping your meals with repetitive flavors, these wonderful flavor enhancers will bring out subordinate tastes from aromatics like cumin, turmeric, coriander, curry leaves, cardamom and asafetida. Because of the current popularity of Mexican, Chinese and Asian food, these ingredients are easy to find.

Fresh vegetables, properly cooked, are the basis of good eating anywhere in the world. They are bursting with energy-giving vitamins, minerals and carbohydrates. Wilted produce is never a bargain, even from your own garden. Vegetables start losing flavor and nutrients from the moment they are picked, so the sooner they are cooked, the more you are assured of tenderness, taste and nutrition.

Use most produce immediately or whisk it into storage. Sturdy tubers and winter squash will do well in paper bags in a cool, dark cupboard, but greens should be sealed in plastic and refrigerated. On the whole, small, slightly underripe produce is more

succulent than oversized giants. The recipes in this chapter offer information on shopping, storage and preparation. Unripe mango or papaya is used while still very firm and
should be kept in paper bags and refrigerated until use.

The peak season for any vegetable varies considerably according to the region,
which makes the menu suggestions tentative. Everything ultimately depends upon the
availability of seasonal produce. The following chart may help you in planning varied
and balanced menus. Select a variety of vegetables from different groupings for color,
texture and taste.

BEAN PODS AND SEEDS:

broad beans	corn
green or snap beans	okra
(stringbeans)	green peas
wax beans	snow peas
butter beans	sprouts
lima beans	

CABBAGE FAMILY:

broccoli	cauliflower
green cabbage	kohlrabi
red cabbage	Brussel sprouts
Savoy cabbage	

LEAFY GREENS AND STALKS:

asparagus	collard greens
celery	mustard greens
fennel	kale
Swiss chard	sorrel
(red or green)	spinach
Belgian endive	vine leaves
beet greens	watercress

SUMMER SQUASH:

zucchini, green or yellow
crooknecks
pattypan (cymling)
cocozelle
cucumber

VEGETABLE FRUITS:

tomatoes: salad, plum, baby, green
bell peppers: red, yellow, green
stuffing peppers: banana, California,
    Anaheim
eggplants: medium or large
Japanese or baby eggplants: narrow or
    small

ROOTS AND TUBERS:

beets
carrots
celeraic
Jerusalem artichokes
parsnips
potatoes: all-purpose (round or long
    white)
        mature baking (Russet or Idaho)
        boiling (round red or white)
        baby new potatoes
yams
sweet potatoes
turnips

WINTER SQUASH:

acorn
Hubbard
butternut
buttercup or Turban
pumpkin
spaghetti

SPECIALTY SELECTIONS:

bittermelon or bittergourd (*karela*)
bottlegourd (*louki*)
sponge gourd (*toray*)
round gourd or squash melon (*tinda*)
green papaya or paw paw
jicama
plaintain
colocasia (*arbi*)
horseradish root
lotus root (*bhain*)
white cooking radish (*mooli* or *daikon*)
water chestnuts (*singhara*)
chayote or vegetable pear

THREE METHODS OF COOKING VEGETABLES

VEGETABLE BASICS: People often ask me how I became involved in Vedic cooking. My first exposure to it was a luncheon hosted by Srila Prabhupada in 1966, an experience that unlocked a floodgate of questions in my mind. By early 1967 I was Srila Prabhupada's fortunate student, attending his small cooking classes every day for three months. As apprentices, his students were exposed to the basics: how to shop, organize, prepare ingredients, measure, use a knife and our hands, clean up and, ultimately, cook. Though I came from a family of serious cooks, some French-trained, this period was the most formative and thrilling of my life.

Our study of vegetable cooking began with the effects of seasoning and cooking methods on texture and taste. Using the world's best-known vegetable—the potato—we spent weeks exploring three basic methods of cooking, learning how to control the taste and appearance of a dish without diminishing its nutritive value. If you are new to Vedic cooking, you might like to start by exploring these three basic methods. When you are conversant with the variables, you can confidently and pleasurably improvise with seasonal fresh produce. Let's take a quick look at these three methods.

METHOD ONE—Sautéed and Braised Dry Vegetables (cooked without water): Small pieces of uniformly cut-up vegetables—dice, julienne, or diagonal slices—are briskly sautéed in seasoned *ghee* or oil in an open pan over brisk heat until they are partially cooked and slightly browned. As they cook they are turned frequently with a spoon, or the pan is shaken, to keep them from browning unevenly or sticking.

From here on, there are two options. The first, for vegetables with a substantial amount of moisture, is to reduce the heat slightly and stir-fry the vegetables until tender-crisp and lightly browned. The second is to cover the pan tightly, reduce the heat to low and cook the vegetables in their own juices.

If you want a crust on the cooked vegetables, raise the heat and quickly brown them, tossing gently. During this final stage you can drizzle in *ghee* or oil to prevent sticking.

Try this method with potatoes, yams, peas, snow peas, asparagus, okra, eggplants, cabbage, new carrots, green beans, bell peppers and spinach.

METHOD TWO—Sautéed and Braised Vegetables (cooked in broth): The vegetables are briskly sautéed and then simmered in an aromatic broth until tender. This method combines several procedures, with options as to the finished texture. The most engaging aspects of this method are the timing and heat control: it is a challenge to cook the vegetables just to the point of tenderness without overcooking. Vegetables cut into medium-sized chunks or cubes are sautéed in seasoned *ghee* or a mixture of oil and butter until partially cooked and slightly browned. At this point the liquid is added, the heat is reduced to low, the pan is covered and the vegetables are simmered to tenderness.

Four finished textures are possible: a vegetable stew, vegetables in a sauce, moist vegetables in a concentrated glaze, or crusty, dry vegetables. If all of the broth is to be cooked off, I find a nonstick pan helpful for putting a crust on the dry vegetables. Small quantities of *ghee* or butter help keep them from sticking to the pan while they become tender. The right heat, timing and pan size all play important parts in controlling the texture of the finished dish. Vegetables suitable for this method include cauliflower, carrots, eggplants, potatoes, winter and summer squash, yams, potatoes, peas, green beans, Swiss chard, broad beans, lima beans, chayote, bottle gourd and Jerusalem artichoke.

METHOD THREE—Precooked Vegetables in Seasoned *Ghee*, Sauce or Broth: In the first two methods, the vegetables are sautéed before being cooked to tenderness. In this method, the vegetables are first cooked to near tenderness, then pan-fried or sautéed in seasonings. Depending on the vegetable and the precooking technique, it can be cooked either whole or cut up, peeled or unpeeled, by boiling, steaming, pressure cooking, oven-baking, coal-baking, deep-frying or shallow-frying. If it has been cooked whole—say, by steaming or baking—it is then cut into uniform pieces and quickly browned with seasonings in *ghee* or a blend of oil and butter. It can be served dry or further finished in a prepared sauce, or it can be added to a light broth. In contrast to Methods One and Two, this method is broad enough to encompass almost any vegetable.

EXAMPLES OF USING THE THREE METHODS

To get a clearer idea of the three methods, let's carry potatoes through the steps. Depending on the spices on your shelves, pick one of the three sample seasoning combinations below and try each method with the same ingredients. You will notice the vast differences created by varying heat, timing and vegetable shape. With variations in seasoning, too, it is easy to see how you can create innumerable dishes from any vegetable.

Sometimes the *chaunk*, or fried spice seasoning, is added to the main ingredients; other times, the main ingredients are added to the *chaunk*. In either case, the seasoning greatly affects the flavor. The *chaunk*'s strength is determined by the heat and how long it is fried: the faster or longer you cook it, the more potent the flavor. Watch the color as it cooks; lightly browned seasonings impart mild flavor, dark brown bracing flavor and black a pungent, extreme taste. It is strictly a matter of personal preference.

Seasoning 1:

3 medium-sized all-purpose potatoes (about 1 pound/455 g)
3 tablespoons (45 ml) *ghee* or peanut oil
½–2 dried red chilies, broken into bits
1 teaspoon (5 ml) cumin seeds
½ teaspoon (2 ml) turmeric
2–4 tablespoons (30-60 ml) water or stock for Method One;
 1–2½ cups (240–600 ml) for Methods Two and Three
1 teaspoon (5 ml) salt
2 tablespoons (30 ml) chopped fresh coriander or minced parsley

Seasoning 2:

3 medium-sized all-purpose potatoes (about 1 pound/455 g)
3 tablespoons (45 ml) *ghee* or sesame oil
½ tablespoon (7 ml) minced green chilies (or as desired)
l teaspoon (5 ml) cumin seeds
½ tablespoon (7 ml) scraped, finedly shredded or minced fresh ginger root
½ teaspoon (2 ml) turmeric
½ tablespoon (7 ml) ground coriander
2–4 tablespoons (30–60 ml) water for Method One;
 1–2½ cups (240–600 ml) for Methods Two and Three
1 teaspoon (5 ml) salt
2 tablespoons (30 ml) chopped fresh coriander or minced parsley

Seasoning 3:

3 medium-sized all-purpose potatoes (about 1 pound/455 g)
3 tablespoons (45 ml) *ghee* or a mixture of oil and unsalted butter
½ tablespoon (7 ml) minced green chilies (or as desired)
1 teaspoon (5 ml) cumin seeds
½ teaspoon (2 ml) black mustard seeds
½ tablespoon (7 ml) scraped, finely shredded or minced fresh ginger root
¼ teaspoon (1 ml) yellow asafetida powder (*hing*)*
½ teaspoon (2 ml) turmeric
½ tablespoon (7 ml) ground coriander
2–4 tablespoons (30–60 ml) water or stock for Method One;
 1–2½ cups (240–600 ml) for Methods Two and Three
1 teaspoon (5 ml) salt
½ teaspoon (2 ml) *garam masala*
2 tablespoons (30 ml) chopped fresh coriander or minced parsley

 *This amount applies only to yellow Cobra brand. Reduce any other asafetida by three-fourths.

Example of Method One
DRY POTATOES (COOKED WITHOUT WATER)

1. Cut the potatoes into ½-inch (1.5 cm) dice. Heat the *ghee* or oil in a heavy non-stick frying pan over moderate heat. When it is hot but not smoking, add the red or green chilies, whole spice seeds (cumin and perhaps black mustard seeds), ginger root and asafetida. Fry until the cumin seeds darken a few shades or the mustard seeds turn gray and pop. If you are using asafetida, add it, and in a few seconds stir in the potatoes. Sauté until they are partially cooked and slightly browned.

2. Reduce the heat to low and sprinkle in the ground spices (turmeric and perhaps coriander). Toss to mix. At this point you can sprinkle in 2–4 tablespoons (30–60 ml) of water or stock. Cover and cook, stirring once or twice, for about 15 minutes or until the potatoes are fork-tender. Uncover and add the salt, *garam masala*, if desired, and fresh herb. Toss to mix, and serve.

Example of Method Two
SUCCULENT BRAISED POTATOES (COOKED IN STOCK)

1. Cut the potatoes into 1-inch (2.5 cm) cubes. Heat 2½ tablespoons (37 ml) of *ghee* or selected alternative in a large heavy nonstick saucepan over moderately high heat. When it is hot but not smoking, drop in the green or red chilies, whole spice seeds— cumin and possibly black mustard seeds—and ginger root. Fry until the cumin seeds darken a few shades or the mustard seeds turn gray and pop. Sprinkle in the asafetida, and a few seconds later stir in the potatoes. Sauté until the cubes are lightly browned.

2. Sprinkle in the ground spices (turmeric and coriander if you are using them). Follow with half of the fresh herbs and 1¼ cups (300 ml) of water or stock. Partially cover, reduce the heat to low and gently cook until the potato cubes are just tender and the liquid has nearly cooked off. You will have to adjust the heat to coordinate these factors. When the potatoes are nearly dry, uncover, add the remaining ½ tablespoon (7 ml) of *ghee* or oil and raise the heat. Shake the pan to keep the potatoes from sticking to the bottom, and cook until a light crust forms. Complete the dish with salt, the remaining herbs and *garam masala* if you are using them.

Example of Method Three
BAKED POTATOES SAUTEÉD IN SEASONINGS (USING NO LIQUID)

1. Bake the potatoes until just tender, peel them, and cut into ¾-inch (2 cm) cubes.
2. Heat the *ghee* or oil in a large heavy frying pan over moderate heat. When it is

hot but not smoking, add the green or red chilies and whole spice seeds (cumin and possibly black mustard seeds) and ginger root. Fry the seasoning until the cumin seeds darken a few shades or the mustard seeds turn gray and pop. Sprinkle in the asafetida, if desired, and in seconds stir in the potatoes. Sprinkle with the ground spices (turmeric and perhaps coriander), and shake the pan or gently toss with a spatula until the potatoes brown slightly. Complete the dish with salt, *garam masala*, if desired, and fresh herb. Stir once before serving.

DRY-TEXTURED VEGETABLES

The vegetable dishes in this section are some of the most frequently prepared in India. In the north and west, they would be served with hot flat breads; in the east and south, with hot rice. These dishes are neither pan-fried nor braised nor sautéed, but prepared by a combination of techniques that yield dry-textured vegetables. Added liquids are reduced during the cooking and become an integral part of the finished dish.

Ghee is considered the most flavorful cooking medium in most regions, though I have indicated when mustard, sesame, peanut or coconut oil is a regional alternative. Butter cannot be used on its own for stir-fried recipes as it burns over even moderate heat. If you do not have *ghee* or the suggested oil in your kitchen, use a mixture of butter and light vegetable oil—sunflower, safflower, or corn.

Glazed Carrots

GAJAR SABJI

In India, carrots are more often used raw in salads, as crisp pickle spears or in sweet *halvas* than as a cooked vegetable. They are brilliant orange-red roots, harvested both young and sweet or oversized as giants. Most Americans have three choices: baby carrots 2–3 inches (5–7.5 cm) long, medium-sized carrots and large tapered carrots with a fibrous core. You can use any of them with slightly different preparation. Finger-thick babies require little preparation: simply trim the ends and slice in half lengthwise. To prepare medium-sized carrots, peel and trim the ends and slice on the diagonal about ½ inch (1.5 cm) thick. When dealing with mature carrots, peel, trim the ends, slice in half lengthwise and remove the core (insert a small pointed knife beneath the core at the thick end of the carrot and pry the core free). Cut the hollow carrots on the diagonal into ½-inch (1.5 cm) lengths.

I first had this dish while traveling through the Punjab. It was prepared in an alkaline Himalayan sparkling water, though still water with a lemon or apple juice yields an equally flavorful cardamom glaze.

Preparation time (after assembling ingredients): 10 minutes
Cooking time: 20–40 minutes Serves: 4 or 5

30 baby carrots, about 1 pound (455 g), 6–8
    medium-sized or 4–5 large, cut as described above
3 tablespoons (45 ml) *ghee* or unsalted butter
2 tablespoons (30 ml) brown sugar or maple syrup
¼ teaspoon (1 ml) turmeric
½ teaspoon (2 ml) coarsely crushed cardamom seeds
½ teaspoon (2 ml) ground coriander
2 tablespoons (30 ml) orange or apple juice
⅔ cup (160 ml) still or sparkling mineral water
½ teaspoon (2 ml) salt
⅛ teaspoon (0.5 ml) freshly ground pepper
    or cayenne pepper
2 tablespoons (30 ml) coarsely chopped fresh coriander
    or minced fresh parsley
1 teaspoon (5 ml) fresh lime or lemon juice
¼ teaspoon (1 ml) freshly grated nutmeg

1. Place the carrots in a single layer in a roomy skillet or sauté pan. Add 2 tablespoons (30 ml) of *ghee* or butter and the sweetener, turmeric, cardamom seeds, ground coriander, orange or apple juice, water and salt. Bring to a boil, cover and reduce the heat to low. Simmer young carrots for as little as 20 minutes, older ones for up to 40 minutes.

2. When almost all of the water has evaporated, uncover and rapidly boil off the remainder. Shake the pan to keep the carrots from sticking. When the carrots are coated with a shiny glaze, remove the pan from the heat and add the remaining 1 tablespoon (15 ml) of *ghee* or butter and the pepper and fresh herb. Shake the pan to mix the ingredients. Just before serving, toss with lime or lemon juice and nutmeg.

Spicy Cauliflower with Braised Tomato
GOBHI TAMATAR SABJI

Snowy cauliflower and ripe tomatoes marry their colors and flavors over gentle heat until the cauliflower is butter-soft and the tomatoes are reduced to a seasoned glaze. The only liquid is the juice from the tomatoes, so the dish must be braised slowly. The result is a dry-textured, succulent everyday dish that can be featured on any lunch or dinner menu.

Preparation time (after assembling ingredients): 10 minutes
Cooking time: 25–30 minutes
Serves: 4 or 5

3–4 tablespoons (45–60 ml) *ghee* or vegetable oil
1-inch (2.5 cm) piece of fresh ginger root,
    scraped and cut into thin julienne
1–2 green jalapeño chilies, cored, seeded and slivered
½ teaspoon (2 ml) black mustard seeds
1 teaspoon (5 ml) cumin seeds
1 large cauliflower (about 3 pounds/1.5 kg), trimmed, cored
    and cut into flowerets 2 x 1 x ½ inches (5 x 2.5 x 1.5 cm)
1 tablespoon (15 ml) ground coriander
½ teaspoon (2 ml) turmeric
1 teaspoon (5 ml) salt
3 medium-sized tomatoes, each peeled and cut into eighths (about 1 pound/455 g)
1 teaspoon (5 ml) *garam masala*
3 tablespoons (45 ml) coarsely chopped fresh coriander or minced parsley
butter (optional)

1. Heat the *ghee* or oil in a large nonstick casserole or sauté pan over moderate to moderately high heat. When it is hot but not smoking, drop in the ginger, chilies, mustard and cumin seeds. Fry until the mustard seeds pop and turn gray and the cumin seeds turn brown. Stir in the cauliflower, ground coriander, turmeric and salt. Stir-fry until the flowerettes are slightly browned, then stir in the tomatoes. Cover and reduce the heat to low. Cook for 15–20 minutes, shaking the pan occasionally to keep the vegetables from sticking, or until the cauliflower stalks are just tender.

2. Uncover, raise the heat and stir-fry to evaporate all the liquid. Just before serving, sprinkle with the *garam masala*, fresh herb, and add a knob of butter, if desired.

Sautéed Cauliflower and Green Peas
GOBHI HARI MATAR SABJI

In all cauliflower dishes, the quality of the vegetable is paramount. Look for crisp, tightly packed white flowerets and bright green leaves. It is important to cut the flowerets into uniform pieces, but the success of the dish really lies in slow, gentle braising; the cauliflower cooks in its own juice and seasonings until the flowerets are butter-soft and the stems tender-crisp. Garden-fresh peas are in a class of their own, but good-quality frozen baby peas are sometimes better than "fresh" peas from the store, and certainly much less work.

This type of dry cauliflower dish is popular for a simple lunch throughout Uttar Pradesh.

Preparation time (after assembling ingredients): 10 minutes
Cooking time: 25–30 minutes
Serves: 4 or 5

4 tablespoons (60 ml) *ghee* or vegetable oil
½ tablespoon (7 ml) scraped, finely shredded or
    minced fresh ginger root
1¼ teaspoons (6 ml) cumin seeds
8–10 curry leaves or 1 bay leaf
1 large cauliflower (about 3 pounds/1.5 kg), trimmed, cored
    and cut into flowerets 1½ x 1 x ½ inches (4 x 2.5 x 1.5 cm)
½ teaspoon (2 ml) turmeric
¼ teaspoon (1 ml) paprika or cayenne pepper
3 tablespoons (45 ml) chopped fresh coriander, parsley or chervil
1 cup (240 ml) fresh peas (about 1 pound/455 g in pods) or frozen baby peas, defrosted
2–4 tablespoons (30–60 ml) water
l teaspoon (5 ml) salt
⅓ cup (80 ml) plain yogurt, sour cream or cream
Brazil nut curls or parsley sprigs for garnish (optional)

1. In a heavy 5-quart/liter nonstick saucepan, heat the *ghee* or oil over moderately high heat until it is hot but not smoking. Fry the cumin seeds until they brown, then drop in the curry leaves or bay leaf, and in a few seconds stir in the cauliflower. Sprinkle with turmeric, paprika or cayenne and half of the fresh herb. Stir-fry until the cauliflower is lightly browned. Add the fresh peas and 2–4 tablespoons (30–60 ml) of water, cover and reduce the heat to low. Stirring occasionally, cook for 15–20 minutes or until the cauliflower is tender. If you are using frozen peas, drain well and add for the last 3–4 minutes of cooking.

2. Before serving, mix in the salt, remaining herb and yogurt, sour cream or cream. If desired, garnish each serving with Brazil nut curls or parsley sprigs.

Curried Cauliflower and Potatoes
GOBHI ALOO SABJI

Potato spears and cauliflower flowerets are browned in spices over strong heat to bring out their rich, deep flavors and are then gently cooked to tenderness with tomatoes. Neither dry nor wet, this dish has a succulent, moist texture that is somewhere in between. You can vary the flavor with tomatoes, using green, Italian plum or ripe reds.

Preparation time (after assembling ingredients): 5 minutes
Cooking time: 30 minutes
Serves: 5 or 6

2 hot green chilies, stemmed, seeded and cut lengthwise into long slivers (or as desired)
½-inch (1.5 cm) piece of scraped fresh ginger root, cut into thin julienne
1 teaspoon (5 ml) cumin seeds
½ teaspoon (2 ml) black mustard seeds
4 tablespoons (60 ml) *ghee* or a mixture of vegetable oil and unsalted butter
3 medium-sized potatoes (about 1 pound/455 g), peeled and cut
    into spears 2½ x ½ x ½ inches (6.5 x 1.5 x 1.5 cm) long
1 medium-sized cauliflower (about 2 pounds/1 kg), trimmed, cored
    and cut into flowerets 2½ x ½ x ½ inches (6.5 x 1.5 x 1.5 cm) long
2 medium-sized red or green tomatoes (about ½ pound/230 g), quartered
½ teaspoon (2 ml) turmeric
2 teaspoons (10 ml) ground coriander
½ teaspoon (2 ml) *garam masala*
1 teaspoon (5 ml) *jaggery* or brown sugar
1¼ teaspoons (6 ml) salt
3 tablespoons (45 ml) coarsely chopped fresh coriander or minced parsley
lime or lemon wedges (optional)

1. Combine the chilies, ginger, cumin seeds and mustard seeds in a small bowl. Heat the *ghee* or oil-butter mixture in a large nonstick saucepan over moderately high heat. When it is hot but not smoking, pour in the combined seasonings and fry until the mustard seeds turn gray, sputter and pop. Drop in the potatoes and cauliflower and stir-fry for 4–5 minutes or until the vegetables pick up a few brown spots.

2. Add the tomatoes, turmeric, coriander, *garam masala*, sweetener, salt and half of the fresh herb. Stir well, cover and gently cook over low heat, stirring occasionally, for 15–20 minutes or until the vegetables are tender. You may want to sprinkle in a few tablespoons (45 ml) of water if the vegetables stick to the bottom of the pan, but stir gently to avoid mashing or breaking them. Serve with the remaining fresh herb and garnish with lemon or lime wedges, if desired.

Crispy Diced Eggplant with Bitter *Neem* Leaves
NEEM BAIGAN

The ingredients for this dish are mentioned in the *Chaitanya Charitamrita*, a fifteenth-century Bengali text describing the pastimes and activities of Sri Chaitanya Mahaprabhu. The author describes a feast prepared in honor of the great saint: "Among the various vegetables offered were newly-grown leaves of *nimba* (*neem*) trees fried with eggplant."

Bitter -tasting vegetable dishes are popular in Bengal. They are known to stimulate a failing appetite and pleasantly contrast with other tastes. I suggest beginning with only a hint of this flavoring agent, enough to enliven and heighten the vegetable. Once overdone, nothing can remedy bitter seasonings. Bitter *neem* leaves (in English, margosa) are rarely, if ever, available at Indian grocery stores. A substitute is dry-roasted fenugreek seeds. Bengalis prefer to cook this dish in mustard oil, but you can use the oil of your choice. Serve the dish in portions of 2–3 tablespoons (30–45 ml) to complement a full lunch or dinner menu.

Preparation time (after assembling ingredients): 15 minutes
Cooking time: 10 minutes
Makes: 5 or 6 small servings

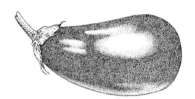

1 medium-sized eggplant (1¼ pounds/570 g)
½ tablespoon (7 ml) salt
1 teaspoon (5 ml) tumeric
¼ cup (120 ml) *ghee*, mustard oil or vegetable oil
¼-½ teaspoon (1-2 ml) powdered bitter *neem* leaves or
¼-1 teaspoon (2-5 ml) powdered roasted fenugreek seeds

1. Dice the eggplant and transfer to a bowl. Sprinkle with 1 teaspoon (5ml) salt and the turmeric, toss and set aside for 15 minutes. Toss again, then remove the eggplant with a slotted spoon and pat dry with paper towels.

2. In a frying pan, heat the *ghee* or oil over moderately high heat until it is hot but not smoking. (If you use mustard oil, let it smoke for 5 seconds before adding the eggplant. This makes the pungent oil docile.) Add the eggplant and stir–fry until browned and crisp. In the last minute of cooking, add the *neem* or fenugreek and the remaining salt. Toss well, drain in a strainer or on paper towels, and serve hot with a sprinkle of lemon or lime juice.

Okra Supreme
BHINDI SABJI

For many cooks okra is an unknown vegetable. If they have ever eaten it, it may have been in the American South as part of a gumbo or stew, or deep-fried in a corn batter. Few, however, would ever buy it and try to serve it to family or guests. Yet this stir-fried okra is easy to make, and so delicious that it will surprise even the reluctant. Okra is a summer vegetable, at its best in June or July, but you may find it as early as April and as late as September. The pods should be small—3–4 inches (7.5–10 cm) long—and the pointed end will snap off if fresh; when the pods are old, the ends will only bend. The cut pods release a glutinous sap, so the rinsed okra must be dried thoroughly on paper towels before it is cut, to prevent excessive stickiness. Since this is a pan-fried vegetable, cooked without water, a nonstick frying pan is ideal, using a minimal amount of oil to yield the lightly browned vegetable. Serve it on almost any Vedic lunch or dinner menu.

Preparation time (after assembling ingredients): 15 minutes
Cooking time: 25 minutes
Serves: 4

1 pound (455 g) fresh okra
3–4 tablespoons (45–60 ml) *ghee* or peanut oil
1½ tablespoons (22 ml) ground coriander
½ teaspoon (2 ml) ground cumin
¼ teaspoon (1 ml) paprika or cayenne pepper
½ teaspoon (2 ml) *garam masala*
½ teaspoon (2 ml) turmeric
1 teaspoon (5 ml) salt

1. Wash the okra and dry *thoroughly* on paper towels. (If it is a warm day, air-dry in the sun.) Trim off the tip and stem, and slice into rounds ⅓ inch (1 cm) thick.
2. In a large, heavy frying pan, preferably nonstick, heat the *ghee* or oil over moderately high heat. When it is hot but not smoking, add the okra in a single layer and reduce the heat to moderate. Cook for about 20 minutes, stirring occasionally to brown the okra evenly. Toward the end, add the ground spices, raise the heat to moderately high and, stirring steadily, fry until golden brown and fully cooked. Remove the pan from the heat, sprinkle with salt, toss to coat the okra evenly, and let it sit, covered, for 1 minute before serving.

Spicy Okra with Coconut
MASALA BHINDI SABJI

Here is another easy and delicious okra dish, pan-fried with whole spices and grated coconut. As the okra browns lightly, the seasoned coconut forms a flavorsome crust. If you do not have fresh or frozen grated coconut on hand, substitute ground almonds—equally delicious. Keep in mind that okra releases a glutinous sap when cut and sweats when salted, so dry it thoroughly and salt after cooking. You can serve this South Indian dish with practically anything.

Preparation time (after assembling ingredients): 15 minutes
Cooking time: 20–25 minutes
Serves: 4

1 pound (455 g) okra, preferably small
    (3–4 inches/7.5–10 cm long)
4 tablespoons (60 ml) *ghee* or sesame oil
1 teaspoon (5 ml) black mustard seeds
1 teaspoon (5 ml) slightly crushed cumin seeds
¼ teaspoon (1 ml) yellow asafetida powder (*hing*)*
½ teaspoon (2 ml) turmeric
¼ teaspoon (1 ml) cayenne pepper or paprika
⅓ cup (35 g) grated fresh coconut or frozen coconut (55 g), defrosted,
    or ½ cup (50 g) ground almonds
1 teaspoon (5 ml) salt

*This amount applies only to yellow Cobra brand. Reduce any other asafetida by three-fourths.

1. Wash the okra and dry *thoroughly* on paper towels. (If it is a warm day, air-dry in the sun.) Trim off the tips and stems and slice into rounds ¼ inch (6 mm) thick.
2. Heat the *ghee* or oil in a 10–12-inch (25–30 cm) nonstick frying pan over moderately high heat. When it is hot but not smoking, add the black mustard seeds and cumin seeds and fry until the mustard seeds turn gray and sputter and pop. Drop in the asafetida and immediately follow with the okra. Spread the okra into a single layer and reduce the heat to moderate. Stir in the turmeric, cayenne or paprika and coconut or almonds and cook for about 20 minutes, stirring occasionally to brown the okra evenly. You may want to add sprinkles of water if the okra dries out too much.
3. When the okra is golden brown and crusty, remove the pan from the heat, add the salt and cover for 1 minute before serving.

White Radish with Chopped Radish Greens
MOOLI SABJI

This typically North Indian radish dish is predominantly seasoned with whole cumin, corian-der and *ajwain* seeds, with a splash of lime juice and sweetener. In Kashmir the likely oil would be mustard; in the Punjab, peanut oil. The distinct appeal of the dish depends on the type of radish you use, as the varieties grown range enormously in pungency, color and size. Radishes, like beets, are at their best pulled fresh from the garden, so you will have to use fresh greens, which means a variety that is available locally—from pink-red round radishes to white icicles. If the commercially grown radishes where you shop come without the greens, fill in with a bunch of Swiss chard, spinach, mustard greens or kale. If you can find good *mooli* radish from Indian or Chinese greengrocers, by all means use it, the flavor is exceptional.

Preparation time (after assembling ingredients): 15 minutes
Cooking time: 15–20 minutes
Serves: 4

6 medium-sized white icicle radishes (about ½ pound/230 g),
    18–20 medium-sized round red radishes or
    4 medium-sized *mooli* or daikon radishes
½ pound (230 g) radish greens, Swiss chard, spinach, or kale,
    washed, trimmed and chopped
1 teaspoon (5 ml) cumin seeds
½ tablespoon (7 ml) coriander seeds
¼ teaspoon (1 ml) *ajwain* seeds
3 tablespoons (45 ml) *ghee*, mustard or peanut oil
½ teaspoon (2 ml) turmeric
¼ teaspoon (1 ml) cayenne pepper or paprika
2 teaspoons (10 ml) maple or brown sugar
1 teaspoon (5 ml) salt
2 teaspoons (10 ml) fresh lime or lemon juice

    1. Wash and trim the radishes, paring the long variety if necessary. Cut white radishes into ¼-inch (6 mm) dice; if using the round variety, thinly slice. Place the radishes in a steaming basket, lay the greens on top and steam for up to 15 minutes or until tender-crisp.
    2. Combine the cumin, coriander and *ajwain* seeds in a small bowl. In a large heavy-bottomed nonstick pan, heat the *ghee* or oil over high heat. When it is hot but not smoking, (unless you are using mustard oil which you let smoke for a few seconds) add the spice seeds and fry until they darken a few shades. Seconds later, add the radishes and greens. Stir in the turmeric, cayenne or paprika and sweetener. Reduce the heat to moderate and fry for 4–5 minutes. Remove from the heat, add the salt and lime or lemon juice and toss to mix well.

Spiced Green Beans
MASALA BARBATTI SABJI

Here is a simple yet delicious way to cook green beans Marawadi style. If you are a gardener, try growing Thompson and Morgan's thin, long asparagus beans; they most resemble the type used in India. Beans are sweet and tender only when harvested immature and full of sugar. They are best cooked within hours after being picked, as are peas. If you are supermarket shopping, try to get locally grown, vividly green beans that break with a snap. Some strains of beans still have strings down the side of the pods, which should be pulled off.

Preparation time (after assembling ingredients): 10 minutes
Cooking time: 15 minutes
Serves: 4 or 5

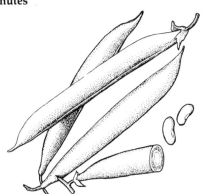

4 tablespoons (60 ml) *ghee* or a mixture of
    light oil and unsalted butter
2 teaspoons (10 ml) black mustard seeds
1 teaspoon (5 ml) cumin seeds
¼–½ teaspoon (1–2 ml) crushed dried chilies
1 pound (455 g) green beans, trimmed and
    cut into ¼-inch (6 mm) pieces
½ cup (120 ml) water
1 teaspoon (5 ml) ground coriander
1 teaspoons (5 ml) salt
1 teaspoon (5 ml) sugar

1. Heat the *ghee* or oil-butter mixture in a large heavy-bottomed frying pan over moderate heat. When it is hot but not smoking, add the mustard seeds, cumin seeds and chilies and fry until the cumin seeds darken and the mustard seeds pop and turn gray. Add the beans and stir-fry for 2–3 minutes. Pour in the water, cover tightly and cook for 10–12 minutes or until the beans are tender-crisp.

2. Uncover, raise the heat and add the remaining ingredients. Raise the heat and boil until the water evaporates and the beans sizzle in the seasoned *ghee* or oil.

Green Beans in Yogurt–Poppy Seed Sauce
BARBATTI TARI SABJI

These beans can be cooked quite some time before needed and the final cooking completed just before serving. They are warmed in a velvety yogurt sauce made rich with puréed white poppy seeds or cashews.

Preparation time (after assembling ingredients): 10 minutes
Cooking time: 5 minutes
Serves: 4 or 5

3 tablespoons (45 ml) white poppy seeds or chopped cashews
2 hot green chilies (or as desired)
½-inch (1.5 cm) piece of fresh ginger root,
   scraped and coarsely chopped
½ teaspoon (2 ml) cumin seeds
¼ cup (60 ml) coarsely chopped fresh coriander or parsley
¾ cup (180 ml) plain yogurt
1 pound (455 g) green beans, trimmed, cut into 3-inch
    (7.5 cm) pieces and steamed until tender- crisp
3 tablespoons (45 ml) *ghee* or unsalted butter
6 curry leaves, preferably fresh, or ½ cassia or bay leaf
1 teaspoon (5 ml) salt
¼ teaspoon (1 ml) freshly ground nutmeg

    1. Put the poppy seeds or cashews in a food processor or blender, cover and pulse until powdered. Add the chilies, ginger, cumin, half of the fresh herb and the yogurt. Process until creamy smooth, then combine with the green beans in a bowl and toss well.

    2. To assemble the dish, heat the *ghee* or butter in a large heavy-bottomed frying pan over moderate heat. Drop in the curry leaves or bay leaf and let sizzle for a few seconds. Pour in the beans and sauce, salt and nutmeg. Stir-fry until the sauce thickens, either slightly or until almost dry. Serve with the remaining herb, piping hot, at room temperature or chilled.

Green Beans with Coconut
BARBATTI NARIYAL SABJI

There are innumerable popular green bean and coconut variations in Hyderabad's Vaishnava kitchens, this one from the home of S.K. Sethi. The contrast of bright green beans against snow-white coconut speckled with black mustard seeds and reddish *urad dal* makes this an attractive yet simple dish. For extra protein, if you do not have *urad dal*, use 3 tablespoons (45 ml) of chopped peanuts. You can steam the beans ahead of time and assemble the dish just prior to serving.

Preparation time (after assembling ingredients): 5 minutes
Cooking time: 10 minutes
Serves: 4 or 5

1 tablespoon (15 ml) each *chana dal* and raw rice
2 minced seeded hot green chilies (or as desired)
3 tablespoons (45 ml) water
5 tablespoons (75 ml) *ghee* or sesame oil
1 tablespoon (15 ml) split *urad dal* or 3 tablespoons
    (45 ml) chopped peanuts or almonds
1 teaspoon (5 ml) black mustard seeds
8–10 curry leaves, if available
¼ teaspoon (1 ml) yellow asafetida powder (*hing*)*
1 pound (455 g) green beans, trimmed and cut into ¼-inch (6 mm)
    pieces and steamed until nearly tender
1 teaspoon (5 ml) salt
⅛ teaspoon (0.5 ml) freshly ground black pepper
1 cup (85 g) grated fresh or defrosted frozen coconut (140 g)
3 tablespoons (45 ml) chopped fresh dill, fennel or coriander

*This amount applies only to yellow Cobra brand. Reduce any other asafetida by three-fourths.

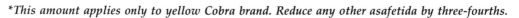

1. Grind the *dal* and rice in a spice mill until powdered. Transfer to a bowl and stir in the green chilies and water. Mix well. Heat the *ghee* or oil in a large heavy-bottomed nonstick frying pan over moderate heat. When it is hot but not smoking, add the *urad dal*, peanuts or almonds and fry for 15 seconds or until they begin to turn light brown. Follow with the mustard seeds and fry until they turn gray and pop. Drop in the curry leaves and asafetida and seconds later, pour in the *dal*-rice mixture. Cook until the mixture is dry, then follow with the green beans, salt and pepper. Sauté, shaking the pan, until the beans are heated through, adding the coconut and fresh herb at the last moment. Toss to mix.

Green Beans with Water Chestnuts
BARBATTI SINGHARA SABJI

The water chestnut is a floating water plant growing in lakes and ponds on several continents. The fruits are angular, with brown skins and a white, floury nut inside—refreshingly crisp and delicious. There are several kinds. *Singhara* nuts, grown in the lakes of Kashmir, are eaten as snacks or blanched, sliced, dried and ground into flour. Chinese water chestnuts, or *pi-tsi*, are not really nuts, but tubers, deriving their name from their resemblance to the water chestnut. They are available in small cans, sliced or whole, in supermarkets. The South American tuber called jicama is a readily available fresh substitute for canned water chestnuts. Use whichever kind you can find easily. To prepare fresh water chestnuts, cut with a sharp knife from the crown to the base and peel away the soft, brownish casing. Blanch, slice and soak in water until used.

Preparation time (after assembling ingredients): 5 minutes
Cooking time: 10 minutes
Serves: 4–6

1 teaspoon (5 ml) black mustard seeds
3 tablespoons (45 ml) melted *ghee* or unsalted butter
1-inch (2.5 cm) piece of fresh ginger root, scraped
    and cut into thin julienne
1 pound (455 g) green beans, trimmed, cut into ½-inch
    (1.5 cm) lengths and steamed until tender-crisp
¼ teaspoon (1 ml) paprika or cayenne pepper
1 teaspoon (5 ml) ground coriander
12 water chestnuts, peeled and sliced; or
    1 small jicama, peeled, trimmed and
    cut into pieces about 1 inch (2.5 cm)
    square by ⅛ inch (3 mm) thick; or
    one 10-ounce (285 g) can of sliced
    water chestnuts, drained and rinsed
2 tablespoons (30 ml) fresh lime juice
1 teaspoon (5 ml) salt
2 tablespoons (30 ml) chopped fresh coriander, basil or parsley

Preheat a large heavy-bottomed frying pan over moderate heat. Drop in the mustard seeds, and when they begin to pop add the melted *ghee* or butter. Drop in the ginger, green beans, paprika or cayenne, ground coriander and water chestnuts or jicama, and sauté until the green beans and water chestnuts are heated through. Add the lime juice, salt and fresh herb at the last moment.

Cubed Potatoes with Fresh Fenugreek
KHATTE ALOO METHI

This everyday vegetable is popular throughout North and Central India. Earth-specked new potatoes—no bigger than marbles—and fresh fenugreek greens are sold in vegetable bazaars from Amritsar to Benares. New potato skins rub away easily during washing, and what little remains is paper thin and negligible. Fresh fenugreek greens vary from source to source—and no matter what the leaf size, be sure to trim off thick stems—they tend to toughen when cooked. The flavor from young leaves is pleasingly bitter, something like the nippy heat from sprouted mustard or cress, and are quite effortless to grow in a kitchen or windowsill herb garden. Fenugreek is usually available fresh at Indian groceries and is always available dried though the packages usually contain more stems than leaves. If you can't get the fresh greens, substitute spinach and add a pinch of powdered roasted fenugreek seeds for flavor. For variation, try the dish using different oils—*ghee*, mustard oil or peanut oil. All three are surprisingly different and tasty.

Preparation time (after assembling ingredients): 15 minutes
Cooking time: 15–20 minutes
Serves: 5 or 6

1½ pounds (685 g) medium-sized waxy red
    new potatoes or walnut-sized baby reds
5 tablespoons (75 ml) mustard oil,
    peanut oil or *ghee*
1 teaspoon (5 ml) cumin seeds
1 teaspoon (5 ml) black mustard seeds
1½ cups (360 ml) chopped fenugreek greens
    or leaf spinach, (washed and trimmed)
¼ teaspoon (1 ml) paprika or cayenne pepper
½ teaspoon (2 ml) turmeric
1 teaspoon (5 ml) salt
1 teaspoon (5 ml) *garam masala*
2 teaspoons (10 ml) lemon or lime juice

1. Wash the potatoes and boil them in their skins until they are just fork-tender. Do not overcook. Drain them and spread out to cool. Peel and cut into ¾-inch (2 cm) cubes.

2. Heat the oil or *ghee* in a heavy 12-inch (30 cm) nonstick frying pan. Let mustard oil reach the smoking point. Sauté the potatoes quickly until they begin to brown, then remove with a slotted spoon and set aside.

3. Add the cumin and mustard seeds to the hot oil and fry until the mustard seeds turn gray and sputter. Stir in the fenugreek greens or spinach, paprika or cayenne, turmeric and a sprinkle of water, cover and reduce the heat to moderately low. Cook for 8–10 minutes, then add the potatoes, salt and *garam masala*. Shake the pan or gently toss to mix, cover and cook until the potatoes are heated through. Sprinkle with lemon or lime juice before serving.

Baby Potatoes with Seasoned Tomato Sauce
ALOO TAMATAR SABJI

If you have a garden and can pull up really small marble-sized waxy-red potatoes, you have the perfect choice for this dish—the delicate skins almost float off during scrubbing. If you use larger new potatoes, red or white, cook them whole and slip off the skins when cool.

Preparation time (after assembling ingredients): 10 minutes
Cooking time: 15–20 minutes
Serves: 4 or 5

1½ pounds (685 g) waxy new potatoes, no
    more than 2 inches (5 cm) in diameter
3–4 whole cloves
6–8 whole black peppercorns
2 teaspoons (10 ml) coriander seeds
1 teaspoon (5 ml) cumin seeds
½ teaspoon (2 ml) fennel seeds
1-inch (2.5 cm) piece fresh ginger root,
    peeled and coarsely chopped
2–3 hot green chilies (or as desired)
3 tablespoons (45 ml) coarsely chopped
    fresh coriander leaves or parsley
2–3 tablespoons (30-60 ml) water
4 tablespoons (60 ml) *ghee*, or 2
    tablespoons (30 ml) each vegetable
    oil and melted unsalted butter
1 teaspoon (5 ml) black mustard seeds
6–8 curry leaves, preferably fresh
1 cup (240 ml) tomatoes, peeled, seeded and
    coarsely chopped (about ¾ pound/340 g)
scant ½ teaspoon (2 ml) turmeric
1 teaspoon (5 ml) *garam masala*
½ teaspoon (2 ml) *chat masala*
½ tablespoon (7 ml) salt

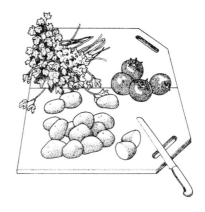

    1. Boil the potatoes in their skins just until fork tender. Cool and peel if necessary and cut into ½-inch (1.5 cm) pieces.
    2. Place the cloves, peppercorns, coriander seeds, cumin seeds and fennel seeds in a mortar or spice mill and grind to a powder. Transfer to a blender, add the ginger, chilies, 1 tablespoon (15 ml) of the fresh herb and the water, and blend until smooth.
    3. Heat the *ghee* or oil in a heavy 12-inch (30 cm) nonstick frying pan over moderately high heat. When it is hot but not smoking, add the black mustard seeds and fry until they pop and turn gray. (If you are using oil, add the butter now.) Drop in the curry leaves and in seconds follow with the tomatoes and turmeric. Reduce the heat and, stirring now and then, cook until the juices cook off and the *ghee* separates from the tomatoes. Add the potatoes, *garam masala*, *chat masala* and salt, gently stir, and cook, covered, until the potatoes are hot. (You may need to add sprinkles of water if you do not use a nonstick pan.) Sprinkle with the remaining fresh herb before serving.

Curried Potatoes with Eggplant
ALOO BAIGAN SABJI

This is an example of the third method of cooking vegetables described in the introduction to this chapter. Both vegetables are steamed until tender. The potatoes are briskly stir-fried in seasoned *ghee* and then coated, along with the eggplant, in a delicately spiced yogurt-coconut sauce. Besides having a lovely flavor, this dish is light because the eggplant is steamed rather than fried.

Preparation time (after assembling ingredients): 5 minutes
Cooking time: 15 minutes
Serves: 5 or 6

⅓ cup (80 ml) plain yogurt
½-inch (1.5 cm) piece of fresh ginger root, scraped and coarsely chopped
2 seeded hot green chilies, broken into bits (or as desired)
¼ cup (25 g) shredded fresh or dried coconut
½ teaspoon (2 ml) *garam masala*
4 tablespoons (60 ml) *ghee* or a mixture
    of vegetable oil and unsalted butter
1 teaspoon (5 ml) black mustard seeds
½ tablespoon (7 ml) cumin seeds
8–10 curry leaves, preferably fresh
¼ teaspoon (1 ml) yellow asafetida powder (*hing*)*
6 medium-sized boiling potatoes (about 2 pounds/1 kg), steamed
    until tender, peeled and cut into ¾-inch (2 cm) cubes
1 teaspoon (5 ml) turmeric
1 tablespoon (15 ml) ground coriander
1 small eggplant (8–10 ounces/230–285 g) cut into
    1-inch (2.5 cm) cubes and steamed until tender
1¼ teaspoons (6 ml) salt
3 tablespoons (45 ml) chopped fresh parsley or coriander
1 tablespoon (15 ml) fresh lemon juice

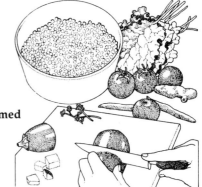

*This amount applies only to yellow Cobra brand. Reduce any other asafetida by three-fourths.

    1. Combine the yogurt, ginger, green chilies and coconut in a food processor or blender, cover and process until smooth. Add the *garam masala* and pulse for a few seconds. Set aside.

    2. Heat the *ghee* or oil-butter mixture in a heavy 4–5-quart/liter saucepan or 12-inch (30 cm) nonstick frying pan over moderately high heat. When it is hot but not smoking, drop in the mustard and cumin seeds and fry until the mustard seeds sputter and the cumin seeds turn golden brown. Stir in the curry leaves and asafetida, and immediately follow with the potatoes. Stir-fry for 3–4 minutes, then pour in the seasoned yogurt, turmeric, ground coriander, eggplant, salt and half of the remaining fresh herb. Gently toss to mix.

    3. Reduce the heat to moderate, then fry, turning the vegetables very gently until they are dry. Before serving, mix in the lemon juice and remaining fresh herbs.

Sesame Yogurt Potatoes
EKADASEE TIL ALOO BHAJI

In the Hindi language, *eka* means "eleventh" and *dasee* means "day." The eleventh day after each full moon and the eleventh day after each new moon are called *Ekadasee*. All Vaishnavas observe *Ekadasee* by minimizing physical needs and increasing spiritual practices. Many Vaishnavas fast the whole day, taking only water or fruits. For practicality, Srila Prabhupada recommended light meals consisting of nuts, root vegetables, seeds and milk products. This dry potato dish was frequently on his *Ekadasee* menu. They are best made in a nonstick frying pan or a well-used cast-iron skillet.

Preparation time (after assembling ingredients): 10 minutes
Cooking time: 30–40 minutes
Serves: 6

6 medium-sized all-purpose potatoes (about 2 pounds/1 kg),
    peeled and cut into ½-inch (1.5 cm) cubes
½ cup (120 ml) plain yogurt, whisked until smooth
½ tablespoon (7 ml) scraped, finely shredded
    or minced fresh ginger root
¼ teaspoon (1 ml) cayenne pepper or paprika
5 tablespoons (75 ml) *ghee* or sesame oil
3 tablespoons (45 ml) sesame seeds
1 teaspoon (5 ml) black mustard seeds
½ tablespoon (7 ml) cumin seeds
½ tablespoon (7 ml) salt
1 tablespoon (15 ml) fresh lemon juice
2 tablespoons (30 ml) chopped fresh coriander or parsley

1. Boil or steam the potatoes until they are fork-tender. Drain them and place in a mixing bowl. Add the yogurt, ginger and cayenne or paprika, and gently fold to coat the potatoes with seasoned yogurt. Set aside for ½–3 hours.

2. Heat the *ghee* or oil in a heavy 10–12-inch (25–30 cm) frying pan over moderate heat. When it is hot but not smoking, drop in the sesame seeds, black mustard seeds and cumin seeds. When the seeds begin to pop, add the potatoes and salt and fry, stirring occasionally, for 3–5 minutes or until the potatoes begin to brown. Sprinkle with lemon juice and fresh herb before serving.

Summer Squash and Green Peas
LOUKI HARI MATAR SABJI

Any young, seedless summer squash—such as green or yellow zucchini, pattypan, bottle gourd or yellow crookneck—will yield good results. Recognizing quality in raw zucchini will make all the difference between a successful dish and a tasteless one. Zucchini should be small, 3–6 inches (7.5–15 cm) long, with a bright color, firm, crisp texture and paper-thin glossy skin. Cooked zucchini is sweet and tender with a fine, distinct yet delicate flavor all of its own. This dish goes well with almost any other vegetable.

Preparation and cooking time (after assembling ingredients): 15–20 minutes
Serves: 5 or 6

3 tablespoons (45 ml) *ghee* or 1½ tablespoons
    (22 ml) each vegetable oil and unsalted butter
2 hot green chilies, stemmed, seeded and cut
    lengthwise into slivers (or as desired)
1 teaspoon (5 ml) cumin seeds
8–10 small zucchini (about 1½ pounds/685 g)
    cut into ½-inch (1.5 cm) cubes
½ teaspoon (2 ml) turmeric
1 tablespoon (15 ml) ground coriander
1½ cups (360 ml) fresh peas (1½ pounds/685 g) in pods or
    one 10-ounce (285 g) package of frozen baby peas, defrosted
3 tablespoons (45 ml) chopped fresh coriander, parsley or mint
1 teaspoon (5 ml) salt

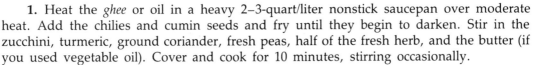

   1. Heat the *ghee* or oil in a heavy 2–3-quart/liter nonstick saucepan over moderate heat. Add the chilies and cumin seeds and fry until they begin to darken. Stir in the zucchini, turmeric, ground coriander, fresh peas, half of the fresh herb, and the butter (if you used vegetable oil). Cover and cook for 10 minutes, stirring occasionally.
   2. Uncover and sauté until the squash softens. If you are using frozen peas, add them 1–2 minutes before serving. Add the salt and the remaining fresh herb, gently stir and serve.

MOIST VEGETABLES

Sautéed Brussels Sprouts with Coconut
CHAUNK GOBHI FOOGATH

Adapted from a recipe cooked by the residents of Udupi, in the South India's Kanada district, this dish may be prepared with either *ghee* or coconut oil. In the fried seasoning, split *urad dal* is browned with spice seeds. Shop for baby Brussels sprouts, bright green and compact. If the sprouts are large, remove the tough outer leaves. If you want a creamy dish, fold in a spoonful of plain yogurt or sour cream just before serving.

Preparation time (after assembling ingredients): 30 minutes
Cooking time : 15-20 minutes
Serves: 4

1½ pounds (685 g) small Brussels sprouts
3 tablespoons (45 ml) *ghee* or coconut oil
1½ teaspoons (7 ml) black mustard seeds
2 teaspoons (10 ml) split *urad dal*, if available
8 curry leaves, preferably fresh
¼ teaspoon (1 ml) cayenne pepper or paprika
½ teaspoon (2 ml) *garam masala*
⅛ teaspoon (0.5 ml) freshly ground nutmeg
1 teaspoon (5 ml) salt
⅓ cup (35 g) shredded fresh coconut

1. Cut off the stem of the Brussels sprouts, along with any wilted, yellow or loose outer leaves. If the sprouts are large, remove the tough, outer leaves and use only the compact center. Cut a small cross in the base of each and soak in salted water for 15 minutes.

2. Drop the sprouts into a large pot of salted boiling water and cook, uncovered, for 5 minutes. Drain well. (These two steps can be done ahead of time.)

3. Heat the *ghee* or oil in a large frying pan over moderately high heat. When it is hot but not smoking, drop in the black mustard seeds and split *urad dal* and fry until the mustard seeds pop and turn gray and the *urad dal* turns reddish – brown. Add the curry leaves, Brussels sprouts, cayenne or paprika, *garam masala* and nutmeg. Sauté for 3–4 minutes, then cover and reduce the heat to low. Cook for 4–5 minutes longer if the sprouts are young, up to 10 minutes if they are old. When they are just tender, add the salt and coconut and gently toss.

Creamed Potatoes with Lemon Pepper
EKADASEE ROGAN ALOO

Root vegetables are popular on *Ekadasee* menus. This substantial variation is ideal for cold winter days, when everyone gravitates to the warmth of the kitchen. With *pooris*, hot rolls or toast, your family will likely find it a welcome change from Sunday hashbrowns. The potatoes can be half-cooked—either steamed or pan-fried the night before or early in the morning—and finished at mealtime.

Preparation time (after assembling ingredients): 10 minutes
Cooking time: 30 minutes
Serves: 6 to 8

12 small boiling potatoes (about 2 pounds/1 kg), peeled
5 tablespoons (75 ml) *ghee* or unsalted butter
½ bay or cassia leaf
3 whole cloves
¾ cup (180 ml) light cream or milk
½ teaspoon (2 ml) black lemon pepper
1 teaspoon (5 ml) freshly ground sea salt
2 tablespoons (30 ml) chopped fresh parsley or coriander
a sprinkle of paprika or cayenne pepper

1. Cut the potatoes into quarters and prick each piece in two or three places with the tip of a sharp paring knife or potato fork. Heat the *ghee* or butter in a large heavy-bottomed nonstick frying pan over moderate heat. Add the bay or cassia leaf and cloves and let them sizzle for several seconds. Add the potatoes and fry, stirring occasionally, until they are half-cooked and turning golden. Alternately, steam the potatoes, along with the bay or cassia leaf and cloves. (This can be done ahead of time.)

2. Pour in the cream or milk, reduce the heat slightly and cook, stirring now and then, until it has reduced by half into a thick sauce and the potatoes are fork–tender. Sprinkle with lemon pepper and salt. Remove the pan from the heat, cover and set aside for 1–2 minutes. Stir gently, remove the cloves and bay or cassia leaf, and serve piping hot sprinkled with the fresh herb and paprika or cayenne.

Sautéed Eggplant and Bell Peppers
BAIGAN SIMLA MIRCH TARKARI

This dish can be made with green, red or yellow bell peppers, all yielding wonderful flavor and color variations. The eggplant is steamed prior to its browning in seasoned *ghee*, a step that cuts calories to the minimum. Fresh *garam masala* puts a mark of distinction on the dish.

Preparation time (after assembling ingredients): 10 minutes
Cooking time: 15–20 minutes
Serves: 4 or 5

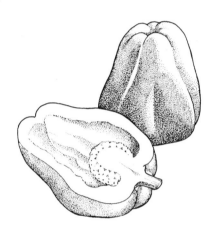

½ teaspoon (2 ml) caraway seeds
¼ teaspoon (1 ml) cardamom seeds
½-inch (1.5 cm) piece of cinnamon stick, crushed
½ teaspoon (2 ml) cumin seeds
½ tablespoon (7 ml) coriander seeds
3 whole cloves
6 black peppercorns
¼ teaspoon (1 ml) freshly ground nutmeg
3 tablespoons (45 ml) *ghee* or vegetable oil
1 teaspoon (5 ml) black mustard seeds
3 green, red or yellow bell peppers (about 1 pound/455 g),
    stemmed, seeded and cut lengthwise into thin strips
1 medium-sized eggplant (1–1¼ pounds/455–570 g) cut
    into ¾-inch (2 cm) cubes and steamed until tender
½ teaspoon (2 ml) turmeric
1¼ teaspoons (6 ml) salt
2 tablespoons (30 ml) chopped fresh coriander or parsley
¼ cup (60 ml) yogurt or sour cream, at room temperature (optional)

1. To make the *garam masala*, combine the caraway seeds, cardamom seeds, crushed cinnamon, cumin seeds, coriander seeds, cloves and peppercorns in a spice or coffee mill and grind to a powder. Add the nutmeg and blend well. Set aside.

2. Heat the *ghee* or oil in a large, heavy nonstick frying pan over moderately high heat. When it is hot, but not smoking, add the mustard seeds and fry until they sputter and turn gray. (You may want to use a lid or spatter screen to prevent the seeds from scattering on the stovetop.) Drop in the peppers and sauté until blistered and wilted (5–7 minutes). Remove and transfer to a plate.

3. Add the eggplant, freshly ground seasonings and turmeric to the pan, then, gently tossing, fry until slightly brown. Add the peppers, salt and fresh herb and toss to mix. If desired, fold in the yogurt or sour cream before serving.

Simple Potato and Green Pea Stew
ALOO HARI MATAR FOOGATH

This dish is popular throughout North India. If you use ¾ cup (180 ml) of water, the texture should be dry. If you want a stewlike consistency, add more water. This is an ideal accompaniment to steamed rice.

Preparation and cooking time: 30–40 minutes
Serves: 6

3 tablespoons (45 ml) *ghee* or vegetable oil
1 tablespoon (15 ml) scraped, finely shredded
    or minced fresh ginger root
2 hot green chilies, seeded and minced (or as desired)
½ tablespoon (7 ml) cumin seeds
1 teaspoon (5 ml) black mustard seeds
¼ teaspoon (1 ml) yellow asafetida powder (*hing*)*
8 curry leaves, preferably fresh
2 medium-sized tomatoes (about ¾ pound/340 g),
    peeled, seeded and chopped
1½ pounds (685 g) waxy new potatoes, peeled
    and cut into ¾ inch (2 cm) thick fingers
¾ teaspoon (3.5 ml) turmeric
1 tablespoon (15 ml) ground coriander
¾ -1½ cups (180–360 ml) water
1½ cups (360 ml) fresh peas (1½ pounds/685 g) in
    pods or one 10-ounce (285 g) package of frozen
    baby peas, defrosted
1¼ teaspoons (6 ml) salt
3 tablespoons (45 ml) chopped fresh coriander or parsley

This amount applies only to yellow Cobra brand. Reduce any other asafetida by three-fourths.

   1. Heat the *ghee* or oil in a heavy-bottomed 5-quart/liter pan, preferably nonstick, over moderate heat. When it is hot but not smoking, add the ginger, chilies, cumin seeds and black mustard seeds and fry until the mustard seeds turn gray and pop. Immediately add the asafetida and curry leaves, and within seconds add the tomatoes. Fry for 2–3 minutes or until the *ghee* separates from the tomato purée.
   2. Add the potatoes, turmeric, ground coriander and water and bring to a boil. Reduce the heat to moderately low, cover and cook for 15 minutes.
   3. Add the fresh peas, salt and half of the fresh herb and continue cooking, partially covered, until the potatoes are soft but not broken down. If you are using frozen peas, add them in the last 2–3 minutes. Garnish with the remaining fresh herb and serve.

Sliced White Radishes with Golden Pumpkin

MOOLI KADDU FOOGATH

White cooking radishes (*mooli*) pleasantly contrast in color and taste with golden-red pumpkin. The flavor of radishes varies enormously, from the mild salad icicle type available in supermarkets to the slightly hot and pungent *mooli* sold in ethnic markets. Use whatever type is easily available, including Oriental *daikon*. When you fry fenugreek seeds in a seasoning, allow them to turn khaki-red but do not let them darken to deep brown, for at that stage flavor is excessively bitter. Quite amazingly, if you continue cooking the seeds until they blacken, they again lose their bitterness.

Preparation and cooking time: 30–40 minutes
Serves: 5 to 6

4 tablespoons (60 ml) *ghee* or corn oil
1 teaspoon (5 ml) scraped, finely shredded
      or minced fresh ginger root
1 teaspoon (5 ml) cumin seeds
½ teaspoon (2 ml) black mustard seeds
scant ½ teaspoon (2 ml) fenugreek seeds
8 curry leaves, preferably fresh
¼ teaspoon (1 ml) yellow asafetida powder (*hing*)*
2 cups (480 ml) ¼-inch (6 mm) thick sliced
      white radishes (about ¾ pound/340 g)
1½ pounds (685 g) peeled yellow pumpkin,
      Hubbard or butternut squash, peeled and
      cut into 1-inch (2.5 cm) cubes
½ cup (120 ml) fresh peas or frozen baby peas,
      (defrosted under hot water and drained)
¼ teaspoon (1 ml) cayenne pepper or paprika
1 teaspoon (5 ml) turmeric
2 teaspoons (10 ml) ground coriander
¼ cup (60 ml) water
½ teaspoon (2 ml) *amchoor* powder or
      2 tablespoons (30 ml) lemon juice
1 teaspoon (5 ml) salt
3 tablespoons (45 ml) coarsely chopped fresh
      coriander or minced parsley

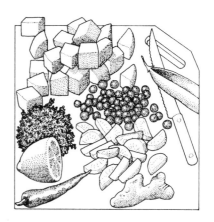

*This amount applies only to yellow Cobra brand. Reduce any other asafetida by three-fourths.

    1. Heat the *ghee* or oil in a heavy-bottomed 5-quart/liter nonstick pan over moderately high heat until it is hot but not smoking. Add the ginger, cumin seeds, black mustard seeds and fenugreek seeds and fry until the fenugreek seeds darken to a golden red. Drop in the curry leaves and asafetida, and in seconds add the radishes. Sauté until they begin to brown, then stir in the pumpkin or squash, fresh peas, cayenne or paprika, turmeric, ground coriander and water. Cover, reduce the heat to low and cook until the pumpkin is fork-tender (anywhere from 20 to 30 minutes).
    2. A few minutes before serving, fold in the *amchoor* or lemon juice, salt, fresh herb and frozen peas.

Lima Beans with Golden Raisins
SEM KISHMISH FOOGATH

Fresh lima beans are usually available as small "butter limas" or larger, as "potato limas." Shop for local produce—dark green pods, tightly closed and bulging with large beans. To free the beans from the pods, cut a strip along the inner edge of the pod, then with your thumbnail remove the beans. June, July and August yield the most profuse crops, yet at some specialty greengrocers the availability extends a month before and after. If you want to try this dish in the dead of winter, you can substitute frozen Fordhook limas. As the raisins plump, they impart a delicate sweetness to this dish.

Preparation and cooking time (after assembling ingredients): 30 minutes
Serves: 4

3 cups (710 ml) water
1½ cups (360 ml) fresh lima beans (about 2 pounds/1 kg in pods) or
    one 10-ounce (285 g) package of frozen Fordhook lima beans, defrosted
2 tablespoons (30 ml) *ghee*, unsalted butter or olive oil
¼ teaspoon (1 ml) paprika or ⅛ teaspoon (0.5 ml) cayenne pepper
¼ teaspoon (1 ml) ground mustard
¼ teaspoon (1 ml) turmeric
3 tablespoons (45 ml) golden raisins or currants
2 teaspoons (10 ml) *jaggery* or brown sugar (optional)
1½ tablespoons (22 ml) lime or lemon juice
½ teaspoon (2 ml) salt
1½ tablespoons (22 ml) finely chopped fresh coriander, dill or parsley
¼ cup (60 ml) water

1. Bring the 3 cups (710 ml) of water to a boil in a 3-quart/liter saucepan, preferably nonstick. Add the beans and cook over low heat for 10 minutes. Pour off the water.

2. Add the *ghee*, butter or oil and remaining ingredients (if you are using frozen beans, add at this stage). Simmer, partially covered, for 10–15 minutes or until the beans are tender. Uncover, raise the heat and reduce the remaining liquid to a glaze.

Note: Cooking times vary considerably depending on the size and freshness of the beans.

FRIED VEGETABLES

Crispy Deep-Fried Eggplant Slices
BAIGAN BHAJI

Though fried potatoes are welcome almost any time of day, fried eggplants are usually part of a meal, because they must be served just after they are fried. If they are held in a warmer, even for 10 minutes, the crispy crust softens and the overall effect is a soggy fritter. If you reuse the *ghee* or oil after frying, be sure to pass it through a fine filter to remove traces of flour; the inevitable residue would burn and shorten the life of the frying medium.

Preparation time (after assembling ingredients): ½ hour
Cooking time: 10 minutes
Serves: 6 to 8

1 medium-sized eggplant (1–1¼ pounds/455–570 g)
    cut crosswise into ¼-inch (6 mm) slices
salt
⅓ teaspoon (1.5 ml) paprika or cayenne pepper
whole wheat flour for dusting
***ghee* or vegetable oil for frying**

   1. Place the eggplant slices on a tray and sprinkle liberally with salt. Let them sit for at least ½ hour to draw out excess moisture. Rinse off the salt, then pat the slices dry with paper towels. Sprinkle the slices with paprika or cayenne.
   2. Place a small quantity of flour in a plastic or paper bag and drop in as many eggplant slices as you will fry in a batch. Shake vigorously, then remove each piece, shake off the excess flour, and set on a plate.
   3. Pour enough *ghee* or oil to measure 2–3 inches (5–7.5 cm) deep into a large, heavy deep-frying pan. Heat the oil to 375°F (190°C) and put in as many eggplant slices as will fit in a single layer. Fry each side until crisp and browned. Remove the slices with a slotted spatula and set aside on paper towels. Repeat for each batch.

Eggplant Fritters

KHASA BAIGAN BHAJI

These are aptly called eggplant sandwich fritters. When I first served them to Srila Prabhupada, much to my delight, he dubbed them "vegetable chops". These fritters can be served hot or at room temperature.

Salting time: ½ hour
Preparation and cooking time: about 30 minutes
Serves: 4 to 6

1 large eggplant (about 2 pounds/1 kg), cut crosswise into ½-inch (1.5 cm) slices
salt
½ cup (50 g) chickpea flour (sifted before measuring)
3 tablespoons (45 ml) self-rising flour or whole wheat pastry
    flour mixed with a generous pinch of baking powder
2 tablespoons (30 ml) cornmeal
⅛ teaspoon (0.5 ml) cayenne pepper or paprika
¼ teaspoon (1 ml) turmeric
3 tablespoons (45 ml) finely chopped fresh coriander, basil or parsley
3 tablespoons (45 ml) water
6 ounces (170 g) mozzarella cheese, thinly sliced
1¼ cups (125 g) fresh or dry bread crumbs or ⅔ cup (115 g) fine semolina
ghee or vegetable oil for shallow-frying

1. Place the eggplant slices on a tray and sprinkle liberally with salt. Let them sit for at least ½ hour to draw out excess moisture.

2. Combine the flours, baking powder, cornmeal, cayenne or paprika, turmeric, fresh herb and ¼ teaspoon (1 ml) of salt with the water in a bowl and whisk into a smooth batter the consistency of thick cream. (You may have to add more water.)

3. Rinse the salt off the eggplant and pat the slices dry with paper towels. To obtain uniform rounds, cut out with biscuit rings about 2 inches (5 cm) in diameter. Pair eggplant slices of the same size, reserving the ends or trimmings for another use. Trim the cheese slices so they are slightly smaller than the eggplant rounds. Place 2 thin slices of cheese between a pair of eggplant slices. Dip the sandwich in the chickpea batter, lightly shake off the excess flour, then coat with bread crumbs or semolina and set aside on waxed paper. Make all the eggplant sandwiches in this way.

4. Heat *ghee* or oil to a depth of ½ inch (1.5 cm) in a large heavy frying pan over moderate heat until it is hot but not smoking. Place the sandwiches in the pan and fry for 10–15 minutes on each side or until the eggplant is fork–tender and nicely browned. Adjust the heat carefully: if the temperature is too high, the cheese tends to burst through the batter–crumb casing; if it is too low, the fritters absorb excessive oil. Serve piping hot.

Butter Soft Eggplant Wedges
BHONA BAIGAN BHAJI

Srila Prabhupada gave us this recipe during his 1967 San Francisco cooking classes. In Bengal, *bhaji* is loosely defined as any fried vegetable, and while this variation has other names, such as Eggplant *Pukki*, one thing is constant: it must be served immediately after cooking, piping hot. To get authentic results, I recommend using fresh *ghee*; my second choice would be a newcomer on the market—avocado oil. It can be heated to a very high temperature without smoking, is very delicious, and one of the lowest of all unsaturated fats—actually helping to lower cholesterol in the blood. Olive oil would be the third choice. I like to use baby white or purple egglants, but large eggplants can be cut into wedges and used as well.

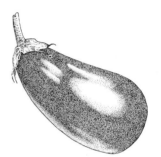

Salting time: 15–30 minutes
Preparation and Frying time: under 15 minutes
Serves: 6 to 8

1½ tablespoons (22 ml) turmeric
1½ tablespoons (22 ml) salt
3 tablespoons (45 ml) water
8–10 baby white or purple eggplants (about 1¼ pounds/570 g)
    or 1 medium-sized eggplant (about 1¼ pound/570 g)
ghee or olive oil for frying

1. Combine the turmeric, salt and water in a bowl. Cut small eggplants in half, or cut larger ones into wedges roughly 2½ inches (6.5 cm) long and 1½ inches (4 cm) wide. Toss the eggplant with the turmeric-salt mixture and set aside for 15–30 minutes.

2. To remove the watery turmeric marinade, drain the eggplant in a paper towel-lined colander. Pour enough *ghee* or oil to reach a depth of ½ inch (1.5 cm) in a large heavy frying pan and place it over moderately high heat. When it is hot and nearly reaches its smoking point, carefully add a single layer of eggplant pieces. Fry, turning the pieces on all sides, until they assume a rich reddish-brown color and are fork-tender.

3. Rinse off the salt from the eggplant slices and pat dry with paper towels. Pour into a large heavy frying pan ½ inch (1.5 cm) *ghee* or oil and place over moderately high to high heat. When it is hot but not smoking, add as many eggplant pieces as will fit in a single layer. Fry on both sides until fork tender, reddish-brown and crisp. Remove with a slotted spoon and drain on paper towels. Fry the remaining eggplant, adding additional *ghee* or oil as necessary.

4. Place the fried eggplant in a single layer on a cookie sheet, brush or spoon on the sauce, and warm under the broiler just to let the flavors mingle. Serve hot.

Cauliflower and Potato Surprise
GOBHI ALOO BHAJI

Although this was one of four cauliflower and potato vegetables served at a recipe testing banquet, it was unanimously voted the favorite. It is indeed popular throughout much of North India, this version a long-time secret from the Shashi Gupta family of Kurukshetra. I noticed that although undeniably rich, it is always one of the first to disappear at holiday dinners. I often use homemade yogurt, or good commercial yogurt like Brown Cow or Nancy's, instead of cream or sour cream. It is every bit as delicious and far less caloric.

Preparation and cooking time (after assembling ingredients): 35 minutes
Serves: 5 or 6

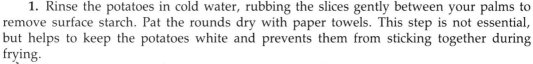

2 large baking potatoes (about 1 pound/455 g) peeled
    and cut into rounds ¼-inch (6 mm) thick
ghee or vegetable oil for frying
1 medium-sized cauliflower (about 2 pounds/1 kg),
    trimmed and divided into flowerets
1 teaspoon (5 ml) dry-roasted coarsely crushed cumin seeds
¼ teaspoon (1 ml) fresh coarsely ground black pepper
⅛ teaspoon (0.5 ml) cayenne pepper or paprika
½ teaspoon (2 ml) turmeric
1 teaspoon (5 ml) salt
1 cup (240 ml) very fresh plain yogurt or sour cream, at room temperature
parsley sprigs for garnishing

    1. Rinse the potatoes in cold water, rubbing the slices gently between your palms to remove surface starch. Pat the rounds dry with paper towels. This step is not essential, but helps to keep the potatoes white and prevents them from sticking together during frying.

    2. Pour in enough *ghee* or vegetable oil to half fill a deep-frying vessel. Place over moderate heat and allow it to slowly reach 375°F (190°C). If you use a roomy wok or *karai*, you can fry all of the potatoes at once; if the pan is small, divide into two batches. Carefully add the potatoes and fry until golden brown (8–10 minutes). Remove the slices with a slotted spoon and drain on paper-towel-lined cookie sheets. Fry each batch of potatoes and cauliflower until tender and golden brown. (I keep the fried vegetables warm in a preheated oven.)

    3. When all of the vegetables are fried and still warm, place them in a large bowl. Sprinkle with the cumin seeds, black pepper, cayenne or paprika, turmeric and salt. Gently toss the delicate vegetables to coat with the spices. Fold in the yogurt or sour cream, garnish with the parsley sprigs and serve piping hot.

    Note: The yogurt or sour cream puts a glistening coat of sauce on the crisp vegetables, which must be served immediately. If the dish is kept warm or held before serving, the vegetables absorb the sauce and the dish becomes dry.

Crisp 'n' Soft Mixed Vegetable Croquettes
EKADASEE ARBI ALOO BADA

This is a unique croquette dish, for it is neither bound with cream sauce nor breaded in crumbs, as are most. Instead, these croquettes are a combination of three starchy vegetables: potatoes, plantains and colocasia or *arbi*. They are cooked individually until soft, mashed or shredded, and blended with little more than salt, pepper, chilies and herbs.

Known as *Ekadasee* croquettes, they are made without the addition of any form of grain. Fried carefully, the mixture is sufficiently starchy to remain intact, but if the temperature is either too high or low, the croquettes tend to disintegrate. To prevent this disaster, you may want to be on the safe side and bind the mixture with a generous spoon of arrowroot. No matter what your choice, do watch the frying temperature—it should not fall below 360°F (180°C)

Preparation time (after assembling ingredients): 45 minutes
Cooking time: about 15 minutes
Serves: 6 or 7

¾ **pound (340 g) colocasia corns (*arbi*), cut into 1-inch (2.5 cm) pieces**
3 medium-sized waxy boiling potatoes (about ¾ pound/340 g), peeled
1 green plantain, about 10 inches (25 cm) long
1 teaspoon (5 ml) cracked black pepper
1 teaspoon (5 ml) salt
2 hot chilies, seeded and minced (or as desired)
1 tablespoon (15 ml) arrowroot (optional)
3 tablespoons (45 ml) chopped fresh coriander
ghee **or oil for deep-frying**

   1. Boil the colocasia for 20–25 minutes or until fork-tender. If you have a tiered vegetable steamer, so much the better. You can cook all the vegetables simultaneously. Increase the cooking time by at least 15 minutes, then check to see if it is done every 5 minutes thereafter. Plunge them into cold water and peel off the starchy skins. Set aside to dry out.
   2. Cut the potatoes into quarters and boil for 20–30 minutes or until fork-tender. Drain and set aside in a folded clean kitchen towel to dry out.
   3. Cut the thick skin from the plantain, removing any fibers. Cut in half and boil for 25–30 minutes or until tender. Drain, and when cool enough to handle, shred through the coarse holes on a hand grater into a mixing bowl.
   4. Mash together the colocasia and potatoes and add the plantain. Knead in the pepper, chilies, salt, arrowroot and coriander.
   5. Wash your hands, rub them with a film of oil and divide the mixture into 14 even pieces. Roll, press and mold into smooth logs about 2 inches (5 cm) long or doughnuts 2 inches (5 cm) in diameter and set aside on waxed paper.
   6. Heat *ghee* or oil to a depth of at least 1½ inches (4 cm) in a deep-fryer until it reaches 370°F (190°C) on a frying thermometer. Add half of the croquettes, making sure not to crowd the pan, and fry until richly browned. Remove with a slotted spoon and drain on paper towels. Serve at once in a napkin-lined basket or fry the remaining batch and serve all together, piping hot.

Deep-Fried Julienne Potatoes and Carrots
ALOO GAJAR BHAJI

This is an easy dish for the kitchen with a good mandoline or a food processor. The peeled vegetables can be hand-cut across the julienne blade to yield perfectly uniform straws. Cuisinart has a blade that makes reasonably fine julienne vegetables in seconds. Without a julienne blade, use a standard 3–4 mm slicing disk. Pre-cut the carrots and potatoes to fit horizontally into the feeding tube. Slice, then remove the slices and stack them, cut side up, in the feeding tube. Process again to yield fine julienne. This is not a main-dish vegetable but rather a little nibbler. Allow 3–4 tablespoons (45–60 ml) per serving.

Preparation time: 30 minutes by hand or 5 minutes with food processor
Soaking time: 30 minutes
Cooking time: about 15 minutes
Serves: 5 or 6

2 large carrots (about 6 ounces/170 g), peeled
2 medium-sized baking potatoes
    (about 12 ounces/340 g), peeled
ghee or vegetable oil for deep-frying
¼–½ teaspoon (1–2 ml) fine salt
¼ teaspoon (1 ml) cayenne pepper or paprika
1 tablespoon (15 ml) lemon juice

1. To cut the vegetables in a food processor, attach the fine julienne blade. Cut the carrots and potatoes into pieces 2½ inches (6.5 cm) long and load them horizontally in the processor chute. This will make 2½ inch (6.5 cm) long julienne.

To cut the vegetables by hand, first cut them lengthwise into slices about ⅛ inch (3 mm) wide. Then cut them crosswise into pieces 2½ inches (6.5 cm) long. Try to make all the pieces uniform in size so that they will take the same time to cook.

2. Soak the cut vegetables in separate bowls of ice water for 30 minutes. Pat thoroughly dry with paper towels.

3. Pour enough *ghee* or oil into a frying vessel to fill it to a depth of 2 inches (5 cm). Place the pan over moderately high heat until the temperature reaches 370°F (190°C) on a deep-frying thermometer. Fry a small handful of julienne carrots until golden brown and crisp. Remove with a slotted spoon and drain on paper towels. In batches, fry all of the carrots and potatoes.

4. Place the crisp straws in a bowl and sprinkle in the salt, cayenne or paprika and lemon juice and serve immediately. The vegetables will soften as they cool. Do not cover.

Shredded Plantain Clusters
KHASA KACHA KELA BHAJI

These little finger foods work well as hor d'oeuvres and appetizers for any social occasion. If you want to try the dish but lack asafetida, omit the first three ingredients and use ¼ cup (60 ml) of *Mint-Lime Butter* instead.

Preparation time (after assembling ingredients): 15 minutes
Cooking time: up to 20 minutes
Makes: 10–12 clusters

4 tablespoons (60 ml) unsalted butter, at room temperature
¼ teaspoon (1 ml) yellow asafetida powder (*hing*)*
⅛ teaspoon (0.5 ml) paprika or cayenne pepper
2 large plantains, 9–12 inches (23–30 cm) long
***ghee* or oil for deep-frying**
5 or 6 lemon or lime twists (optional)

*This amount applies only to yellow Cobra brand. Reduce any other asafetida by three-fourths.

1. Mix the butter, asafetida and paprika or cayenne in a bowl and set aside.

2. Peel the plantains with a knife, removing the tough green skins and stray strings. Shred through the large holes on a hand grater or in a food processor fitted with a coarse shredding disk. Press ¼ cup (60 ml) of shredded plantains firmly between your palms to flatten and mold into a tight 2-inch (5 cm) cluster. Arrange them on a plate in a single layer.

3. Pour *ghee* or oil into a large, heavy frying pan to a depth of 1½ inches (4 cm). Place over moderate heat until it reaches 365°F (185°C) on a deep-frying thermometer. When it is hot, place the clusters one at a time into the oil in a single layer. Fry on both sides until golden brown and crisp, about 3 minutes per side. Remove with a slotted spoon and drain on paper towels. Fry the remaining clusters. While they are still quite warm but not steaming hot, smear the top of each cluster with the seasoned butter.

Crispy Plantain Wafers
SADA KACHA KELA BHAJI

In South India these are as popular as potato chips are in America. It is a national snack pastime, and in much of the south, is almost always fried in coconut oil. This tasty oil is also highly saturated, and should be avoided if you are on a cholesterol reduced diet; try sunflower, safflower or soybean oil instead. South Indians, from roadside cooks to housewives, swear by a special frying treatment for the wafers. Since it involves sprinkling water in hot oil, it breaks all safety rules. To avoid splattering, use a spray bottle set on the finest mist. It will cause the oil to foam, but splatter no more than when adding potato straws for frying.

Preparation time (after assembling ingredients): 10 minutes
Soaking time: 30 minutes
Cooking time: 15 minutes
Serves: 4 or 5 as a nibbler

2 large unripe plantains, each 9–12 inches (23–30 cm) long
½ tablespoon (7 ml) salt
¼ teaspoon (1 ml) turmeric
2 tablespoons (30 ml) hot water
melted coconut or vegetable oil for frying

1. Cut away the hard skins from the plantains with a paring knife and slice cross-wise, slightly on the diagonal, as thinly as possible. Soak the plantain in ice water for at least ½ hour, then drain and pat thoroughly dry with paper towels.

2. Dissolve the salt and turmeric in the hot water and place it in a spray bottle. Pour 2 inches (5 cm) of oil into a deep-frying vessel. Place the pan over moderate heat and slowly heat to 370°F (190°C) on a deep-frying thermometer. When it is hot, drop in enough plantain slices to float to a layer on top of the oil. The oil will froth and foam. Fry for about 2 minutes. Holding the spray bottle well above the pan, spray a fine mist into the pan. The oil will froth, but not splatter. (Experts feel this is the means to the crispiest wafers.) Fry, turning to cook on both sides, until they are very crisp, still yellow-colored, for another 1–2 minutes. Transfer with a slotted spoon to paper towels to drain. Fry the remaining wafers in the same way. Serve hot, or let cool and store in airtight containers. These wafers stay crisp indefinitely but are considered stale after a week or two.

Bitter Melon Chips with Coconut
BHONA KARELA NARIYAL

Srila Prabhupada was so fond of bitter melons that he requested them in one form or another nearly every day for lunch. Like most Bengalis, he regarded the vegetable as both a digestive aid and appetite stimulator. Because they are not always easily available, he requested his personal cook to keep a stock of dehydrated sliced bitter melons on hand for world wide traveling. To this day, I try to keep a jar of dried bitter melon slices in the larder, used primarily for this recipe. Dried bitter melon is less pungent than fresh, and deep-fried, it is far crunchier. The wafers fry in seconds, and even for newcomers, are quite irresistible.

Bitter melons, also called bitter gourds or balsam pears, are an important vegetable in eastern and southern cuisines. They are spiny melons, 4–8 inches (10–20 cm) long, thickish in the middle and pointed at both ends. Always look for small melons, picked immature, that are dark green in color and heavy for their size. In Bengal the bitter melons are fried in mustard or peanut oil until dark brown and crisp. To tone down the bitterness, the chips are coated with powdered fresh coconut and seasonings. Serve 4–6 chips per person as an appetizer-relish with a dab of pickle or chutney.

Preparation and salting time: 30 minutes
Cooking time: 10–15 minutes
Serves: 4 to 6

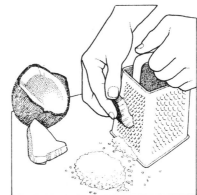

4 small or 2 medium-sized bitter melons
   (about ½ pound/230 g)
4 tablespoons (60 ml) mustard or peanut oil
¼ teaspoon (1 ml) turmeric
¼ teaspoon (1 ml) paprika or cayenne pepper
¼ cup (25 g) grated fresh or dried coconut
½ tablespoon (7 ml) lemon or lime juice
salt

1. Trim the ends off the bitter melons and slice crosswise into rounds ¼ inch (6 mm) thick. Place them in a bowl, sprinkle liberally with salt and place a weight on them. Set aside for at least ½ hour. Rinse under running water, drain, and pat dry with paper towels.

2. Heat the oil in a 7–9 inch (17.5–22.5 cm) frying pan over moderate heat. (If using mustard oil, allow it to reach the smoking point before adding the vegetables. This makes the pungent oil docile.) When it is hot, add the bitter melon rounds and stir-fry, cooking on both sides, until crisp and reddish-brown, from 10–15 minutes. Remove the pan from the heat, add the remaining ingredients and ¼ teaspoon (1 ml) salt, and toss well. Serve hot or at room temperature.

Fried Bitter Melon with Ground Almonds
BHONA KARELA BHAJI

Aside from the fact that no Bengali meal is complete without a bitter dish, Bengalis also assert that bitter melon dishes aid digestion, cleanse the blood and encourage a failing appetite. Because most Americans feel that bitter foods are akin to medicines, this version tones down the bitterness. The cut vegetables are parboiled in salted water before they are fried and then liberally coated with ground almonds, nut butter and a touch of seasoning. The finished product is perfect for newcomers to fresh bitter melon cookery. Serve as you would a little mound of seasoned potatoes, more as an appetizer than a vegetable dish, on a full lunch or dinner menu.

Preparation and blanching time: 30 minutes
Cooking time: 10–15 minutes
Serves: 4 to 6

4 small bitter melons, up to 4½ inches (11.5 cm)
    long, or 2 medium-sized bitter melons, up to
    6 inches (15 cm) long (about ½ pound/230 g)
2 tablespoons (30 ml) salt
3 cups (710 ml) warm water
4 tablespoons (60 ml) *ghee* or vegetable oil
2 tablespoons (30 ml) ground almonds or cashews
2 tablespoons (30 ml) almond or cashew butter
⅛ teaspoon (0.5 ml) paprika or cayenne pepper
⅛ teaspoon (0.5 ml) freshly ground nutmeg

1. Trim the ends off the bitter melons, slice lengthwise in half, then into quarters, and scoop out the yellow-orange seeds and pulp. Now cut crosswise at ¼-inch (6 mm) intervals. Combine the salt and water in a small saucepan and add the bitter melon. Set aside for 25 minutes, then bring to a boil over high heat. Parboil for 3 minutes, then rinse in a strainer under running water. Drain and pat dry with paper towels.

2. Heat the *ghee* or oil in a 7–9-inch (17.5–22.5 cm) frying pan over moderate heat. When it is hot but not smoking, add the bitter melon pieces and stir-fry until two-thirds cooked, about 8 minutes. Stir in the remaining ingredients and continue to cook for up to 5 minutes until well browned. Serve hot or at room temperature.

Sliced Okra in Seasoned Yogurt
BHINDI BHAJI

This typically Kashmiri dish, from the Srinagar kitchen of Dr. Karan Singh, is served at room temperature and assembled just before serving. For entertaining, I like to serve it garnished with toasted almonds or pine nuts.

Preparation time (after assembling ingredients): 15 minutes
Cooking time: under 15 minutes
Serves: 4 to 6

1 pound (455 g) okra
1 teaspoon (5 ml) salt
⅛ teaspoon (0.5 ml) yellow asafetida powder (*hing*)*
1 teaspoon (5 ml) *garam masala*
3 tablespoons (45 ml) finely chopped fresh coriander
⅔ cup (160 ml) plain yogurt, or half yogurt
　　and half sour cream
2 tablespoons (30 ml) finely chopped toasted almonds
　　or pine nuts
⅛ teaspoon (0.5 ml) freshly ground pepper
2 tablespoons (30 ml) toasted sliced almonds or pine nuts, as a garnish
melted *ghee* or vegetable oil for frying

*This amount applies only to yellow Cobra brand. Reduce any other asafetida by three-fourths.

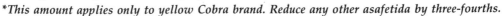

1. Wipe the okra with a slightly damp kitchen towel to brush off any dirt. Dry thoroughly with paper towels, then cut off the stems and tails and slice crosswise into rounds ½ inch (1.5 cm) thick. Pour *ghee* or oil to a depth of 1½ inches (4 cm) into a deep-frying vessel. Place over moderate heat until it reaches 365°F (185°C) on a deep-frying thermometer. Add the okra and fry until golden brown and crispy. Remove the okra with a fine-mesh frying spoon and transfer to a cookie sheet lined with paper towels. Sprinkle with ¾ teaspoon (3.5 ml) salt, and the asafetida, *garam masala* and coriander, and toss to mix.

2. Combine the yogurt with the chopped pine nuts, black pepper and the remaining ¼ teaspoon (1 ml) salt in a bowl and stir until creamy.

3. Drizzle portions of the fried okra with the yogurt sauce and garnish with whole pine nuts, or fold the okra into the sauce and gently blend.

Pumpkin Wafers
KADDU BHAJI

You can use any winter squash—butternut, acorn, banana, or Hubbard.

Preparation and salting time: 30 minutes
Cooking time: about 20 minutes
Makes: 4 to 6 small servings

1 pound (455 g) peeled, seeded pumpkin or
    squash, cut into wafers ¼ inch (6 mm)
    thick and 1½ inches (4 cm) across
1 teaspoon (5 ml) salt
1 teaspoon (5 ml) turmeric
¼ teaspoon (1 ml) cayenne pepper
3 tablespoons (45 ml) ground rice (coarse flour)
    or sifted chickpea flour
ghee or vegetable oil for deep-frying

    1. Place the pumpkin wafers in a single, slightly overlapping layer on a tray, sprinkle with salt, turmeric and cayenne, and set aside for ½ hour.

    2. Pat the slices dry with paper towels, place them in a paper or plastic bag containing the flour, and shake the bag to dredge the slices. Shake off the excess flour by slapping each piece sharply and then divide them into three batches.

    3. Pour 2 inches (5 cm) of *ghee* or oil into a deep frying pan. Place over moderately high heat until the temperature reaches 360°F (180°C) on a deep-frying thermometer. Fry one batch for 4–5 minutes or until the slices turn a rich golden brown, then transfer with a slotted spoon to paper towels. Fry the remaining two batches in the same way. Sprinkle with additional salt, if desired.

Deep-Fried Stuffed Hot Green Chilies
HARI MIRCH BHAJI

Fresh hot green jalapeños, averaging 2½ inches (6.5 cm) long and 1 inch (2.5 cm) wide, are available in most areas. If their skin has begun to turn red but is still shiny and firm, they are still quite usable. Smaller chilies are inevitably the hottest, especially serranos, and they are next to impossible to seed and stuff. Use jalapeños or the conical fresnos (usually limited to California markets). Srila Prabhupada once commented to his servant-cook Srutakirti das, "Chili *pakori* and fried chilies are cooling in hot climates; they actually reduce the body temperature." They are also recognized as appetite stimulators by inhabitants of the tropics. If you fancy hot foods, by all means give this dish a try on a full Vedic menu. Warn the unseasoned newcomer, and, depending on personal tolerance, allow 1 or 2 per person.

Preparation time: 15 minutes
Cooking time: 10 minutes
Makes: 12 chilies

12 hot green jalapeño chilies, each about 2½ inches (6.5 cm) long
½ teaspoon (2 ml) ground mustard
½ teaspoon (2 ml) turmeric
¼ teaspoon (1 ml) salt
¼ teaspoon (1 ml) ground cumin
¼ teaspoon (1 ml) *garam masala*
1 tablespoon (15 ml) chickpea flour
about 1 tablespoon (15 ml) plain yogurt
1 cup (240 ml) *ghee* or vegetable oil for deep-frying

1. Wash the chilies and pat them dry. With a sharp paring knife, make a cut from the top to the bottom of each chili, cutting halfway through. Carefully pry out the seeds and membrane, then wash the cavity under running water and pat dry.
2. Combine the mustard, turmeric, salt, cumin, *garam masala*, chickpea flour and enough yogurt to make a paste. Mix well. Spread the paste evenly into the cavity of each chili.
3. Heat the *ghee* or oil in a 1-quart/liter saucepan over high heat until it reaches 360°F (180°C) on a deep-frying thermometer. Fry the chilies 4 at a time for 2–3 minutes or until they blister and turn brown. Remove with a slotted spoon and drain on paper towels.

LEAFY GREEN VEGETABLES

Greens, including the tops of root vegetables, the leaves of cabbages and grapevines, and, in warm climates, the fifty-plus species grown especially for tender leaves, constitute the basis of a group of loved dishes called *sak*. In India, these usually center around a strain of spinach called Malabar nightshade. In addition, mustard greens, fenugreek greens, collard greens, escarole and radish greens, to name a few, are added for seasonal variation. They offer a range of tastes from sweet to bitter, and textures from purées to wilted salads. Depending on regional customs, *sak* can be cooked in scantily seasoned *ghee*, mustard oil, sesame oil or ground nut oil. On one occasion when I served *sak* to Srila Prabhupada, he captivated me with histories detailing Lord Chaitanya's love for it. He related the *Shri Chaitanya Charitamrita* pastime in which Lord Chaitanya traveled from Jagannatha Puri to Vrindavan through the vast Jharikanda forests. His servant, Bala-bhadra Battacharya, would collect all kinds of forest greens, edible shoots and roots, and with only spices and oil prepare delicious *sak* for the Lord. Indeed, *sak* was so dear to the Lord that all the Vaishnavas receiving Him would invariably prepare *sak* as part of His meals.

The *sak* recipes in this section hail from several regional cuisines and illustrate variety in tastes and textures. So long as half of the greens are spinach, feel free to add fresh turnip, beet or radish tops, kale, collard or mustard greens, or cress, sorrel or stemmed Swiss chard. If possible, buy locally grown unpackaged leaves so you can examine what you purchase. Select brightly colored, crisp leaves that appear young and tender. Usually old greens are outsized, with thick stems and coarse veins on the leaves. Avoid yellow, spotted, wilted or bruised plants. Once picked, the leaves should be used as soon as possible. If you must keep them for up to 2 days, refrigerate, unwashed, in a plastic bag.

All greens must be trimmed and washed before cooking. Cut or tear off any bruised parts of the leaf, then remove the stem. Fold each leaf in half, glossy top side in. Grasp the thick stem at the base of the leaf and pull it off toward the tip, removing coarse veins. Plunge the leaves into a large bowl of cold water; press and swish to loosen the clinging sandy grit. Change the water 2 or 3 times, depending on quantity. If the leaves are mud-caked, they must be individually washed in cold water. Shake off excess water before placing them in a colander. (Do not try to wash them in a colander; the grit will remain nestled on the textured surfaces.) Avoid cooking greens in aluminum or cast iron, for they tend to discolor and absorb flavors from the pan. Stainless steel, enamel on iron or a nonstick surface is ideal.

Buttery Spinach
SAK

There are so many ways to season a simple *sak* that I find it difficult to select just one recipe to represent the possibilities. This variation could come from any region, from almost any kitchen, garnished with fried currants and cashew nuts. In Punjab and Gujarat, *sak* is routinely accompanied with corn dishes.

Preparation time (after assembling ingredients): a few minutes
Cooking time: 15 minutes
Serves: 4

2 pounds (1 kg) fresh spinach, trimmed and washed
5 tablespoons (75 ml) *ghee* or unsalted butter
1–2 hot green chilies, cored, seeded and slivered
1½-inch (4 cm) piece of fresh ginger root,
    scraped and cut into thin julienne
2 whole cloves, crushed
¼ teaspoon (1 ml) each fennel seeds, black mustard
    seeds, and cumin seeds, crushed
1 teaspoon (5 ml) salt
¼ cup (35 g) raw cashew bits
⅓ cup (45 g) dried currants, soaked in warm water
    for 30 minutes, drained and dried on paper towels
½ teaspoon (2 ml) *garam masala*
a few butter pats (optional)
lemon or lime twists (optional)

1. Plunge the spinach into a large pot of salted boiling water. Cook for 8 minutes. Drain in a colander, pressing firmly with the back of a spoon to extract as much water as possible. Coarsely chop.
2. Melt 2½ tablespoons (37 ml) of the *ghee* or butter in a wide heavy casserole or sauté pan over moderate heat. Add the green chilies, ginger, cloves and spice seeds, and fry for about 1 minute. Stir in the spinach and salt and heat through. Cover and set aside.
3. Heat the remaining 2½ tablespoons (37 ml) of *ghee* or butter in a small saucepan over moderately low heat. Toss in the cashew bits and fry, stirring constantly, until they begin to color. Add the currants and continue to fry until they plump and brown. Remove the pan from the heat. Stir in the *garam masala* then pour the contents over the spinach. Finish with an additional pat of butter and lemon or lime twists, if desired.

Seasoned Spinach with Julienne Potatoes

ALOO SAK

India's city dwellers have been influenced by numerous international cuisines, but the villagers are slow to accept change, if at all, and this recipe is real village-style cooking—simple and straightforward. Spinach is often coupled with mustard greens, kale or collard greens in this dish, and because of the potatoes, it is a good way to be introduced to new flavors. This is a "dry" dish, and the fried potatoes are added to the cooked greens just before serving to prevent them from losing their shape.

Preparation time (after assembling ingredients): 10 minutes
Cooking time: 30 minutes
Serves: 6 to 8

4 medium-sized new boiling potatoes (about
    1 pound/455 g), cooked until nearly fork-tender
½ teaspoon (2 ml) turmeric
½ teaspoon (2 ml) *garam masala*
½ teaspoon (2 ml) ground cumin
¼ teaspoon (1 ml) cayenne pepper or paprika
2 teaspoons (10 ml) ground coriander
1 teaspoon (5 ml) sugar
1½ tablespoons (22 ml) lemon juice
2½ tablespoons (37 ml) water
5 tablespoons (75 ml) *ghee* or sesame oil
1 pound (455 g) fresh spinach, trimmed, washed and coarsely chopped, or one
    10-ounce (285 g) package of frozen chopped spinach, defrosted and pressed dry
⅓ pound (150 g) each fresh collard greens, mustard greens and kale, stemmed,
    washed and chopped, or one 10-ounce (285 g) package of frozen mixed greens,
    defrosted and pressed dry
1–1½ teaspoons (5–7 ml) salt
6–8 lemon or lime wedges

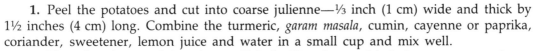

    1. Peel the potatoes and cut into coarse julienne—⅓ inch (1 cm) wide and thick by 1½ inches (4 cm) long. Combine the turmeric, *garam masala*, cumin, cayenne or paprika, coriander, sweetener, lemon juice and water in a small cup and mix well.

    2. Heat the *ghee* or oil in a heavy 12-inch (30 cm) nonstick frying pan or sauté pan over moderately high heat. Add the potatoes and fry, gently turning, until they are golden brown. Remove with a slotted spoon and set aside.

    3. Reduce the heat to low, add the spice blend and fry until all of the liquid has evaporated. Stir in the greens, cover and cook for 10–15 minutes; you may add a sprinkle of water during the cooking if the excess on the leaves has evaporated. Uncover, add the salt and stir well to blend in the spices.

    4. Add the potatoes, cover and let them warm through, about 5 minutes. Gently fold the potatoes into the greens. Accompany each serving with a lemon or lime wedge, or arrange on a warmed platter garnished with citrus wedges.

Curried Greens and Eggplant

BAIGAN SAK

.The "heat" in this *sak* should be noticeable. Fresh green chilies, though unpredictable in strength, are usually milder than dried red chilies. If you are very sensitive to chilies, try fresh Anaheims or yellow wax. To be authentic, this dish should be a bit hot and spicy. Bengalis sauté the greens quickly over high heat, allowing them to wilt, then soften, but still retain exuberant color and fresh flavor.

Preparation time (after assembling ingredients): a few minutes
Cooking time: 10–15 minutes
Serves: 4 or 5

4 tablespoons (60 ml) peanut oil plus
    2 tablespoons (30 ml) mustard oil, or
    6 tablespoons (90 ml) vegetable oil
1 small eggplant (8–10 ounces/230–285 g),
    cut into ¾-inch (2 cm) cubes
½ teaspoon (2 ml) *garam masala*
½ teaspoon (2 ml) turmeric
1–2 whole green jalapeño chilies, dried
    whole red chilies, Anaheim chilies or
    yellow wax chilies (or as desired)
1 teaspoon (5 ml) each crushed fennel seeds,
    coriander seeds and cumin seeds
½ cassia or bay leaf
1 pound (455 g) fresh spinach, trimmed, washed
    and coarsely chopped, or one 10-ounce (285 g)
    package of frozen chopped spinach, defrosted
    and pressed dry
1 teaspoon (5 ml) *jaggery* or maple syrup
½ tablespoon (7 ml) salt
1 tablespoon (15 ml) lemon or lime juice
4 or 5 lemon or lime wedges

    1. Heat 4 tablespoons (60 ml) of peanut or vegetable oil in a nonstick wok or large frying pan over moderately high heat. When it is hot but not smoking, drop in the eggplant and stir-fry until reddish-brown and crisp. Remove with a slotted spoon and drain on paper towels. Sprinkle with *garam masala* and turmeric, and toss to coat the cubes with spices.
    2. Add the mustard oil or the remaining 2 tablespoons (30 ml) vegetable oil to the pan. Heat the mustard oil to the smoking point for a few seconds, but only allow the vegetable oil to become hot. Immediately add the chilies, spice seeds and cassia or bay leaf, and in a few seconds add the greens, sugar and salt. Reduce the heat to moderate and cook for about 4 minutes, stirring frequently.
    3. Add the lemon or lime juice and fried eggplant, toss gently and reheat the eggplant. Serve immediately, garnished with lemon or lime wedges.

Bengali Spinach

BADAAM SAK

Srila Prabhupada encouraged me to observe cooking techniques from the expert chefs at the C. L. Bajoria household in Calcutta. On one occasional visit, I arrived just after Mr. Bajoria had returned from his hill station resort and jute plantations in Bihar. He had brought back kilos of hand picked raw almonds. Each was encased in a soft, greenish skin with a texture somewhere between those of crisp apples and water chestnuts. They were served at breakfast as nibblers, accompanied by several varieties of seasonal fruit. For the evening meal, the ingenious cooks chose to contrast the crisp almonds with stir-fried spinach. As an alternative to almonds, try peanuts or pistachios.

Preparation and nut soaking time: at least 4 hours
Cooking time: 25 minutes
Serves: 4 or 5

⅔ cup (100 g) raw almonds, peanuts or pistachios, with skins
2 cups (480 ml) warm water
3 tablespoons (45 ml) *ghee* or sesame oil
1 teaspoon (5 ml) black mustard seeds
½ teaspoon (2 ml) cumin seeds
⅛ teaspoon (0.5 ml) fenugreek seeds
1½ tablespoons (22 ml) *jaggery* or dark brown sugar
½ tablespoon (7 ml) scraped, finely shredded or minced fresh ginger root
1 teaspoon (5 ml) seeded and minced hot green chilies
2 pounds (1 kg) fresh spinach, trimmed, washed and coarsely chopped, or two
    10-ounce (570 g) packages frozen chopped spinach, defrosted and pressed dry
⅓ cup (35 g) freshly shredded coconut, lightly packed
1 teaspoon (5 ml) salt
2 tablespoons (30 ml) heavy cream
⅛ teaspoon (0.5 ml) freshly ground nutmeg
butter and lemon twists for garnishing

1. Soak the nuts in warm water for 4 hours or overnight. Drain and slip off the loose skins. Wash in fresh water, then drain.

2. Heat the *ghee* or oil in a 5-quart/liter nonstick pan over moderate heat. When it is hot but not smoking, add the spice seeds and sugar and fry until the seeds darken and the sugar caramelizes. Add the ginger, chilies, spinach, nuts, coconut and salt, cover, reduce the heat to low, and cook for 10 minutes. Uncover and turn the spinach over with two forks, so that the cooked leaves on the bottom change places with those on the top. Add water if necessary, and cook for another 10 minutes.

3. Stir in the cream and nutmeg and heat for 1–2 minutes. Serve immediately. Garnish each serving with a pat of butter and a lemon twist.

Greens and Plantain with Toasted Almonds

KACHA KELA SAK

Plantains, unlike their ubiquitous smaller cousins, bananas, must be cooked before eating. When they are not available, a good alternative is parsnips. Choose young, tender parsnips—about 8 inches (20 cm) long. In the North Indian style, the coarsely shredded plantains or parsnips and greens are cooked separately, then assembled. They are then thickened into a purée and flavor-enriched with spices and fine cornmeal or chickpea flour.

Preparation time (after assembling ingredients): 10 minutes
Cooking time: 30 minutes
Serves: 4 or 5

1 large plantain or two 8-inch (20 cm) parsnips
1 pound (455 g) fresh spinach, trimmed and washed,
    plus 1 pound (455 g) mixed fresh greens, trimmed
    and washed; or one 10-ounce (285 g) package of
    frozen leaf spinach plus one 10-ounce (285 g)
    package of frozen mixed greens
4 cups (1 liter) water
5 tablespoons (75 ml) *ghee* or corn oil
3 tablespoons (45 ml) fine cornmeal or chickpea flour
1 teaspoon (5 ml) coarsely crushed black mustard seeds
1 teaspoon (5 ml) coarsely crushed cumin seeds
½ teaspoon (2 ml) turmeric
¼ teaspoon (1 ml) cayenne pepper or paprika
1 teaspoon (5 ml) *jaggery* or brown sugar
1 teaspoon (5 ml) salt
3 tablespoons (45 ml) toasted slivered almonds
4 or 5 lemon or lime wedges for garnishing

1. Cut off the skin from the plantain with a sharp paring knife, or peel the parsnips with a potato peeler. Shred through the coarse holes on a grater. Steam or blanch until soft. Drain well.

2. If you are using fresh spinach and mixed greens, bring the water to a boil in a large stockpot. Pack in the greens, reduce the heat, cover and simmer for 15 minutes. Drain well in a colander, pressing out excess moisture. Using two sharp knives scissors fashion, finely chop. Alternatively, cook the frozen spinach and greens according to package directions, drain and press out excess moisture.

3. Heat the *ghee* or oil in a large, heavy-bottomed nonstick frying pan or wok over moderate heat. Add the cornmeal or chickpea flour, black mustard seeds and cumin, and fry, stirring constantly, until the meal or flour darkens a few shades. Stir in the plantain or parsnip and stir-fry for 2 minutes. Add the turmeric, cayenne or paprika, sweetener, salt and greens. Gently stir until hot throughout. Serve on a warmed platter or on individual dishes with a sprinkle of almonds and a citrus wedge.

Spiced Creamed Spinach
MALAI SAK

Throughout India, districts, towns, even individual homes have their own distinct cuisines. This delicious creamed spinach hails from the community of Vaishnava *brahmins* of Delhi, and the final texture and richness are determined by the milk product you select: cream, sour cream, crème fraîche, cream cheese or plain yogurt.

Preparation time (after assembling ingredients): 5 minutes
Cooking time: 15 minutes
Serves: 4 or 5

⅛ teaspoon (0.5 ml) cayenne pepper
½ tablespoon (7 ml) ground coriander
¼ teaspoon (1 ml) freshly ground pepper
⅛ teaspoon (0.5 ml) freshly grated nutmeg
¼ teaspoon (1 ml) turmeric
1 teaspoon (5 ml) *garam masala*
3 tablespoons (45 ml) water
4 tablespoons (60 ml) *ghee* or unsalted butter
⅛ teaspoon (0.5 ml) yellow asafetida powder (*hing*)*
2 pounds (1 kg) fresh spinach, trimmed, washed and coarsely chopped
1 teaspoon (5 ml) salt
½ cup (120 ml) of any of the following: heavy cream, cream cheese
    (cut into cubes), crème fraîche, sour cream or stirred yogurt

*This amount applies only to yellow Cobra brand. Reduce any other asafetida by three-fourths.

1. Combine the cayenne, coriander, black pepper, nutmeg, turmeric and *garam masala* in a small bowl, add the water, and mix well. Melt the *ghee* or butter in a 5-quart/liter nonstick pan over moderate heat. Add the asafetida and let it sizzle for a few seconds, then pour in the spice mixture. Fry for about 2 minutes.

2. Pack in the spinach and sprinkle with the salt. Cover and reduce the heat. Cook for 6–8 minutes, then turn the leaves over so that the uncooked layer on the top changes places with the cooked leaves underneath. Cook for an additional few minutes.

3. Remove the pan from the heat and stir in the desired milk product. Return the pan to the heat and rewarm briefly. (If the yogurt is allowed to simmer, it will curdle.) Serve immediately.

SEASONED VEGETABLE PURÉES

Why do potatoes baked in an oven and potatoes baked in ashes taste so different? Both are cooked by dry heat, but the latter allows charcoal flavors to permeate the skins, resulting in a smoky flavor that is incomparable. It is this taste that is essential to authentic *bhartas*, or vegetable purées.

Few vegetables can stand exposure to open heat without protective covers. Classic *bhartas* are therefore made from those limited few: mature potatoes, yams or sweet potatoes, winter squash and eggplants. If you have a hibachi, fireplace, campfire or pile of fall leaves that has been burning for some time and is covered with white ash, by all means take the opportunity to ash-bake a vegetable and try a *bharta*. Here are three methods of preparing the vegetables—in ashes, in an oven, or over open flame. Potatoes, sweet potatoes, yams and squash are ash- or oven-baked, while eggplant is best ash-baked or gas flame-roasted. Of course, they all can also be baked in an electric or gas oven.

Ash-Baked Vegetables: Wash and dry the vegetable and pierce the skin in a few places. Bake the root vegetables or squash, nestled in a bed of hot white ash. Cook yams and sweet potatoes for 1–1¼ hours, mature baking potatoes for 1½–1¾ hours, and squash, depending on size, for about 2½ hours. The eggplant should be laid on the ash and rotated intermittently until the outside is charred and the inside has become butter-soft throughout, anywhere from 45 minutes to 1 hour. Wearing thick gloves, dig out or lift off the vegetables, then brush off the ashes. Vegetables are done when they easily yield to pressure or can easily be pierced with a fork, offering no resistance. Cut in half, discarding seeds and fiber in squash, and scoop out the soft pulp.

Oven-Baked Vegetables: Wash and dry the vegetable, then pierce the skin in a few places. I like to rub butter on the root vegetables and eggplant and then rub with smoked salt before baking. Bake in a preheated 425°F (220°C) oven, allowing about 1 hour for mature baking potatoes, 45–50 minutes for yams or sweet potatoes, about 45 minutes for eggplants resting on a baking sheet. Remove the root vegetables or squash with a mitt. They are done when they easily yield to pressure or when the thick skins can be easily pierced with a fork. The eggplant is done when butter soft. Cut the baked squash in half, discarding the seeds and fibers, and scoop out the soft pulp.

Roasted or Broiled Eggplants: Wash and dry medium-sized eggplants, then prick the surface in seven or eight places. To roast on top of the stove, line the burner with aluminum foil. Turn the heat on low and set an eggplant, stem side up, directly on the burner. Roast for 5–6 minutes or until the skin is charred. Lay it on its side and cook until charred, then give it a quarter-turn and char, bit by bit, for 20 minutes or until the entire eggplant is blistered and charred and the flesh is butter-soft. To broil in an oven, preheat the broiler and lay the eggplant on a foil-lined tray. Broil until the skin is charred, then rotate and broil the eggplant, bit by bit, for about 15–20 minutes or until the entire skin is charred and the flesh is butter soft. Let cool briefly, then rinse with water and pat dry. Split open and scoop out the eggplant, discarding the skin.

Zesty Mashed Potatoes
ALOO BHARTA

Mature potatoes—large russets or Idahos, mealy and dry-fleshed, are ideal for mashing. Bake or boil them, mash them while hot, and season, allowing a little "heat" from the green chilies. I sometimes imitate ash-baked flavor by adding a sprinkle of smoked salt rather than using all sea salt. This is a good place to introduce *Ginger Ghee* or flavored butters.

Preparation time: (after assembling ingredients): a few minutes
Serves: 4

5–6 mature baking potatoes (about 2 pounds/1 kg),
    freshly ash- or oven-baked (page 89),
    or freshly boiled or steamed potatoes
3–4 tablespoons (45–60 ml) seasoned or plain
    butter or *ghee*
1 teaspoon (5 ml) salt
⅛ teaspoon (0.5 ml) freshly ground pepper
1–2 seeded and minced hot green chilies
3 tablespoons (45 ml) scalded cream or milk
fresh parsley or coriander sprigs for garnishing

1. Cut the warm baked potatoes and scoop out the pulp, or peel the skins from boiled or steamed potatoes. Mash with a potato masher or force through a food mill or potato ricer. Add the remaining ingredients and whisk with a fork until creamy and blended. Serve immediately or keep warm in a double boiler.

Mashed Potato Balls with Horseradish
MASALA ALOO BHARTA

Horseradish, a pungent tap root, is used primarily in Bengali and Orissan cuisines, though occasionally elsewhere. You can find the roots at Oriental and Indian grocery stores and sometimes even in supermarkets. Peel off the brownish skin and finely grate the outer part; discard the tough woody core. Since you are likely to use only a little at a time, you can freeze the unused portion in plastic bags for up to two months. At room temperature, freshly ground horseradish loses its "punch" within eight hours. In England, and in some American gourmet shops, plain grated horseradish is sold in small bottles.

This side dish is meant to be nose-tingling and buttery. It is served in smooth balls, 2 or 3 per person, at room temperature, with a wedge of lime. If you are considering a full-course Bengali meal, do give this delightful potato dish a try. It is also delicious for breakfast, spread on whole grain toast sprinkled with shredded cheese and broiled.

Preparation time (after assembling ingredients): a few minutes
Serves: 6 or 7

3 large baking potatoes (about 1½
    pounds/685 g) freshly ash- or oven-baked
    (page 89) or freshly boiled or steamed
4–5 tablespoons (60–75 ml) unsalted butter
2–3 teaspoons (10–15 ml) grated fresh horseradish
1 teaspoon (5 ml) salt
⅛ teaspoon (0.5 ml) freshly ground white pepper
⅛ teaspoon (0.5 ml) paprika or cayenne pepper
6 or 7 lime wedges, preferably Key lime

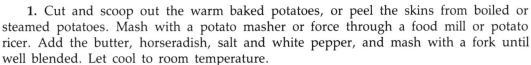

1. Cut and scoop out the warm baked potatoes, or peel the skins from boiled or steamed potatoes. Mash with a potato masher or force through a food mill or potato ricer. Add the butter, horseradish, salt and white pepper, and mash with a fork until well blended. Let cool to room temperature.

2. Divide into 12–15 portions and roll between buttered palms into smooth balls. Sprinkle with paprika or cayenne and serve at room temperature with lime wedges.

Note: This dish may be assembled up to 6 hours before serving, kept covered and refrigerated. Bring to room temperature before serving.

Baked Eggplant Purée with Seasoned Yogurt
BAIGAN BHARTA

Eggplant *bharta*, in one form or another, is a national favorite of India. I learned to make this variation during my first Bombay residence in the kitchen of the Kailash Seksaria family. The cooks excel at several regional cuisines, and this Punjabi-style presentation was a favorite of hosts and guests alike. Baby white eggplants were ever-so-slowly ash-baked on a nearly burned-out *neem* wood fire until they nearly fell apart. Chilies and seasonings gave the dish a feisty punch, and the yogurt added creamy distinction.

Preparation time (after assembling ingredients): 5 minutes
Cooking time: 15 minutes
Serves: 4

1 medium-sized eggplant (1–1¼ pounds/455–570 g),
    freshly baked, roasted or broiled (page 89)
2 tablespoons (30 ml) *ghee* or vegetable oil
1–2 teaspoons (5–10 ml) hot green chilies,
    seeded and minced
¼ teaspoon (1 ml) yellow asafetida powder (*hing*)*
1 teaspoon (5 ml) cumin seeds
1 teaspoon (5 ml) ground coriander
1 teaspoon (5 ml) salt
2 tablespoons (30 ml) each finely chopped
    fresh coriander and mint
⅔ cup (160 ml) plain yogurt or sour cream
1 teaspoon (5 ml) *garam masala*

*This amount applies only to yellow Cobra brand. Reduce any other asafetida by three-fourths.

1. Slice the eggplant in half lengthwise and carefully scoop out the pulp. Discard the skin and coarsely chop the pulp.

2. Heat the *ghee* or oil in a large nonstick frying pan over moderate heat. When it is hot but not smoking, add the green chilies, asafetida and cumin seeds and fry until the cumin seeds darken. Add the eggplant, ground coriander and salt, and cook, stirring frequently, until the mixture is dry and thick, about 10 minutes.

3. Remove the pan from the heat and let cool to room temperature. Stir in the fresh herbs, yogurt or sour cream and *garam masala*. (You may want to add a sprinkle of smoked salt if you baked the eggplant in an electric or gas oven.) Serve hot, at room temperature or chilled.

Butternut Squash Purée with Coconut
KADDU BHARTA

Pumpkin is the most popular winter squash in India. It is sold in cut pieces. This bright orange squash is more often boiled than baked. In the West, we can ash- or oven-bake whole smaller varieties, such as butternut, acorn, Hubbard or buttercup. Flavor and nutrition are locked within the tough, thick skin. A delicate blend of cardamom, fennel and lime juice beautifully offsets the sweet purée. Garnish with toasted coconut and/or hazelnuts.

Preparation time (after assembling ingredients): a few minutes
Cooking time: 15 minutes
Serves: 4

1 large butternut squash (about 1 pound/455 g), freshly baked or steamed
4 tablespoons (60 ml) unsalted butter
2 teaspoons (10 ml) fennel seeds, crushed
½ teaspoon (2 ml) cardamom seeds, crushed
1–2 teaspoons (5–10 ml) hot green chilies, seeded and minced
2–3 tablespoons (30–45 ml) *jaggery*, maple sugar or syrup
3 tablespoons (45 ml) cream (optional)
1 teaspoon (5 ml) salt
¼ cup (25 g) shredded coconut and/or chopped hazelnuts,
    toasted in a 300°F (150°C) oven until golden
2 tablespoons (30 ml) lime juice

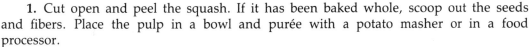

    1. Cut open and peel the squash. If it has been baked whole, scoop out the seeds and fibers. Place the pulp in a bowl and purée with a potato masher or in a food processor.
    2. Heat 3 tablespoons (45 ml) of the butter in a 12-inch (30 cm) nonstick frying pan over moderate heat. When it is hot and frothing, add the fennel seeds, cardamom seeds and green chilies. Within seconds add the squash purée, sweetener, cream, if desired, and salt. Cook, stirring frequently, until thickened, about 5 minutes. Before serving, garnish with coconut or hazelnuts, the remaining butter and sprinkle with lime juice.

Buttery Sweet Potato Purée with Tomato Bits
SHAKARKAND BHARTA

For this dish you can use either yams or sweet potatoes, depending on the degree of sweetness or moisture you prefer. It is little more than a seasoned mashed root vegetable dish, and is nice with a Vedic or Western dinner menu. To keep calories to a minimum, rely on the orange juice to make a buttery consistency. The sweet, firm flesh of Italian plum tomatoes is ideal for this *bharta*, though you can use any type; even green tomatoes are delicious.

Preparation time (after assembling ingredients): a few minutes
Cooking time: about 10 minutes
Serves: 6

6 medium-sized yams or sweet potatoes
   (about 2 pounds/1 kg) freshly ash-
   or oven-baked (page 89)
1 teaspoon (5 ml) salt
½ teaspoon (2 ml) turmeric
¼ teaspoon (1 ml) paprika or
   ⅛ teaspoon (0.5 ml) cayenne pepper
¼ teaspoon (1 ml) ground nutmeg or mace
   or ⅛ teaspoon (0.5 ml) ground ginger
4 tablespoons (60 ml) orange juice
½ teaspoon (2 ml) orange zest
3 tablespoons (45 ml) *ghee* or butter
1½ tablespoons (22 ml) brown sugar or *jaggery*
2 medium-sized Italian plum tomatoes (about
   ¾ pound/340 g), seeded and coarsely chopped
2 tablespoons (30 ml) sliced almonds, toasted

1. Cut and scoop out the yam or sweet potato pulp and mash with a potato masher or force through a food mill or potato ricer. Add the salt, turmeric, paprika or cayenne, nutmeg, mace or ginger, orange juice and orange zest, and whisk with a fork until well blended.

2. Heat the *ghee* or butter in a 12-inch (30 cm) frying pan over moderate heat. Add the sweetener and cook until it caramelizes and turns reddish-brown. Drop in the tomatoes and cook, gently tossing, just until they soften and glisten.

3. Add the yams or sweet potatoes and, using the back of a wooden spoon, mash and blend the ingredients. When warmed throughout, serve on a warmed platter, garnished with toasted almonds.

STUFFED VEGETABLES

Baked Bananas Stuffed with Tamarind–Flavored Coconut
NARIYAL BHARA KELA

Bananas are native to India and are one of the most popular fruits of the nation. There are said to be staggering 400 varieties of bananas. Even so, they are divided into only two categories: eating and cooking. In this dish, a small, very sweet eating banana, either yellow or red–skinned, is preferred. Known as lady fingers or golden fingers, they are often available in Mexican or Indian grocery stores. Though they are traditionally baked in softened banana leaf wrappers on a coal–fed oven, I find that they bake wonderfully in any oven and in almost any type of baking dish.

Preparation time (after assembling ingredients): 15 minutes
Cooking time : 20 minutes
Makes: 8 side dish servings

2 tablespoons (30 ml) instant tamarind concentrate (available at Indian groceries)
1½ tablespoons (22 ml) water
1 tablespoon (15 ml) minced fresh mint or ½ teaspoon (2 ml) dried mint
⅛ teaspoon (0.5 ml) cayenne pepper or ¼ teaspoon (1 ml) paprika
3 tablespoons (45 ml) grated fresh or dried coconut
1 teaspoon (5 ml) *garam masala*
½ teaspoon (2 ml) *ajwain* seeds or fennel seeds, crushed
¼ teaspoon (1 ml) salt
8 small firm ripe bananas, no more than 6–7 inches (15–18.5 cm) long, preferably
    "finger" bananas, red or yellow, 4–5 inches (10–12.5 cm) long
3 tablespoons (45 ml) slivered almonds
½ cup (120 ml) maple syrup
2 tablespoons (30 ml) finely chopped crystallized ginger
1 tablespoon (15 ml) each lime and orange juice
2 tablespoons (30 ml) melted butter

1. Combine the tamarind concentrate with water and whisk with a fork until blended. Add the mint, cayenne or paprika, coconut, *garam masala, ajwain* or fennel seeds and salt, and toss to mix.

2. Preheat the oven to 375°F (190°C). Peel the bananas and, using a sharp paring knife, cut a slit about two–thirds through the flesh lengthwise, leaving ¼ inch (6 mm) uncut at each end. Very carefully ease the tamarind–coconut mixture evenly into the slits. Arrange in a single layer in a baking dish and scatter slivered almonds over the bananas.

3. Combine the maple syrup, crystallized ginger, lime and orange juice and butter in a bowl and stir until blended. Pour the syrup over the bananas and bake for about 20 minutes, basting occasionally to keep them moist. Serve with a drizzle of the thickened syrup, either warm or at room temperature.

Pishima's Stuffed Okra
BHARA BHINDI

This is my favorite stuffed okra recipe, and I have stuck as close as possible to the original version I learned from my well-wishing Vaishnava teacher and cooking inspiration, Pishima.

Preparation time (after assembling ingredients): 30 minutes
Cooking time: 20–30 minutes
Serves: 6

1½ pounds (685 g) tender okra, preferably 4-inch
    (10 cm) pods, washed and thoroughly dried
2 tablespoons (30 ml) coarsely crushed coriander seeds
1 tablespoon (15 ml) coarsely crushed cumin seeds
2 teaspoons (10 ml) fennel seeds
½ teaspoon (2 ml) freshly ground pepper
1 tablespoon (15 ml) *garam masala*
¼ teaspoon (1 ml) cayenne pepper or paprika
¼ teaspoon (1 ml) yellow asafetida powder (*hing*)*
½ teaspoon (2 ml) turmeric
1 tablespoon (15 ml) ground almonds
½ teaspoon (2 ml) *amchoor* powder or
    ½ tablespoon (7 ml) lemon juice
5 tablespoons (75 ml) *ghee* or sunflower oil
½ tablespoon (7 ml) salt

*This amount applies only to yellow Cobra brand. Reduce any other asafetida by three-fourths.

1. Slice off the stem end and ⅛ inch (3 mm) off the tip of each okra pod. Slit each one lengthwise, leaving ¼ inch (6 mm) unslit at both ends, taking care not to cut the pods in half.

2. Combine the crushed coriander seeds, cumin seeds, fennel seeds, black pepper, *garam masala*, cayenne or paprika, asafetida, turmeric, ground almonds and *amchoor* powder if you're using it. After mixing the ingredients together, drizzle in the lemon juice (if you haven't used *amchoor*) and 2 teaspoons (10 ml) of *ghee* or oil, and crumble through your fingers to blend well into a dry, oatmeal like consistency.

3. Using a teaspoon or butter knife, ease about ¼ teaspoon (1 ml) of the stuffing evenly into each slit. Working one at a time, stuff, then press the cut edges closed and set aside, covered, until ready to cook.

4. When you are ready to fry the okra, place the *ghee* or oil in a heavy-bottomed 12-inch (30 cm) frying pan over moderately high heat. When it is hot but not smoking, add the stuffed okra and spread the pods into one layer. Cover, reduce the heat to moderate and cook for about 5 minutes. Remove the lid, gently turn the okra to ensure even browning, and fry, turning frequently, for 20–25 minutes or until the okra is tender, golden brown and crisp. Depending on the size of the pods, cooking time will vary. Transfer the okra to paper towels, salt and gently toss. Serve piping hot.

Pan-Fried Baby Eggplants Stuffed with Ground Almonds
BADAAM BHARA BAIGAN

Eggplant is a native of India and is prepared in almost every conceivable way. As a side-dish vegetable, baby white or purple eggplants are slit, spread with spices and pan-fried until butter soft. Although baby whites (which look like large eggs) are only available at specialty greengrocers in large cities, the seeds are sold through numerous mail order and retail outlets. They are as easy to grow as tomatoes. You could also use small, narrow Japanese eggplants for this dish.

Preparation time: 15–20 minutes
Cooking time: about 30 minutes
Serves: 6

12 baby white or purple eggplants (2 ounces/60 g each)
3 tablespoons (45 ml) ground almonds
1 tablespoon (15 ml) ground coriander
1 teaspoon (5 ml) ground cumin
1 teaspoon (5 ml) *garam masala*
½ teaspoon (2 ml) turmeric
¼ teaspoon (1 ml) cayenne pepper
½ teaspoon (2 ml) *amchoor* powder or ½
   tablespoon (7 ml) lime juice
¼ teaspoon (1 ml) yellow asafetida powder (*hing*)*
½ tablespoon (7 ml) salt
4 tablespoons (60 ml) *ghee* or vegetable oil
2 coin-sized slices of peeled fresh ginger root
6 sprigs fresh coriander or parsley for garnishing

This amount applies only to yellow Cobra brand. Reduce any other asafetida by three-fourths.

1. Almost halve the eggplants, cutting from the rounded base end to within ½ inch (1.5 cm) of the stem and cap. Soak in cold water for 10 minutes or until they open up slightly. Drain in a colander, then pat the outsides dry with paper towels.

2. Combine the almonds, spices and salt in a small dish and mix well. Smear the stuffing on the cut surfaces of the eggplants until all the mixture is used. Gently press the eggplants together to reshape them, then bind them closed by winding 2 or 3 rounds of ordinary white sewing thead around the thick end, and twist to knot.

3. Combine the *ghee* or oil and sliced ginger root in a heavy-bottomed 12-inch (30 cm) nonstick frying pan. Place the pan over moderate heat and when the *ghee* or oil is hot but not smoking, drop in the eggplants and cook, gently tossing, for about 8 minutes or until they are glossy and lightly browned. Reduce the heat to low, cover and cook for about 20 minutes, turning the eggplants 3 or 4 times to brown evenly on all sides. Remove the threads and garnish with herb sprigs before serving.

Pan-Fried Whole Bitter Melons with Cashew Stuffing

KAJU BHARA KARELA

Salting and preparation time: about 1 hour
Cooking time: 30 minutes
Makes: 8 stuffed bitter melons

8 baby bitter melons (about 12 ounces/340 g
    each), 2½–3 inches (6.5–7.5 cm) long
1½ tablespoons (22 ml) salt
½ tablespoon (7 ml) sugar
3 cups (710 ml) water
½ cup (75 g) cashew halves, blanched
    almonds or hazelnuts
3 tablespoons (45 ml) shredded fresh coconut
    or shredded frozen coconut, defrosted
½ tablespoon (7 ml) dark brown sugar
½ teaspoon (2 ml) fennel seeds
1 teaspoon (5 ml) cumin seeds
l tablespoon (15 ml) coriander seeds
½ teaspoon (2 ml) turmeric
¼ teaspoon (1 ml) cayenne pepper or paprika
¼ cup (60 ml) plain yogurt
5 tablespoons (75 ml) *ghee* or vegetable oil
lime wedges for garnishing

1. Wash and dry the bitter melons. With a sharp paring knife, slit lengthwise, cutting halfway through each. Using a small melon baller, scoop out the pulp and seeds and discard. Rub each melon inside and out with salt and sugar, and set aside for 30 minutes. Bring the water to a boil in a 2-quart/liter saucepan and partially cook for 10 minutes. Remove them with a slotted spoon and plunge into cold water. After cooling for 5 minutes, drain and pat thoroughly dry, inside and out.

2. To make the stuffing, place the nuts, coconut, brown sugar, fennel seeds, cumin seeds and coriander seeds in a blender or food processor fitted with a metal blade. Cover and pulse until the nuts are powdered. Transfer to a bowl and add the turmeric, cayenne or paprika and enough of the yogurt to make a moist stuffing. Divide into 8 portions.

3. Using a butter knife, stuff each bitter melon, handling them carefully to avoid tearing the uncut side. Press the two cut melon edges together until they meet, then bind each one closed, wrapping them from one end to the other 5 or 6 times around with ordinary white sewing thread.

4. Heat the *ghee* or oil in a 8–9-inch (20–22.5 cm) frying pan over moderate heat. When it is hot but not smoking, add the melons in a single layer. After 2 minutes, reduce the heat slightly, then pan-fry, turning them as they brown, so that they are crisp and richly colored, about 20–25 minutes.

5. Remove with a slotted spoon and drain on paper towels. Snip the thread and unwind, removing all loose pieces. Serve hot and crispy with lime wedges.

Dairy Products

Perhaps you have traveled to India and, sitting in the back of a speeding cab, experienced something like this: Moving at a breakneck pace, the car approaches a trio of lotus-eyed white cows sleeping smack in the middle of the street. The driver toots his horn, people scatter, the driver deftly swerves, misses the cows and weaves on through a labyrinth of city congestion. That was no mere stroke of good luck. No one, taxi drivers included, would ever disturb the cows. In India, cows, calves and bulls are free to wander through the streets of cities and villages. Further, millions of residents, many very poor, share their meager sustenance with a pet cow or calf. Naturally, you may ask, why does an entire country maintain such reverence for cows?

The answer can be traced to the vast religio/philosophical texts of India known as the *Vedas*. Comprising voluminous *Puranas* (histories) and *Upanishads* (philosophic treatises), the *Vedas* detail the laws, morals and knowledge required to lead one to the ultimate stage of spiritual perfection. Each level of development, from social to intellectual to spiritual, is meticulously detailed so as to give the best chance for rapid spiritual development. The first stage of spiritual progress comes in learning to live in harmony with the land. India—still very much an agrarian culture—acknowledges the vital part cows play in the well-being of the community; indeed, the Sanskrit word *go* means both "cow" and "land." Protecting both is considered a religious duty and the secret to peace and prosperity. Both are also the basis of a vegetarian diet for hundreds of millions in India, providing milk products, grains, legumes, vegetables and fruits.

Milk is considered to be a perfect, complete food that nourishes the brain and calms the nerves, thus facilitating *yoga* practice. To own a cow is to possess great wealth, and despite suggestions by uninformed observers that reverence for cows impedes India's economic self-sufficiency, no one is willing to give up owning them.

The Puranic text *Srimad Bhagavatam* tells us something of cow protection in former ages. The First Canto describes the shock, anger and decisive reaction of Pariksit Maharaj, one of the last great kings of the Vedic period, when he discovered someone attempting to butcher a cow. Elsewhere in the *Bhagavatam*, The Eleventh Canto pays tribute to Nanda Maharaj of Vrindavan, whose immense wealth stemmed from his unflagging protection of the cows under his care: "The bodies of the cows, bulls and calves were painted with a mixture of oil and turmeric mixed with varieties of precious minerals. Their heads were bedecked with peacock feathers, and they were each garlanded with flowers and covered with cloth and golden ornaments." The cows sensed that they were protected, and in their happiness they saturated the pasturing fields with their milk.

The *Vedas* compare milk to nectar, and the cooks in India's Vedic times made full use of the creative possiblities of milk and its three main products—butter, fresh unripened cheeses and yogurt—both as raw ingredients and as the basis for thousands of sweet and savory dishes. The ancient process of sterilizing milk was very simple: twice a day, morning and evening, all of the milk was quickly brought to a boil three times. Milk was so abundant that it was considered stale at half a day old! Every drop was used; the whey left over from freshly churned butter, called *chaach*, was fed to domestic animals.

The milk most of us buy starts out as it always has, with the cow, but then it is subjected to the intricacies of modern processing technology. First, the milk is no longer drawn from the cows by hand but by machine, and pumped directly into 37°F (3°C) holding tanks, pending pasteurization and then homogenization. Then the milk is labeled according to its percentage of butterfat. Most American milk comes from Holstein cows and is pale and bland. Store-bought skim milk contains less than 0.5 percent butterfat; low-fat milk, 2 percent; whole milk, about 3.25 percent; extra-rich milk, 4 percent; half-and-half, at least 10.5 percent; light cream, at least 18 percent; whipping or heavy cream, 30–36 percent; and catering heavy cream, up to 40 percent. Certified raw milk—with the highest butterfat content of all—is available in Oregon and California. California's Alta Dena is the nations largest raw milk producer.

British milk has color-coded metallic caps on the bottle tops. Green means certified raw milk; silver, pasteurized; red, homogenized; blue, sterilized; and gold, pasturized rich Guernsey or Jersey (at least 4 percent butterfat). Some outstanding European specialty milk products, such as England's Cornish clotted cream with 60 percent butterfat, and double cream, with 48 percent, as well as French crème fraîche, with 40 percent butterfat, are now sold at supermarkets in large cities.

Milk is dried or powdered by spray drying or roller drying. Spray-dried milk is made by spraying whole or skim milk into a large chamber of hot air. Powder forms and falls to the bottom of the chamber. Then it is processed (at temperatures lower than those for roller drying) into nutritious powdered milk. Roller-dried milk is made by putting a film of milk on a heated steel roller and scraping it off when dried. Although spray-dried non-fat, non-instant powdered milk is best for adding body to yogurt, it does not work well in quick and easy milk fudges. British whole milk powder is excellent for making shortcut milk fudge, but is not available in America. No matter what your choice, check the expiration date on powdered milks. If it is sold in bulk, give it a sniff: it should have virtually no smell. If it is old, it will have a "milky" odor.

Because milk and its products are as perishable as they are valuable, keep them refrigerated at 35–40°F (1–5°C). For each hour that milk is kept over 45°F (7°C), it loses one day of freshness.

Since most Vedic dishes call for milk that is heated at least to the boiling point, equipment is also important. Milk is sensitive to bacteria, and porous utensils such as wooden spatulas absorb bacteria easily. Heavy-bottomed thick stainless steel, enamel-covered cast iron, and nonstick heavy aluminum cookware are all better choices. If you delve into making *ghee*, yogurt or fresh cheese on a regular basis, buy one or two pans and reserve them exclusively for milk.

HOMEMADE BUTTER AND SEASONED
VARIATIONS

Understandably, village life in India centers on land and cows; but even in urban areas, the majority of households make their own fresh butter and *ghee* weekly. I was first inspired to make my own butter when living in southern Oregon's Rogue Valley. Fresh from a five-year stay in India, I settled into a small farm complete with garden plot, orchards and a family pet Guernsey cow named Bhimala. With the arrival of her first calf, Bhimala produced an astounding 4½ gallons (18 liters) of milk daily for three years non-stop—enough to supply five families and a local restaurant with whole and skimmed milk, yogurt, crème fraîche and seasoned butters. I am no longer on a farm. Gone are the milk separator and butter churn. Now I use cartons of store-bought heavy cream and a food processor.

Where I live now, heavy cream costs roughly $3.00 a quart/liter. That quart/liter churns into 1¼–1¾ pounds (570–795 g) of butter. As of this writing, a pound (455 g) of unsalted butter costs about $2.40 and it costs me $1.70–$2.40 a pound to make it at home. The savings are not great—maybe enough for a new food processor attachment or a knife now and then—but I much prefer the quality of the homemade. If you use fresh cream, the pure skim buttermilk that is left over will be sweet; if you use ripened cream, it will be tart. I prefer the sweet, but both are usable in breads, muffins, some soups and fruit drinks. So far as the cream is concerned, I find that the flavor depends mainly on the kind of pasture where the cows grazed. Bhimala grazed in alfalfa fields full of buttercups and wild lavender, and her milk was the sweetest imaginable. But no matter what your source, you are sure to be delighted with homemade fresh unsalted butter.

Homemade Butter

MAKHAN

In Indian homes, butter is churned today much as it has been for thousands of years. A large earthen pot called a *ghara* is half-filled with several days worth of ripened cream. By using a system of interconnected sticks and ropes, hand-agitation makes a wooden paddle whirl butter flecks into butter blobs. Our modern wonder the food processor has more than simplified the procedure. Depending on the size of your work bowl, you can process 1–2 quarts/liters at a time.

Preparation time (after ingredients are assembled): 10–20 minutes
Makes 1¼–1¾ pounds (570–795 g)

1 quart/liter heavy cream
½ cup (120 ml) ice water
2 ice cubes, cracked

Bring the refrigerated cream to about 60°F (15°C). Fit the food processor with a metal blade, add the cream, cover and process. That's all! As it is whipped, the cream gets thicker and thicker—like custard—then finally separates into flecks of butter. Add the ice water and cracked ice at this point to encourage the butter to form into large lumps. Strain off the buttermilk and, using your hands, knead the butter and squeeze out the milky whey. (Alternatively, work the butter with two grooved wooden butter paddles.) When it is clean and compact, rinse under very cold running water, then store in a well-sealed container. You can add salt or seasoned salt to taste, if desired. Well sealed, the butter can be kept frozen for up to 3 months.

Cardamom-Orange Butter
ELAICHE MAKHAN

This butter can be made with either orange juice concentrate or orange marmalade, both yielding vibrant results. Equally delicious is a variation made with rose petal jam. Both orange and rose are compatible with cardamom. Best served on morning breads, muffins or crackers.

Preparation time (after ingredients are assembled): a few minutes
Makes 1¼–1¾ pounds (570–795 g)

1–1½ pounds (455–685 g) unsalted butter, preferably
    homemade (page 104), at room temperature
3 tablespoons (45 ml) frozen orange or
    orange-pineapple juice concentrate or
1½ tablespoons (22 ml) Seville orange marmalade
    or rose petal jam
1 tablespoon (15 ml) coarsely crushed cardamom seeds
1½ tablespoons (22 ml) orange flower or rose water (optional)

Cut the butter into 1-inch (2.5 cm) pieces and put them in a food processor fitted with a metal blade. Add the juice concentrate, marmalade or jam, cardamom and optional orange flower or rose water. Cover and process until the cardamom is ground and the butter is light and fluffy. May be used at room temperature or chilled, in molds or a butter crock. Well sealed, the butter can also be kept frozen for up to 3 months.

Mint-Lime Butter
PODINA MAKHAN

I feel that a splash of lime or lemon juice livens up almost any food, and for those who are cutting down on salt it is a flavor booster and natural salt substitute. The limes in India are most like our Key limes: yellowish-skinned, very juicy and sour. The dark green-skinned limes from Florida are quite acid by comparison. If you wish to control flavors, use lemon or lime juice for sourness, the zest for concentrated taste, and fresh lemon verbena or lemon balm leaves for a milder suggestion of a flavor. I like to serve this butter on almost any *dal* dish, wet or dry.

Preparation time (after ingredients are assembled): a few minutes
Makes: 1 pound (455 g)

1 pound (455 g) unsalted butter, preferably
    homemade (page 104), at room temperature
¼ cup (60 ml) chopped fresh mint
3 tablespoons (45 ml) lime or lemon juice or
    1 tablespoon (15 ml) grated lime zest or 3 tablespoons
    (45 ml) chopped fresh lemon verbena or lemon balm

Cut the butter into 1-inch (2.5 cm) pieces and put them in a food processor fitted with a metal blade. Add the mint leaves and citrus flavoring and process until the butter is fluffy and the leaves are finely chopped. Well sealed, it can be kept refrigerated for 1–2 weeks or frozen for up to 3 months.

Basil-Nutmeg Butter
JAIPHAL MAKHAN

I like to serve this butter with whole grain dishes—from steamed rice to cracked wheat, buckwheat, kasha or millet pilaf. It is equally a natural over blanched *paparh* or *pappadam* noodles. The possibilities are endless. Flavored butters are eye-catching when molded, dressing up even everyday dishes. For entertaining, take time to make individual molds, and keep any leftovers frozen for quick occasional garnishing of steamed vegetables.

Preparation time (after ingredients are assembled): a few minutes
Makes: 1 pound (455 g)

1 pound (455 g) unsalted butter, preferably
    homemade (page 104), at room temperature
⅓ cup (80 ml) chopped fresh basil
1 tablespoon (15 ml) freshly ground nutmeg
1 tablespoon (15 ml) chopped fresh coriander
1 teaspoon (5 ml) salt
1 tablespoon (15 ml) black poppy seeds (optional)

Cut the butter into 1-inch (2.5 cm) pieces and put them in a food processor fitted with a metal blade. Add the basil, nutmeg, coriander and salt. Cover and process until the leaves are finely chopped. For additional flavor, stir in the poppy seeds. Well sealed, the butter can be kept frozen for up to 3 months.

Mango–Maple Syrup Butter
AAM MAKHAN

For this recipe you can use mango, papaya, even peaches or pears. Maple syrup has a flavor reminiscent of *jaggery* from Bengal's date palm trees. This elegant butter is a natural for company brunch with assorted tea breads, muffins or biscuits.

Preparation time (after ingredients are assembled): a few minutes
Makes: about 1½ pounds (680 g)

2 tablespoons (30 ml) sugar
5 strips of orange zest, each 4
    inches x ½ inch (10 x 1.5 cm)
1 pound (455 g) unsalted butter, preferably
    homemade (page 104), slightly chilled
    and cut into 1-inch (2.5 cm) pieces
one 3½-ounce (100 g) package of cream cheese
    or neufchatel, brought to room temperature
    and cut into 1-inch (2.5 cm) pieces
1½ cups (360 ml) chopped mango,
    papaya, peach or pear
½ cup (120 ml) maple syrup

Fit a food processor with a metal blade. Add the sugar and orange zest and pulse the machine off and on until the zest is finely minced. Add the butter and cream cheese and process until smooth. Add the fruit and maple syrup and pulse until the fruit is finely chopped but not puréed. Well covered, the butter can be kept refrigerated for up to 3 weeks.

HOMEMADE *GHEE* AND SEASONED
VARIATIONS

For centuries *ghee* has been a sign of wealth in India, and in the Vedic times one who had ample stocks of *ghee* was said to possess liquid gold. Vedic literature actually refers to *ghee* as "food for the brain," a source of protein and energy. Though other oils are used for specific purposes—Bengalis use mustard oil for pickles and green leafy vegetables, coconut oil is favored in Gujarati and Maharastrian cooking, and ground nut or sesame oil is excellent in many dishes—*ghee* is the choice for those who wish to delve into the true Vedic tradition.

Unless you have particular dietary restrictions, cooking in moderate quantities of *ghee* is no more harmful than cooking in any other oil—in fact better, according to some researchers—and the taste cannot be imitated. Some describe it as "nutty and sweet," which I find an elusive description at best. There is something quite wonderful, however, about the caramel-like aroma of a pot of *ghee* simmering on the kitchen stove.

Though butter is an obvious choice for serving at the table and for baking, it cannot be used on the stove for most sautéing or frying. This is because it is composed of about 80 percent pure butterfat, 18 percent water and 2 percent protein solids, and above 250°F (120°C) the solids begin to burn. *Ghee* is the better choice, for it is free of the solids. French clarified butter (which comes closer than butter to being an acceptable sautéing or frying medium) is made by melting unsalted butter and separating the clear yellow butterfat from the milky protein solids. *Ghee* is made by further simmering the melted butter until the protein solids harden and darken slightly. All of the water evaporates, and the concentrated golden butterfat is carefully strained. Not only does the flavor intensify by this method, but the smoking point rises to nearly 375°F (190°C), at which frying and sautéing are fully possible.

Just as flavored butters lend character to the table, *ghee* is often simmered with curry leaves, fresh ginger root, turmeric, peppercorns or green chilies to add suggested flavors. These flavors, when added to the *ghee*, are the simplest way to liven up steamed vegetables, needing only the addition of a splash of lemon juice. You can purchase ready-made *ghee* at Indian and Middle Eastern grocery stores and many gourmet stores. Dutch *ghee* is excellent, Norwegian and Australian *ghee* are also very good, but these are much more costly than homemade. A six-month supply of homemade *ghee* takes very little effort and only a short time to make. For little more than the few minutes it takes to strain and bottle the *ghee* and label the containers, you can have a pure, golden oil that will keep for up to two months in a cool kitchen larder, up to four months if refrigerated, and six months or more when frozen.

In larger cities, health food stores and gourmet stores handle certified raw unsalted butter made from unpasteurized cream—about as close as you can get to the good old days. Because people are becoming more and more cautious about excess salt in their diet, most supermarkets now sell unsalted butter, either fresh or frozen. The third option is to make your own unsalted butter, using heavy cream and a food processor (see page 104). Making *ghee* is neither difficult nor complicated, but the larger the quantity, the longer the cooking time. There are no shortcuts in preparing pure *ghee*. Only by slow cooking over gentle heat is all of the water driven off and the lactose sugar slightly caramelized, lending a sweet flavor to the butterfat.

You can make *ghee* either on the stove or in an oven. If you are in the kitchen anyway and have a free burner, up to 5 pounds (2.5 kg) can conveniently simmer on a back burner. Should you wish to make a stockpile or want to prepare for quantity cooking, you can make two, four, even six times that amount in a large oven overnight, with the *ghee* almost taking care of itself. The chart below gives you an idea of how long it takes to make various amounts by both methods. You will be amazed at how batch yields will vary, mostly because different butters have different liquid contents.

GRADE AA UNSALTED BUTTER	OVEN METHOD	STOVE METHOD	APPROXIMATE YIELD
1 pound (455 g)	1¼–1½ hours	1 hour	1⅔ cups/¾ pound (400 ml/340 g)
2 pounds (900 g)	1¾–2¼ hours	1½ hours	3 cups/1½ pounds (710 ml/685 g)
3 pounds (1.4 kg)	2¾–3¼ hours	2 hours	5 cups/2¼ pounds (1.25 lt/1 kg)
5 pounds (2.3 kg)	3½–4 hours	3 hours	9 cups/4 pounds (2.25 lt/1.8 kg)
10 pounds (4.5 kg)	6½–7 hours	5–5½ hours	17 cups/7¾ pounds (4.25 lt/3.5 kg)
11–20 pounds (5–9 kg)	8–10 hours	6–7½ hours	32 cups/15 pounds (8 lt/7 kg)

Stove-Top *Ghee*
SADA GHEE

Because the procedure is the same for making 1 pound (455 g) or 10 pounds (4.5 kg) of *ghee*, the equipment will be the same. Only pan size, heat regulation and storing containers vary. For safety, allow at least 3 inches (7.5 cm) of empty pan above the surface of the melted butter, no matter how much you make at one time.

For example, to turn 5 pounds (2 kg) of butter into *ghee*, you will need a 5-quart/liter heavy casserole, pressure cooker or stockpot; a fine-mesh wire skimmer or large metal spoon; a small jar; a ladle; a large sieve, lined with a linen towel or four layers of cheesecloth, resting over another pan; and a clean jar, canister or earthenware crock with a tight-fitting lid.

1–5 pounds (½–2 kg) unsalted butter, preferably homemade (page 104)

1. Put the butter, in ¼-pound (115 g) pieces, in the casserole. Melt it over moderate heat, turning it about to ensure that it melts slowly and does not sizzle or brown at any time. When the butter has melted, increase the heat and bring it to a boil. When the surface is covered with a frothy foam, stir gently and reduce the heat to very low. Simmer, uncovered and undisturbed, until the gelatinous protein solids have settled on the bottom of the pan and turned from white to golden brown, and the thin crust on the surface of the near-motionless butterfat is transparent.

2. With the skimmer, remove the thin dry crust resting on the *ghee* and set it aside in the small jar. At this point, note the color and fragrance of the clear *ghee*. If the solids on the bottom of the pan are darker than golden brown, if the fragrance is intense, or if the color is dark—like toasted sesame oil—the butter has cooked too long or over too high a heat. If this is the case, I would suggest discarding the solids. The *ghee* is still usable, but next time adjust the heat or the cooking time.

Oven-Method *Ghee*
CHOOLA GHEE

This is the best method for making a stockpile of *ghee*. Because the heat surrounds the *ghee*, rather than contacting only the bottom of the pan, the cooking is slower but almost effortless. More of a crust will harden on the surface, and the solids at the bottom of the pan will remain soft and somewhat gelatinous. Adjust the pan size to the quantity of butter you are turning into *ghee*. Always allow 3 inches (7.5 cm) of pan above the surface of the melted butter.

1. Preheat the oven to 300°F (150°C). Place the desired quantity of unsalted butter, in ¼-pound (115 g) portions, in a heavy-bottomed, thick-walled pan. Allow the butter to melt and slowly clarify, uncovered and undisturbed, until there is a layer of solid foam on the surface, clean amber-gold *ghee* in the middle and lumps of pale gold solids on the bottom. Remove the pan from the oven. Depending on quantity, 1 pound (455 g) could take as little as 1 hour; 30 pounds (15 kg) could take 12 hours or more.

2. Skim off the crusty foam on the surface with a fine-mesh wire skimmer or a large metal spoon. Place the foam in a small container.

3. Ladle the clear *ghee* into a strainer lined with a linen towel or four layers of cheesecloth. When you have removed as much as you can without disturbing the solids, skim off the last 1 inch (2.5 cm) with a large spoon. When the *ghee* has cooled somewhat, pour it into storage containers, label and, when at room temperature, cover with a tight-fitting lid.

4. Add the remaining *ghee* and lumps of golden solids to the reserved foam, and use it for anything from creamed soups to sandwich spreads. Keep covered and refrigerated for up to 3–4 days.

Cumin-Flavored *Ghee*
JEERA GHEE

The use of seasoned *ghee* is perhaps the subtlest way to introduce flavor to simple steamed, baked or raw foods. If you have ever tasted the brownish sesame oil used in Oriental cooking, you can get an idea of how even a few teaspoons of cumin *ghee* can lend flavor and aroma to unseasoned dishes. Because this *ghee* is not as strong as the thick sesame oil, you can use it both as a cooking oil and for subtle flavoring.

Prepare this *ghee* just as you would in the stove-top or oven method *ghee* in the previous two recipes, with the following additions for every 3 pounds (1.5 kg) of butter:

3 tablespoons (45 ml) cumin seeds
6–8 fresh or dried curry leaves

Wrap the seasonings in a small piece of cheesecloth to make a bouquet garni. When the butter has melted, add the bouquet garni, and then cook, strain and label as directed on page 111.

Black Pepper *Ghee*
KALA MIRCH GHEE

Black and white pepper both come from the same plant. In large cities, one might purchase unripened dark green berries, which, as they dry, darken into black pepper. No matter what form you use, the volatile oil will lend a touch of pungency without heat.

Prepare *ghee* by either the stove-top or oven method, with the following addition for every 3 pounds (1.5 kg) of butter:

2 tablespoons (30 ml) black, white or dark green peppercorns

Wrap the pepper in a small piece of cheesecloth and add it to the melted butter. Cook, strain and label as directed on page 111.

Clove-Sesame *Ghee*
LAUNG GHEE

This is a delicately flavored *ghee* that I have found excellent for sautéed green vegetable dishes—broccoli, asparagus, green beans and spinach.

Prepare the *ghee* by either the stove-top or oven method, with the following additions for every 3 pounds (1.5 kg) of butter:

25 whole cloves
2 tablespoons (30 ml) whole sesame seeds
¼ whole nutmeg

Wrap the seasonings in a small piece of cheesecloth and add to the melted butter. Cook, strain and label as directed on page 111.

Ginger *Ghee*
ADRAK GHEE

My friend Saragini Devi, whose cooking has always fascinated me, includes ginger in many of her dishes. The first time she deep-fried pastries in ginger *ghee*, I became aware of the nuances possible with this wonderful oil. It is, hands down, my favorite of all seasoned *ghees*.

Prepare *ghee* by either the stove-top or oven method, with the following addition for every 3 pounds (1.5 kg) of butter:

2-inch (5 cm) piece of ginger root, peeled and sliced into 4 pieces

Add the ginger when the butter has melted, then cook, strain and label as directed on page 111.

HOMEMADE YOGURT AND YOGURT
CHEESE

The following milk products are indispensable in Vedic cooking, for India utilizes homemade yogurt and cheese just as often as vegetables, grains and legumes. When it comes to milk products, one cannot overstate the merits of freshness: once made, they lose flavor and nutrients as rapidly as uprooted plants. The closer you are, therefore, to using fresh, homemade yogurt and cheese, the more vibrant and exciting your cooking will be. Though all of the following staples are made from milk, there is a wide diversity in flavors and textures, and it would take several cookbooks to cover the multitude of ingenious ways that milk products are used in the Vedic kitchen.

Homemade Yogurt
DAHI

When I refer to "plain yogurt" as an ingredient, I mean the kind that has been made for thousands of years in Vedic kitchens using whole milk, sometimes even thin cream or top milk, and a starter—nothing else. Most supermarket yogurt is made from low-fat milk, skimmed milk and even reconstituted powdered milk, and does not even resemble the custard-like smooth yogurt found in India, Greece and the Middle East. Yogurt is easy to make, it is economical, and it lends real character to a multitude of Vedic dishes. If you are pressed for time and prefer to use commercial yogurt, many health food stores and delicatessens carry whole milk yogurt, and some, like Brown Cow and Columbo, are very good. They also make the best starters.

Because yogurt is no more than a transformation of milk, it possesses the same food value. Although the importance of fresh milk cannot be emphasized enough, it is the butterfat content that makes for the appreciable differences in body and texture. Whole cow's milk averages 3.25–3.8 percent butterfat, Guernsey and Jersey milk tops 4.2 percent, while half-and-half runs about 12 percent. In India today, buffalo milk, with about 8.2 percent butterfat, is widely used for commercial yogurt. Because I was never fond of its cloying strong taste, I preferred to make my own by boiling cow's milk to reduce it to three-quarters its original volume, ending up with a consistency similar to thick buffalo yogurt. Any yogurt made from unpasteurized milk has a creamy top layer of *malai*—a crust that solidifies on the surface of the milk—which is delicious and can be used a number of ways. When I want to make a firm-bodied yogurt, without the extra calories of whole milk, I add non-fat, non-instant powdered milk to 2 percent milk; the milk powder lends a touch of both sweetness and body. Homemade yogurt is not sweetened, but is both so mild and mellow that many refer to it as tasting sweet. It is a far cry from the often tangy, watery, tart commercial yogurt loaded with unnecessary stabilizers and fillers such as gelatin, locust bean gum, cellulose and carrageenan.

Yogurt has always been a guardian of good health. It is a source of calcium, protein, fat, carbohydrates, phosphorus, vitamin A, the B complex vitamins and vitamin D. It encourages the growth of benign intestinal bacteria that aid digestion and help to destroy the harmful bacteria that are alleged to spawn a variety of illnesses. The lactic acid content helps to digest and assimilate calcium and phosphorus, and yogurt is certainly easier to digest than milk. In one hour, 32 percent of milk can be digested, compared to 91 percent of yogurt. As a rule, yogurt beverages and salads are taken during the hot summer months, and when the fire of digestion increases in the winter, the frequency of milk dishes is increased in the diet.

The starter is nothing more than a little homemade or commercial plain yogurt. It is live bacteria, and must be fresh and sweet; tart and sour starters will yield tart and sour yogurt. Most starters combine *Lactobacillus bulgaricus* and *Streptococcus thermophilus*, but I prefer a culture including *L. acidophilus*, which yields a mild yogurt known to be beneficial.

Yogurt not only flavors, it thickens, enriches and tenderizes. It is the basis of a multitude of Vedic dishes, from creamy chilled *lassi* beverages to nutritious yogurt salads called *raitas*. Drained of its whey, it turns into a low calorie cream cheese called *dehin*, which, sweetened, becomes an elegant Maharashtran dessert known as *shrikhand*.

Preparation time (after assembling ingredients): 20 minutes
Setting time: 4–10 hours
Makes: 1 quart/liter

½ cup (65 g) non-instant, non-fat dry milk powder (optional)
⅓ cup (80 ml) milk, at room temperature (optional)
1 quart/liter milk
3 tablespoons (45 ml) plain yogurt

1. If you want a spoonable firm yogurt, combine the milk powder with the room-temperature milk in a blender and process until lump-free and frothy. Set aside.

2. Bring the milk to a boil quickly in a heavy 3 quart/liter pan, stirring constantly to prevent it from sticking to the pan. Set aside to cool to about 118°F (48°C) or quick-cool by half-submerging the pan in a sink partially filled with cold tap water. While the milk is cooling, rinse a 1½–2-quart/liter container with boiling water, then dry. When the milk has cooled to about 115°F (46°C), pour ½ cup (120 ml) into the sterilized container, add the yogurt starter and whisk until smooth. Pour in the remaining milk and the powdered milk mixture, if you are using it, and blend well. The milk temperature should now be near 112°F (44°C), the ideal temperature for starting plain yogurt. Cover with a clean towel or lid and quickly put the container in a warm place, 85°–110°F (29°–43°C). If the environment is too warm, the yogurt will sour before it sets; if it is not warm enough, the yogurt will not set at all. I use an oven with a gas pilot light, or an electric oven preheated at 200°F (95°C) for 1½ minutes, then turned off. You could also use a large styrofoam picnic cooler, warmed with an open jar of hot water, then tightly covered. Another possibility is a heavy terry towel, blanket or foam rubber pouch resting near a central heater, boiler or heating duct. Any warm nook will do.

3. Check after 5–6 hours. It should be just thick and firm, for as it cools it will further set up considerably. The longer you allow the yogurt to set once it is firm, the stronger and more tart it will be. If it is not set, check every hour for up to 12 hours. If the yogurt has not set by then, there are several possible causes: stale or insufficiently sterilized milk, inadequate blending of starter in the milk, inadequate insulation during setting, or worn-out starter.

4. Refrigerate, covered, once it is set. It is best used within 3 days, though it will last for 4–5. After that, it is considered "old" yogurt and can be used in special recipes.

Yogurt Cheese

DEHIN

Unlike some cultured milk products in this chapter, yogurt cheese is not yet sold commercially in America. I think it could become as popular as neufchatel or cream cheese. It is a revelation in light cheese, with an intriguing flavor. If you like yogurt, you will love *dehin*. It is nothing more than whole milk yogurt, or even low-fat yogurt, drained of whey and thickened until solid. It requires little more than a colander in the way of equipment, and requires only intermittent attention. Homemade, smooth whole milk yogurt makes the best cheese. If you prefer to use commercial yogurt, make sure it is sweet, and use well before the expiration date on the carton. Tart yogurt is often old, and as the yogurt flavor concentrates as it thickens, the cheese will become sharp and sourish as well. If you are using the cheese for a sweet dish, leave it plain; for eating or cooking, add up to ½ teaspoon (2 ml) of seasoned or herb salt.

Preparation time (after assembling ingredients): a few minutes
Draining time: 12–18 hours for soft cheese or 24–36 hours for firm cheese
Makes: 2 cups (480 ml) soft cheese or 1½ cups (360 ml) firm cheese

6 cups (1.5 liters) plain whole milk yogurt
up to ½ teaspoon (2 ml) herb or sea salt (optional)

1. Line a colander with clean muslin or several thicknesses of cheesecloth and set it in a sink. If desired, stir the salt into the yogurt, then place it in the colander and spread it up the sides of the cloth to hasten the absorption of whey. Fold the ends of the cloth over the yogurt.

2. Set the colander on a rack in a dish at least 2 inches (5 cm) deep. (Leave at least 1 inch/2.5 cm between the rack and the bottom of the dish, for the drained-off whey.) Cover the whole unit with clear plastic wrap, sealing it to make it airtight.

3. Refrigerate to drain for 12–18 hours for a soft cheese or 24–36 hours for a firm cheese. Unwrap and store, sealed, for up to 3 days.

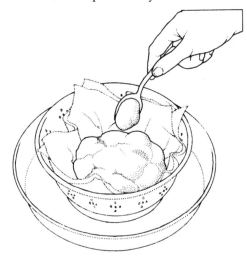

Salads

L ittle salads, loosely called *kachambers*, are light servings of freshness. Unlike Western main-dish or mixed-green salads, which are usually a rich composite of colors, tastes and textures, these are little more than one, two or three ingredients in a light coating of oil, lime or lemon juice and seasoning. They may be as simple as sun-ripe tomato wedges or cucumber spears sprinkled with salt and dry-roasted crushed cumin. In some regions, shredded white radish or red-orange carrots are favorites, bound only with a mustard-scented fried seasoning and traces of fresh herbs. Whether the vegetables and fruits are raw or blanched, dried, sliced or shredded, they are meant to be refreshing contrasts to the other dishes in the meal. Making successful *kachambers* depends more on obtaining really fresh, seasonal produce than on anything else. After glancing at the recipes, take advantage of the season's bounty and improvise. Keep it simple, and assemble it just before serving. *Kachambers* are not separate-course dishes: they go on the dinner plate in small 2–4-tablespoon (30–60 ml) amounts.

All vegetarians know that a balanced, varied diet of grains (breads, cereals, rice), legumes (*dals*, dried beans and peas), dairy products (yogurt, buttermilk, cheese and tart cream) and fruits and vegetables is the necessary key to good health. *Raitas* are an excellent way to introduce cultured milk products into your meals. They are meant to be cool and refreshing on the plate alongside spicier, hot dishes. By yogurt I do not mean skimmed milk yogurt, which is too watery and thin to be authentic in these salads. Rather, if at all possible, make your own (it almost makes itself). Homemade yogurt is marvelously velvety, thick and delicate—a far cry from anything in a carton, which is often tangy and watery. You can appreciate it as a nutrition dynamo: ½ cup (120 ml) of whole milk yogurt has about 7 grams of protein, 10 grams of carbohydrates, 8 milligrams of cholesterol and only 83 calories. Some health food stores carry outstanding whole milk yogurts; just be sure to purchase them well ahead of the expiration date. If you want to add extra body, combine soured or tart cream (similar to crème fraîche) with the yogurt. If you must minimize calories, substitute a creamy cultured buttermilk, usually only 1 percent butterfat.

Rai means black mustard seeds, and for Gujaratis *raita* must contain them. In North India, *raita* usually has dry-roasted coarsely crushed cumin seeds. Fresh herbs are always a part of this dish; although fresh coriander is the most common, you can use those that best complement the menu.

The side dish salads can be served as the basis of a light meal, or as room temperature starters or appetizers.

LITTLE SALADS

Chickpea and Ginger Root Salad
KABLI CHANA ADRAK KACHAMBER

Whole chickpeas are soaked overnight, sometimes even slightly sprouted, before being used in this salad. Two types of rhizomes are suitable here: young camphor ginger or ginger-like mango ginger (a member of the turmeric family). Their flesh should be virtually fiber-free, with a thin skin. Because they are only found sporadically, look for young or "green" fresh ginger at the corner produce store or supermarket.

This salad was a constant on my breakfast menus for Srila Prabhupada. He taught it to me in 1967 and commented that ginger root for breakfast aided his digestion all day. Eight years later, when I forgot to soak the chickpeas one day and had to omit the dish, he again reminded me how important this "digestive" breakfast salad was for his health. Later, another of his cooks, Palika Dasi, related that he also favored another variation using soaked mung *dal* instead of chickpeas—a variation he simply called chutney.

Try this dish with seasonal fresh fruits for a light breakfast, or include it as a "salad-chutney" with lunch or dinner.

Dal soaking time: 8 hours or overnight
Preparation time (after assembling ingredients): 10 minutes
Serves: 4 to 6

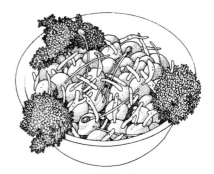

⅓ cup (50 g) whole chickpeas, sorted and soaked
    in 1½ cups (360 ml) water overnight
1½-inch (4 cm) piece of fresh ginger root
1½ tablespoons (22 ml) fresh lime or lemon juice
½ teaspoon (2 ml) *chat masala* (optional)
¼ teaspoon (1 ml) freshly ground black pepper

Drain the chickpeas. Peel the ginger and slice into paper-thin rounds, then paper-thin julienne. Combine all of the ingredients in a small bowl and toss well. Serve directly on the dinner plates in small mounds.

Banana and Pomegranate Salad
KELA ANAR KACHAMBER

This is an appropriate year-round *kachamber* to serve on a buffet or salad table. I first saw it at a North Indian wedding, among numerous small salads. The smooth and sweet golden banana slices make a vivid contrast with the sharp and sweet red pomegranate seeds.

Preparation time (after assembling ingredients): 15 minutes
Serves: 4

1 medium-sized pomegranate
2 medium-sized firm ripe bananas
2 tablespoons (30 ml) fresh lime juice
1 tablespoon (15 ml) maple or date sugar
¼ teaspoon (1 ml) salt (optional)

1. Cut the pomegranate into quarters and twist each wedge to loosen the cells. Gently shake, tap, scoop and coax the cells onto a serving plate and arrange them in a neat mound in the center.

2. Peel the bananas and slice them on the diagonal into ¼-inch (6 mm) rounds. Arrange them in a circle around the pomegranate cells. Sprinkle with the lime or lemon juice, sweetener and salt, if desired, and serve immediately.

Shredded Carrot and Cashew Nut Salad
GAJAR KAJU KACHAMBER

You can use almonds, hazelnuts or pistachios instead of cashews for this dish, and yellow bell peppers in place of red.

Preparation time (after assembling ingredients): 5 minutes
Serves: 6

1 cup (240 ml) scraped finely shredded carrots, pressed dry
⅓ cup (80 ml) finely chopped red bell peppers, stemmed and seeded
⅓ cup (50 g) chopped cashew nuts, toasted
½ teaspoon (2 ml) salt
2 tablespoons (30 ml) yogurt or crème fraîche (optional)
1½ tablespoons (22 ml) *ghee* or vegetable oil
1 teaspoon (5 ml) black mustard seeds
1 tablespoon (15 ml) coarsely chopped fresh coriander
     or minced parsley

1. Combine the carrots, bell peppers, nuts, salt, and yogurt or crème fraîche (if desired) in a mixing bowl.

2. Heat the *ghee* or oil in a small saucepan over moderate heat until it is hot but not smoking. Add the mustard seeds and fry until they sputter, pop and turn gray. Pour the seasoning into the salad, add the fresh herbs and toss to mix.

Apple Salad
SEB KACHAMBER

Outside of Kashmir, where most of India's apples are grown, the texture tends to be mealy—a sure sign of overripening due to long storage at warm temperatures. On the whole, I do not find them as good as most American varieties. Use any crisp salad or all-purpose apple: for example, Newton, Pippin or McIntosh, which are crisp, sweet and juicy, with a tangy overtone; anything from sweet Red or Golden Delicious to tart Granny Smith will do as well. With the grapes and mint-almond dressing, this is an elegant mid-winter fruit *kachamber*.

Preparation and chilling time (after assembling ingredients): 30 minutes
Serves: 6

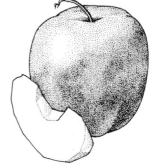

¼ cup (60 ml) plain yogurt or sour cream
2 tablespoons (30 ml) chopped fresh mint
3 tablespoons (45 ml) ground blanched almonds
¼ teaspoon (1 ml) cardamom seeds, crushed
2 tablespoons (30 ml) orange or lemon juice
3 medium-sized apples, cored and diced
½ cup (120 ml) seedless grapes, halved

Blend the yogurt or sour cream, mint, almonds, cardamom seeds and orange or lemon juice in a mixing bowl. Fold in the apples and grapes, cover, and chill for at least ½ hour before serving.

Cucumber and White Radish Salad
KHEERA MOOLI KACHAMBER

This simple salad contrasts crisp raw vegetables with a creamy pine nut dressing. Spooned into a shallow dish and garnished with a decorative pattern of paprika, minced parsley and roasted cumin and sesame seeds, this is an eye-catcher for a buffet.

Preparation and draining time (after assembling ingredients): 30 minutes
Serves: 6

2 small cucumbers (about 12 ounces/340 g), peeled, halved,
    seeded and coarsely shredded
salt
2 white icicle salad radishes (about 6 ounces/170 g),
    scraped and coarsely shredded
¼ cup (60 ml) sour cream or yogurt
2 tablespoons (30 ml) powdered pine nuts or almonds
1 tablespoon (15 ml) olive or sesame oil
¼ teaspoon (1 ml) paprika or cayenne pepper
2 tablespoons (30 ml) minced parsley
½ tablespoon (7 ml) dry-roasted coarsely crushed cumin seeds
2 tablespoons (30 ml) dry-roasted white sesame seeds

Place the cucumbers in a strainer resting over a bowl and sprinkle with salt. Drain for at least ½ hour and then press between your palms to extract excess liquid. Combine the cucumbers, radishes, sour cream or yogurt, nuts and oil in a mixing bowl and blend well. Transfer to a shallow serving dish and sprinkle decoratively with paprika or cayenne, parsley and cumin and sesame seeds. Serve at room temperature or chilled.

Minted Cucumbers and Strawberries
KHEERA KACHAMBER

Though mint and cucumber are a year-round favorite salad combination in India, strawberries are a rare treat. The first time I savored them, they were hand-delivered—carefully wrapped in a *khus* leaf parcel—and perhaps the importance of the occasion made them the sweetest I had ever eaten. Because they are such a rarity in India, they are almost always relished on their own or in this type of simple salad. In England I take advantage of red or black currants, and in America I might use golden raspberries, loganberries, lingonberries or blueberries. Though not available in India, hazelnut oil is perfect for a delicate fruit salad, but you could use almond or walnut oil, or leave out the oil entirely.

Preparation time (after assembling ingredients): 15–20 minutes
Serves: 6

2 long European-type cucumbers (about ½ pound/230 g each)
2 pints (480 ml) strawberries, rinsed and drained
2 tablespoons (30 ml) lemon juice
3 tablespoons (45 ml) orange juice
¼ cup (60 ml) finely chopped fresh mint
⅛ teaspoon (0.5 ml) cayenne pepper or paprika
2 tablespoons (30 ml) hazelnut or alternative oil

1. Peel the cucumbers and cut them crosswise into two or three pieces. Cut each piece lengthwise into four sections. Arrange the wedges in a pattern on a large salad plate. Remove the leaves and core from the strawberries by gathering up the leaves and stem cap and pulling away with a twist. Slice each one in half from cap to tip. Arrange in a decorative pattern between the cucumber wedges.

2. Whisk together the lemon juice, orange juice, mint, cayenne or paprika and oil until emulsified. Pour over the salad just before serving.

SIDE-DISH SALADS

Whole Cauliflower Crowned with Creamy Avocado
GOBHI SALAAD

India's intense heat prevents the widespread use of salad greens—both for home gardeners and on a commercial scale. During northern winters, some green thumbs are successful with a few hardy types. In my search for salads with staying power, using available ingredients, I happened on this variation. It is eye-catching on a salad buffet, and often the first to disappear.

Preparation time (after assembling ingredients): 10 minutes
Cooking time: 25 minutes
Chilling time: 3 hours
Serves: 4 to 6

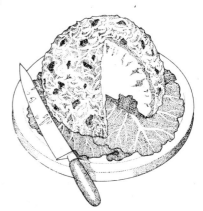

1 large cauliflower (2½ pounds/1.25 kg), trimmed
1 large tomato, peeled, seeded and finely chopped
2 teaspoons (30 ml) olive oil
1 tablespoon (15 ml) lemon or lime juice
½ teaspoon (2 ml) cayenne pepper or paprika
1 teaspoon (5 ml) ground coriander
¼ teaspoon (1 ml) salt
⅛ teaspoon (0.5 ml) freshly ground pepper
2 medium-sized avocados, peeled, pitted and mashed
3 tablespoons (45 ml) sour cream

1. Slice the base off the stem end of the cauliflower so it can sit on a flat surface. Fill a large pan with water to a depth of at least 1 inch (2.5 cm) and place a steaming rack or trivet inside. Bring the water to a boil and place the cauliflower in the steamer. Cover, reduce the heat slightly, and steam until the cauliflower is barely tender, ½ hour or more; avoid overcooking. Let cool, cover, and chill for 3 hours or more.

2. Combine the remaining ingredients in a bowl and mix well. Spread the mixture over the chilled cauliflower, and serve on a bed of cabbage or outer cauliflower leaves on a serving dish. Cut into wedges and serve.

Sprouted Mung Bean Salad with Water Chestnuts and Toasted Almonds

SABAT MOONG SALAAD

You can use any sprouted bean mixture for this salad, but avoid the supermarket, water-logged giant sprouts intended for oriental, stir-fry dishes. These beans should be barely sprouted (¼–½ inch/6 mm-1.5 cm) at most. Assemble this salad just before serving, as the sprouts soften and become watery once exposed to heat or combined with other ingredients.

Preparation time (after assembling ingredients): 10 minutes
Serves: 6

2 cups sprouted mung or aduki beans (page 23)
    (made from 1 cup/195 g whole beans)
¾ cup (180 ml) sliced water chestnuts
1 small yellow or red bell pepper (about
    4 ounces/115 g), stemmed, seeded and diced
½ cup (120 ml) chopped celery
2 tablespoons (30 ml) olive or avocado oil
1 tablespoon (15 ml) lemon juice
⅓ cup (80 ml) plain yogurt or a
    mixture of yogurt and sour cream
½ teaspoon (2 ml) herb or celery salt
1 teaspoon (5 ml) dry-roasted crushed cumin seeds
¼ teaspoon (1 ml) cayenne pepper or paprika
¼ cup (30 g) toasted sliced almonds
6 small tomatoes, cut into flower garnishes

Combine the sprouts, water chestnuts, bell pepper and celery in a salad bowl. (If you want to remove the raw taste from the sprouts, steam them for 5–7 minutes first.) Combine the remaining ingredients (except the almonds and tomatoes) in a screw-top jar, cover and shake until creamy. Just before serving, pour the dressing over the salad and gently toss. Sprinkle with toasted almonds and garnish with tomato flowers.

Lemon Stuffed with Almond-Chickpea Pâté
KABLI CHANA BADAAM SALAAD

Inspired by a dish served at Robert Carrier's Hintelsham Hall in England, these appetizer salads are perfect for small parties, brunches or late-night dinners: hollowed-out lemons filled with hummous-like chickpea pâté, served with decorative vegetable crudités and/or crackers.

Preparation time (after assembling ingredients) 15 minutes
Chilling time: at least 1 hour
Serves: 4

4 large lemons
¾-inch (2 ml) piece of scraped fresh ginger root, sliced
1-2 seeded jalepeño chilies
3 ounces (85 g) cream cheese or fresh
      cheese, cut into small pieces
2 cups (480 ml) drained cooked chickpeas
      (1 cup/100 g when dried)
3 tablespoons (45 ml) toasted sesame seeds
6 tablespoons (90 ml) sour cream or crème frîche
½ teaspoon (2 ml) salt
3 tablespoons (45 ml) olive oil or melted *ghee*
½ teaspoon (2 ml) yellow asafetida powder (*hing***)***
¼ teaspoon (1 ml) freshly ground pepper
1 teaspoon (5 ml) coarsely crushed dry-roasted cumin seeds
1 tablespoon (15 ml) minced fresh parsley or chervil
4 watercress sprigs
bibb lettuce leaves
crudités such as radish flowers, cucumber twists, or tomato flowers (optional)

*This amount applies only to yellow Cobra brand. Reduce any other asafetida by three-fourths.

   1. Cut off the tops of the lemons and reserve. Scoop out the pulp with a grapefruit spoon or knife until the shells are empty. Squeeze the pulp through a strainer and save the juice; discard the membranes and seeds. Trim a thin slice off the bottom of the lemons so they stand upright. Cover and chill until needed.
   2. Fit a food processor with the metal blade. Turn on the motor, drop the ginger and chilies through the feed tube and mince. Add the cheese and process until smooth. Drop in the chickpeas, sesame seeds, sour cream or crème fraîche, salt, oil or *ghee*, asafetida and pepper. Process until smooth, adding up to 2 tablespoons (30 ml) of the reserved lemon juice for flavor and to obtain a uniform, spoonable consistency. Add the cumin seeds and pulse 2 or 3 times to crush them.
   3. Fill the lemon cups, using a pastry bag fitted with a large star nozzle, or simply spoon in the pâté, slightly piling it up over the edge of the cup. Sprinkle with the fresh herbs and top with the reserved caps. Place some bibb lettuce on each plate and add the vegetable garnishes. Chill until you are ready to serve.

Spiced Chickpea Salad with Spinach
KABLI CHANA PALAK SALAAD

As an alternative to spinach, try red or green swiss chard leaves–they are delicious. Because chard is not as tender as spinach, blanch or steam it for a minute or two before assembling the salad.

Soaking time: 8 hours or overnight
Cooking time (after assembling ingredients): about 2 hours
Chilling time: at least 2 hours
Serves: 6

1½ cups (290 g) chickpeas, soaked in water
    8 hours or overnight, then drained
1 teaspoon (5 ml) black mustard seeds
½ teaspoon (2 ml) celery seeds
4 tablespoons (60 ml) lemon juice
6 tablespoons (90 ml) olive or nut oil
scant ½ teaspoon (2 ml) cayenne pepper or paprika
¼ teaspoon (1 ml) yellow asafetida powder (*hing*)*
2 tablespoons (30 ml) tomato paste
2 tablespoons (30 ml) maple syrup or honey
½ teaspoon (2 ml) salt
¼ teaspoon (1 ml) freshly ground pepper
1 large ripe tomato, diced
1 small cucumber, peeled, halved, seeded and diced
½ of a yellow bell pepper, seeded and diced
½ pound (230 g) fresh spinach, washed,
    trimmed, coarsely chopped and patted dry

*This amount applies only to yellow Cobra brand. Reduce any other asafetida by three-fourths.

1. Place the chickpeas in a heavy saucepan with 4 cups (1 liter) of water and simmer over low heat for 1½–2 hours or just until tender. Keep an eye on the chickpeas during the last ½ hour to prevent them from overcooking. Drain and let cool.

2. Crush the mustard seeds and celery seeds with a mortar and pestle. Place them in a salad bowl with the lemon juice, oil, cayenne or paprika, asafetida, tomato paste, sweetener, salt and pepper, and beat with a fork or wire whisk until emulsified. Add the chickpeas, tomato, cucumber and bell pepper. Gently toss, cover and chill for 2–4 hours. Thirty minutes before serving, remove the salad from the refrigerator. Add the spinach, toss, and bring back to room temperature.

Cracked Wheat Salad

DALIA SALAAD

The South Indians' enthusiasm for rice dishes is equaled only by that of the North Indians for wheat. Wheat is eaten in some form every day in the North. During the India-Pakistan skirmish in 1971, I was residing in Vrindavan, tending a friend with a fever. Her resident homeopathic physician insisted that she recuperate on this salad. He knew nothing of Lebanese tabbouleh salad, yet this variation resembles it remarkably. It is full of flavor and nutrition (parsley is loaded with vitamin C). Cracked wheat and bulgur are processed differently but can be used interchangeably. They are available at gourmet, health food and Indian grocery stores. This room temperature salad is good in any season.

Preparation and cooking time (after assembling ingredients): 40 minutes
Serves: 4 to 6

1½ cups (360 ml) water
1 cup (240 ml) cracked wheat or bulgur
½ cup (120 ml) fresh peas or sliced snow peas
½ teaspoon (2 ml) salt
½ teaspoon (2 ml) freshly ground pepper
1 cup (240 ml) minced fresh parsley
¼ cup (60 ml) finely chopped fresh mint or
      1 tablespoon (15 ml) dried mint
2 medium-sized tomatoes, each cut into eighths
      or 8 tomatillos, husked and quartered
¼ cup (60 ml) olive or sesame oil
1–2 seeded and minced hot chilies,
      preferably yellow or red

Bring the water to a boil in a 2-quart/liter saucepan. Add the cracked wheat or bulgur, peas or snow peas, salt and pepper. Remove the pan from the heat and set aside for ½ hour. Most of the water will be absorbed into the grains. If there is any excess, drain it off or place the pan over low heat and cook until it is absorbed. When thoroughly cool, transfer to a serving bowl and gently toss with the remaining ingredients. Serve at room temperature or chill. If you want a showy presentation for a salad buffet, line the serving container with cabbage leaves, spoon in the salad and garnish with yellow bell pepper rings.

Papaya, Avocado and Jerusalem Artichoke Salad
PAPITA SALAAD

The creaminess of papaya and avocado and crispness of Jerusalem artichokes are pleasantly set off by the sweetish coriander-lime vinaigrette. You may prefer mango instead of papaya, or celeriac instead of Jerusalem artichokes. Also called sunchokes, the peeled Jerusalem artichokes may be blanched before use or left raw, depending on your preference. This light salad goes well on any menu from lunch to late supper.

Preparation time (after assembling ingredients): 15 minutes
Serves: 4

3 tablespoons (45 ml) maple syrup or honey
¼ cup (60 ml) lime juice
⅓ cup (80 ml) olive oil, or a mixture of two
    parts almond oil to three parts sunflower oil
½ teaspoon (2 ml) salt
¼ teaspoon (1 ml) yellow mustard powder
¼ teaspoon (1 ml) freshly ground pepper
3 tablespoons (45 ml) chopped fresh coriander
1 medium-sized papaya (about 2½ pounds/1.5 kg),
    peeled, halved lengthwise, seeded, sliced
    crosswise into ⅓-inch (1 cm) slices and sprinkled
    with lemon juice
2 medium-sized ripe avocados, peeled, seeded, cut into
    ½-inch (1.5 cm) cubes and sprinkled with lemon juice
4 Jerusalem artichokes, peeled, cut lengthwise into
    julienne and sprinkled with lemon juice

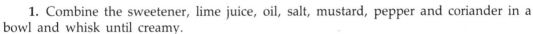

1. Combine the sweetener, lime juice, oil, salt, mustard, pepper and coriander in a bowl and whisk until creamy.
2. Arrange the salad decoratively on a platter or individual plates; for example, overlap papaya slices around the edges, mound the avocado in the center and sprinkle the julienne artichokes between the two. Pour on the salad dressing and serve at once.

Whole Cabbage Stuffed with Carrot Coleslaw
BANDHGOBHI SALAAD

A large, crinkly-leafed Savoy cabbage makes an ideal cabbage bowl, though red or green cabbage can be used as well. In this variation, the cut-away inner portion is trimmed, shredded and jazzed up with herbs, spices, carrots and a creamy dressing. The outer shell serves as a salad bowl. For a summer backyard salad banquet, select several types of cabbage, vary the fillings and use small cabbages for dressings—they are sure crowd pleasers.

Preparation time (after assembling ingredients): 30 minutes
Serves: 6 to 8

1 oversized Savoy or stuffing-type cabbage
4 medium-sized carrots, scraped and shredded
1–2 hot green chilies, seeded and minced
½ tablespoon (7 ml) scraped fresh ginger root, minced
2 tablespoons (30 ml) chopped fresh coriander or dill
salt and freshly ground pepper
½ cup (120 ml) buttermilk or yogurt
½ cup (120 ml) heavy cream
3 tablespoons (45 ml) fresh lime juice
2 tablespoons (30 ml) *ghee* or vegetable oil
1 teaspoon (5 ml) black mustard seeds

1. Trim off all large bruised cabbage leaves and take a slice off the base so the cabbage stands flat on its own. Slice off the top third of the cabbage and cut around the edge, leaving a 1-inch (2.5 cm) border. Hollow out the center, and shred enough of it to equal the amount of carrots.

2. Combine the carrots, cabbage, chilies, ginger, fresh herbs, salt and pepper in a large bowl and toss to mix. In another bowl, combine the buttermilk or yogurt and the cream. Stirring constantly, slowly pour in the lime juice. Whisk until creamy, then pour over the carrot slaw.

3. Place the *ghee* or oil in a small pan over moderate heat. When it is hot but not smoking, add the black mustard seeds and fry until they sputter and turn gray. Pour the seasoning into the salad and toss well. Spoon the salad into the cabbage shell and serve at room temperature or chill.

Creamy Potato Salad Surprise
ALOO SALAAD

Global potato salad variations take many directions: warm and chilled, sweet 'n' sour, mustardy, rich and unadorned. The surprise in this "American-in-Delhi" salad is the addition of crunchy bits of fried *moong dal badi*, sold at most Indian grocery stores.

This potato salad with a Punjabi twist is worth taking on any outing.

Preparation and cooking time (after assembling ingredients): about 45 minutes
Serves: 6

7–8 medium-sized red-skinned boiling potatoes (about 2 pounds/1 kg)
4 tablespoons (60 ml) *ghee* or peanut oil
⅓ cup (30 g) *moong dal badis* (cracked with a kitchen
     mallet into pea-sized bits) or cashew pieces
3 tablespoons (45 ml) each chopped fresh coriander and parsley
¼ teaspoon (1 ml) freshly ground pepper
1¼ teaspoons (6 ml) salt
2 tablespoons (30 ml) lime juice
½ tablespoon (7 ml) coarsely crushed dry-roasted cumin seeds
1 cup (240 ml) sour cream or rich yogurt
about ⅓ cup (80 ml) buttermilk
a sprinkle of cayenne pepper or paprika

1. Boil the potatoes in their skins until they are just fork-tender; take care not to overcook them. Cool slightly, peel and cut into ½-inch (1.5 cm) dice. Place in a salad bowl.

2. Heat the *ghee* or oil in a frying pan over moderate heat. Add the *badi* pieces or cashews and, stirring constantly, fry until golden brown. Pour them and the cooking oil over the potatoes. Add the remaining ingredients and gently mix, using your hands or a wooden spoon, until the salad is coated with dressing. Serve at room temperature or slightly chilled, sprinkled with cayenne or paprika.

Sweet Potato Salad in Maple-Lemon Vinaigrette
SHAKARKAND SALAAD

You can prepare this salad up to 8 hours before serving. Though it is light and healthy, it is also substantial and filling, perfect as a fall or winter salad. The maple-lemon dressing is barely sweet, pleasantly warmed by candied ginger.

Cooking time: about 45 minutes
Preparation and marinating time (after assembling ingredients): about 1 hour
Serves: 6

6 medium-sized sweet potatoes (about 2 pounds/1 kg), washed but not peeled
4 tablespoons (60 ml) maple syrup or honey
3 tablespoons (45 ml) orange or tangerine juice
3 tablespoons (45 ml) lemon or lime juice
¾ teaspoon (3.5 ml) salt
¼ teaspoon (1 ml) freshly ground black pepper or
     ⅛ teaspoon (0.5 ml) cayenne pepper
½ cup (120 ml) olive oil, or 2 tablespoons (30 ml)
     almond oil and 6 tablespoons (90 ml) sunflower oil
⅓ cup (80 ml) finely chopped fresh coriander or parsley
2 tablespoons (30 ml) chopped candied or stem ginger
3 medium-sized tomatoes, peeled, seeded and cut into ½-inch (1.5 cm) cubes

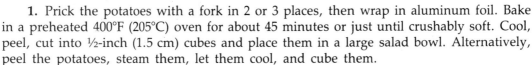

   1. Prick the potatoes with a fork in 2 or 3 places, then wrap in aluminum foil. Bake in a preheated 400°F (205°C) oven for about 45 minutes or just until crushably soft. Cool, peel, cut into ½-inch (1.5 cm) cubes and place them in a large salad bowl. Alternatively, peel the potatoes, steam them, let them cool, and cube them.
   2. Combine the sweetener, juices, salt, cayenne or black pepper, oil, fresh herbs and ginger in a jar, cover and shake until emulsified. Pour the dressing over the potatoes, toss gently, cover and set aside, refrigerated, for 1–8 hours.
   3. Before serving, add the tomatoes, gently toss and serve on a bed of mixed greens.

YOGURT SALADS

Chopped Spinach in Smooth Yogurt
PALAK RAITA

This richly marbled yogurt salad is nutritious and very delicious. Blanched chopped spinach is combined with minced fresh herbs, fresh lemon juice, lemon zest and white pepper. You could use a mixture of greens instead of spinach—mustard greens, chard, watercress, kale or collards— each combination varying the taste.

Preparation time (after assembling ingredients): 15 minutes
Serves: 4 to 6

½ pound (230 g) fresh spinach, washed, patted dry, trimmed and coarsely chopped,
  or ½ package of frozen chopped spinach, defrosted and pressed dry (140 g)
1 tablespoon (15 ml) unsalted butter
2 cups (480 ml) plain yogurt, or 1½ cups (360 ml)
  yogurt and ½ cup (120 ml) tart cream
3 tablespoons (45 ml) minced fresh herbs (coriander,
  dill, tarragon, chervil, parsley)
½ teaspoon (2 ml) grated lemon zest
2 teaspoons (10 ml) lemon juice
½ teaspoon (2 ml) salt
¼ teaspoon (1 ml) white pepper

1. Place the spinach, with any water clinging to the leaves or a sprinkle of water, in a large nonstick pot, add the butter, cover, and cook over moderate to moderately high heat for 5 minutes or until a sizzling sound comes from the pot. Turn the leaves over so the uncooked ones on top change places with the soft cooked ones on the bottom. Cover and cook for another 4–5 minutes. Take off the lid and cook off any excess water. Remove the spinach from the pan and let cool to room temperature. Alternately, cook the defrosted spinach in a dab of butter for a few minutes.

2. Meanwhile, combine the yogurt or yogurt–cream mixture, herbs, lemon zest, lemon juice, salt and pepper in a 1-quart/liter bowl and whisk with a fork until creamy. If you are ready to serve the salad, add the spinach and blend well. Otherwise, chill the yogurt mixture and spinach separately.

3. Just before serving, combine the yogurt mixture and spinach and stir to blend. Serve in small custard-cup-sized bowls.

Tomatoes in Smooth Yogurt
TAMATAR RAITA

Tomato is probably the most popular *raita* selection in India, vying for first position with cucumber. It is simple, unadorned refreshment, with each region having its own slight nuance in seasoning. The contrast between the brilliant red tomatoes and the snowy yogurt is vivid and appealing. To take advantage of the colors, use firm-fleshed or seeded tomatoes. I like to use marble-sized cherry or sugar-lump tomatoes, cut into quarters. You can use either fresh coriander, basil or dill for a garnish—a single leaf or feathery ½-inch (1.5 cm) pieces of dill.

Preparation and cooking time (after assembling ingredients): 10 minutes
Serves: 4 to 6

2 cups (480 ml) plain yogurt, or 1⅔ cups (400 ml)
    yogurt and ⅓ cup (80 ml) sour cream
¾ teaspoon (3.5 ml) salt
⅛ teaspoon (0.5 ml) white pepper
3–4 medium-sized firm ripe tomatoes or cherry
    tomatoes (about 1 pound/455 g), stems removed
1 tablespoon (15 ml) vegetable or peanut oil
1 teaspoon (5 ml) black mustard seeds
1 hot green chili, seeded and finely minced (or as desired)
1–2 sprigs fresh coriander, basil or dill for garnishing

1. Combine the yogurt or yogurt and sour cream, salt and pepper in a 1-quart/liter bowl. Whisk with a fork until smooth and creamy. Wash and dry the tomatoes and cut into ½-inch (1.5 cm) cubes, or quarter the cherry tomatoes; drop into the yogurt mixture, without stirring. The mixture can be covered and refrigerated for several hours or assembled at room temperature.

2. Heat the oil in a small pan over moderate heat. When it is hot but not smoking, add the mustard seeds and green chili and fry until the seeds crackle and turn gray. Pour into the salad and gently blend. Serve immediately, garnishing with fresh herb sprigs.

Fried Okra in Smooth Yogurt
BHINDI RAITA

Chilled yogurt salads are popular throughout India, and in Gujarati homes they are served with almost every summer lunch. This became one of my favorite dishes from the first time I tasted its delightful combination of textures and flavors. Though the ingredients can be prepared ahead of time, the salad is assembled just before serving. Crunchy fried okra is added to a toasted chickpea flour and yogurt sauce. The creamy sauce is seasoned with roasted cumin seeds and fresh coriander or parsley, and finally garnished with a dash of paprika. Since the okra softens as it sits in the sauce, and the chickpea flour both thickens and darkens the color, it can also double as a creamy room-temperature vegetable dish.

Preparation and cooking time (after assembling ingredients): about 30 minutes
Serves: 4 to 6

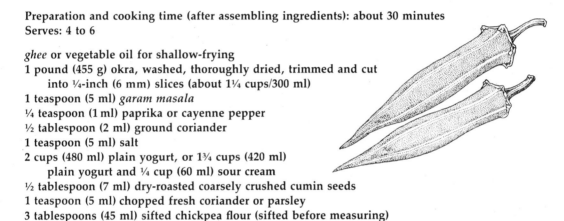

ghee or vegetable oil for shallow-frying
1 pound (455 g) okra, washed, thoroughly dried, trimmed and cut
    into ¼-inch (6 mm) slices (about 1¼ cups/300 ml)
1 teaspoon (5 ml) *garam masala*
¼ teaspoon (1 ml) paprika or cayenne pepper
½ tablespoon (2 ml) ground coriander
1 teaspoon (5 ml) salt
2 cups (480 ml) plain yogurt, or 1¾ cups (420 ml)
    plain yogurt and ¼ cup (60 ml) sour cream
½ tablespoon (7 ml) dry-roasted coarsely crushed cumin seeds
1 teaspoon (5 ml) chopped fresh coriander or parsley
3 tablespoons (45 ml) sifted chickpea flour (sifted before measuring)

1. Pour the *ghee* or oil to a depth of 1 inch (2.5 cm) in an 8-inch (20 cm) frying pan. Set over moderate heat, and when it is hot but not smoking, add the sliced okra. Fry for 15–20 minutes or until crisp and browned. Remove with a slotted spoon and drain on paper towels. While the okra is hot, sprinkle it with *garam masala*, paprika or cayenne, ground coriander and ½ teaspoon (2 ml) of the salt. Toss to mix.

2. Place the yogurt or yogurt and sour cream in a 1-quart/liter bowl and add the remaining ½ teaspoon (2 ml) salt and all but ½ teaspoon (2 ml) each of the cumin seeds and fresh herbs. Whisk with a fork until smooth and creamy.

3. Dry-roast the chickpea flour in a small heavy pan over moderate heat, stirring constantly to prevent scorching. When it darkens a few shades and smells nutty, transfer to a bowl to cool.

4. If you do these steps 1–2 hours ahead of assembling the salad, refrigerate the yogurt and leave the okra uncovered in a 200°F (95°C) oven. Before serving, add the okra to the yogurt, sprinkle with the chickpea flour, and gently stir. Transfer to a serving dish or individual bowls, garnish with the remaining cumin seeds and fresh herbs and a dash of paprika, and serve immediately.

Shredded Cucumbers in Smooth Mint-Flavored Yogurt
KHEERA RAITA

There are so many ways to make this, India's most popular *raita*, that I am presenting two of my favorite recipe variations. In this one, we discover how mint and cucumbers were made for each other. With a touch of lemon or lime zest, you have one of the most refreshing salads possible. Though avocado oil is not available in India, I find it perfect for delicate salads and *raitas*. You must use crisp, seedless young cucumbers. If all you can find are overgrown, out-of-season giants, seed them before shredding. This makes a terrific cold rice salad: simply fold it into room-temperature or chilled cooked rice.

Preparation time (after assembling ingredients) about 30 minutes
Chilling time: 1-2 hours
Serves: 6 to 8

2 medium-sized cucumbers (about 1 pound/455 g)
½ tablespoon (7 ml) salt
1½ cups (360 ml) plain yogurt, or 1¼ cups (300 ml)
      plain yogurt and ¼ cup (60 ml) sour cream
¼ teaspoon (1 ml) cayenne pepper or paprika
2 tablespoons (30 ml) finely chopped fresh mint
1 teaspoon (5 ml) grated lemon or lime zest
2 tablespoons (30 ml) avocado or sesame oil
1 teaspoon (5 ml) black mustard seeds
cucumber flowers and paprika for garnishing

1. Peel and coarsely shred the cucumbers, then place them in a bowl. Sprinkle with salt and toss. Let the cucumbers sit at room temperature for 20-30 minutes. Pour them into a strainer, press out the liquid, then pat them dry with paper towels.

2. Place the yogurt or yogurt-sour cream mixture, cayenne or paprika, mint and citrus zest in a 1-quart/liter bowl and whisk with a fork until smooth and creamy. Stir in the cucumbers. Heat the oil over moderate heat in a small pan. When it is hot but not smoking, add the mustard seeds. Fry until the seeds sputter and turn gray (if the oil is very hot, you may need to use a spatter screen to keep the seeds from jumping out of the small pan). Pour the fried seeds and oil into the cucumber-yogurt mixture, and stir to blend.

3. Refrigerate for 1-2 hours to allow the mint and seasoning to release their flavors. Serve with a garnish of twisted cucumber flowers and a sprinkle of paprika.

Carrots, Cashews and Dates in Smooth Yogurt
GAJAR KAJU RAITA

This colorful *raita* comes from my good friend Mandakini Devi, an accomplished cook. The cashew and date combination can be replaced by almonds and golden raisins or pecans and currants. The yogurt is drained for 2–3 hours before being mixed into the salad to make a thick, rich sauce without the extra calories of added cream.

Preparation and draining time (after assembling ingredients): 2–3 hours
Serves: 4 to 6

2 cups (480 ml) plain yogurt, preferably homemade (page114)
3 medium-sized carrots (about ½ pound/230 g), peeled and shredded
6 pitted dates, sliced into thin rounds, or 2 tablespoons (30 ml) raisins
    or currants soaked in hot water for 10 minutes, then drained
3 tablespoons (45 ml) dry roasted chopped cashews, almonds or pecans
1 teaspoon (5 ml) grated orange or lime zest
2 tablespoons (30 ml) fresh orange juice, strained
2 tablespoons (30 ml) granulated maple or date sugar
¼ teaspoon (1 ml) cardamom seeds, coarsely crushed

1. Line a colander with three thicknesses of cheesecloth (about 16 inches/40 cm square) or a white handkerchief. Place the yogurt in the cloth, gather up the four corners, and tie closed with a piece of kitchen twine. Hang the yogurt from a knob on a kitchen cabinet or a sink faucet where it can drip and drain into a bowl or sink. Let it drain undisturbed for 2–3 hours.
2. Press the carrots between your palms to extract excess juice. Place the drained yogurt in a 1-quart/liter bowl and whisk with a fork until smooth and creamy. Add the remaining ingredients, and stir until blended. Serve at room temperature or chill for 1–2 hours.

Shredded Radish, Coconut and Carrot Salad
MOOLI NARIYAL KACHAMBER

Try this dish when you have leftover fresh coconut on hand, or if you have frozen shredded coconut. In large cities, frozen shredded coconut is sold in 1-pound (455 g) bags at many Cuban and Spanish grocery stores, and for occasional use it is a convenient alternative. Use any fresh radish—little round pinks as a vivid color contrast to the carrots, for example.

Preparation time (after assembling ingredients): 10 minutes
Serves: 6

½ cup (120 ml) shredded radishes
⅓ cup (35 g) shredded fresh coconut
⅓ cup (80 ml) shredded scraped carrots
¼ teaspoon (1 ml) salt
¼ teaspoon (1 ml) paprika or cayenne pepper
2 tablespoons (30 ml) chopped fresh coriander or parsley
1½ tablespoons (22 ml) *ghee* or avocado oil
¼ teaspoon (1 ml) *ajwain* seeds or celery seeds
¼ teaspoon (1 ml) fennel seeds
¼ teaspoon (1 ml) cumin seeds

1. Combine the radishes, coconut and carrots in a strainer and press out the excess liquid. Place them in a bowl and add the salt, paprika or cayenne and fresh herbs.
2. Heat the *ghee* or oil in a saucepan over moderate heat. When it is hot but not smoking, add the *ajwain*, fennel and cumin seeds and fry until they darken a few shades. Pour the seasoning into the salad and toss well.

Chutneys

Chutneys, both fresh and cooked, are piquant, palate-teasing relishes that serve as accents to other dishes. From the simplest lunch of rice, vegetables and yogurt to a lavish spread of 108 preparations, a meal is often considered incomplete without a dab of chutney or pickle to liven it up. In some cases, chutneys play more than a supporting role, for they can be essential to the character of a dish. For example, South Indian *dosas* and *iddlis* are practically never served without some type of fresh coconut chutney, and North Indian *dahi baras* are inevitably served with a spoonful of sweet and sour tamarind chutney. Heat intensity ranges from fiery to pleasantly nippy; texture varies from thinnish sauces to jam like conserves; and taste spans spicy to mild.

In most Indian households, fresh chutneys are ground daily on large stone mortars. With a consistency similar to that of Genoese pestos, they are often little more than pounded fresh herb pastes or purées. Because fresh chutneys thicken and darken during storage, they are usually made within hours of use, even though they remain delicious for several days, and with the help of a food processor or blender one can make fresh chutneys effortlessly in minutes.

Supporting ingredients not only add flavor but also act as stimulating digestives. They include fresh ginger, hot green chilies, lemon juice, coconut, nuts, sour fruits and spice seeds. Glancing through the recipes, you will quickly note the absence of vinegar, curry powder, garlic or onions, ingredients often used in commercial Indian condiments but considered tamasic and therefore unacceptable to Vedic cooks.

Like fresh chutneys, cooked chutneys are invariably hot and spicy. Some, such as green tomato chutney, are unsweetened, while pineapple-raisin chutney is almost a hot, spicy conserve. Cooked chutneys keep well; covered and refrigerated, they can be used for a week or so. While fresh chutneys are everyday condiments, cooked chutneys are invariably served on holiday, festival, wedding and banquet menus. Jam-like cooked fruit chutneys are loved picnic and traveling companions, served with breads, pastries or crackers. Serving sizes for both are small and, depending on the selection, vary from 1–4 rounded spoonfuls. For example, a 2 teaspoon (10 ml) serving of nose-tingling hot coriander chutney will do for starters, while you could begin with ¼ cup (60 ml) of creamy cashew chutney.

Both types of chutney call for some type of hot chilies. How much and what kind you use are entirely matters of personal preference, though I would suggest that you allow enough for the heat to be recognizable. Indians like their chutneys hot, and I have seen many a cook drop two handfuls of fresh chilies and two spoons of cayenne into chutney meant to serve four! The recipes here have been tested with jalepeño chilies, unless stated otherwise. They are moderately hot and easy to seed. If your skin is sensitive, use rubber gloves when handling fresh chilies; normal skin will need little more than a film of oil for protection. Other chilies worth trying include tabasco, banana, cherry, poblano, serrano and Hungarian yellow, to name a few. The smallest varieties are usually the hottest.

FRESH CHUTNEYS

Fresh Coconut and Mint Chutney
NARIYAL PODINA CHATNI

Most people become addicts with their first taste of coconut chutney, and several South Indian dishes are never served without it. In this variation, fresh mint lends both flavor and a soft green hue to the creamy consistency.

Frozen grated coconut is convenient and quite acceptable, and the only alternative to fresh. It is available at some supermarkets and many Hispanic grocery stores.

Preparation time (after assembling ingredients): 15 minutes
Makes: about 1¼ cups (300 ml)

1–2 hot jalepeño chilies, seeded and chopped
½-inch (1.5 cm) scraped fresh ginger root, sliced
10 whole almonds or cashews, blanched
⅓ cup (80 ml) water
2 tablespoons (30 ml) lemon or lime juice
1 tablespoon (15 ml) raw sugar or maple syrup
1 teaspoon (5 ml) salt
⅓ cup (80 ml) trimmed fresh mint, lightly packed
1 cup (85 g) grated fresh or defrosted (140 g)
    frozen coconut, lightly packed

Fit a food processor with the metal blade, or use a blender. With the machine running, drop in the chilies and ginger and process until minced. Add the nuts, pulse four or five times, then process until ground. Add the water, juice, sweetener, salt and mint, and process until smooth. Stop the machine, add the coconut, and continue to process until the chutney is creamy and smooth. (For a thinner consistency, add plain yogurt or milk as desired.) To accompany South Indian dishes, the consistency should be fairly thick; as a dipping sauce, it can be thinner. Serve at room temperature or chilled. Well covered and refrigerated, the chutney can be kept for 1–2 days.

Fresh Coconut and Tamarind Chutney with Fresh Coriander
NARIYAL IMLI CHATNI

Tamarind pulp has a fruity, sour taste and is frequently used in South Indian cooking. In this recipe, a touch of raw sugar is added to bring out a sweet and sour contrast of flavors. This chutney selection from Hyderabad goes well with virtually any savory.

Preparation time (after assembling ingredients) and cooking time: about 30 minutes
Makes: 1½ cups (360 ml)

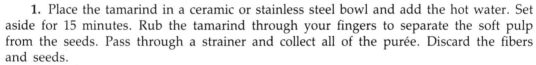

1½-inch (37 g) ball of seeded dried tamarind pulp
½ cup (120 ml) hot tap water
2 tablespoons (30 ml) each chopped fresh mint and coriander
3 tablespoons (45 ml) crumbled *jaggery* or date sugar
2–3 hot green chilies, seeded and chopped
½ teaspoon (2 ml) salt
1¼ cups (105 g) grated fresh coconut, lightly packed
3 tablespoons (45 ml) *ghee* or sesame oil
1 teaspoon (5 ml) black mustard seeds
¼ teaspoon (1 ml) yellow asafetida powder (*hing*)*
10 curry leaves, preferably fresh

*This amount applies only to yellow Cobra brand. Reduce any other asafetida by three-fourths.

1. Place the tamarind in a ceramic or stainless steel bowl and add the hot water. Set aside for 15 minutes. Rub the tamarind through your fingers to separate the soft pulp from the seeds. Pass through a strainer and collect all of the purée. Discard the fibers and seeds.

2. Combine the tamarind purée, herbs, sweetener, chilies and salt in a food processor fitted with the metal blade, or a blender. Cover and process to a smooth purée. Add the coconut and process until well mixed. Transfer to a non-metallic bowl or ceramic dish.

3. Heat the *ghee* or oil in a saucepan over moderate heat. When it is hot but not smoking, add the black mustard seeds and fry until they begin to sputter and turn gray. Remove the pan from the heat, add the asafetida and curry leaves, and after several seconds pour the seasonings into the chutney. Stir well. Serve at room temperature or chilled. Tightly covered and refrigerated, the chutney can be kept for 1–2 days.

Date and Raisin Chutney
KHAJUR KISHMISH CHATNI

Dates are the candy-like fruits of date palm trees, and raisins are sun-dried grapes. Both are intensely sweet and, combined, have considerable nutritive value, especially in concentrated iron. Dates are sold in several states, from very soft and fresh to hard and dry. If possible, use soft organic dates in this recipe.

Preparation time (after assembling ingredients): 2½ hours
Makes: 1½ cups (360 ml)

½ teaspoon (2 ml) fennel seeds
1 teaspoon (5 ml) cumin seeds
½ tablespoon (7 ml) coriander seeds
1 cup chopped pitted dates (about 4 ounces/115 g)
⅓ cup (50 g) raisins, preferably muscat
¼ cup (60 ml) fresh lime juice
2 tablespoons (30 ml) fresh orange juice
½-inch (1.5 cm) piece of peeled fresh ginger root, sliced
2–3 hot green jalepeño chilies, seeded and chopped
¼ teaspoon (1 ml) salt
⅛ teaspoon (0.5 ml) freshly ground nutmeg
2 tablespoons (30 ml) chopped fresh coriander

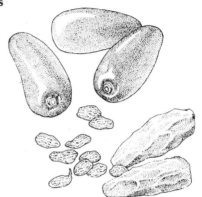

1. Slowly dry-roast the spice seeds in a heavy pan over low heat. When they darken a few shades, remove from the heat and cool. Combine the dates, raisins and citrus juice in a small bowl and set aside for 2 hours.

2. Fit a food processor with the metal blade, or use a blender. With the machine running, drop the ginger and chilies through the feed cap and process until minced. Add the soaked fruits and juices and the spice seeds, and pulse several times until coarsely ground. Transfer to a bowl. Stir in the salt, nutmeg and fresh coriander. Covered tightly and refrigerated, the chutney can be kept for 5–6 days.

Fresh Coriander Chutney
DHANIYA CHATNI

Fresh herb chutney is as popular in the Punjab as pesto is in Genoa. In one of its simplest forms, fresh herb chutney might be a handful of trimmed leaves, several green chilies, salt, lemon juice and water, stone-ground to a wet pulp. This type of chutney is sharp, hot and nose-tingling. Chutney aficionados highly prize a subtle play of supporting flavors, balancing astringent, acid and sweet overtones. They might add unripened gooseberries or mango for a sharp contrast. Most newcomers prefer a tempered version, much like pine nut pesto, cut with coconut, nuts or sour cream to subdue the bite. Serve it as a dipping sauce for a fried savory.

Preparation time (after assembling ingredients): 10 minutes
Makes: 1 cup (240 ml)

1 teaspoon (5 ml) cumin seeds
3 tablespoons (45 ml) sesame seeds
¼ cup (25 g) freshly grated coconut or
    ¼ cup (40 g) chopped almonds
1 cup (240 ml) trimmed fresh coriander, slightly packed
1–2 hot green chilies, seeded
½-inch (1.5 cm) piece of peeled fresh ginger root, chopped
2 tablespoons (30 ml) water
¼ cup (60 ml) sour cream or yogurt (optional)
1 tablespoon (15 ml) raw sugar or *jaggery*
1 teaspoon (5 ml) salt

1. Combine the cumin seeds, sesame seeds and coconut or nuts in a heavy frying pan and place over low heat. Dry-roast, stirring frequently, until the coconut or nuts darken a few shades.

2. Combine the coconut mixture and the remaining ingredients in a food processor fitted with the metal blade, or a blender, and process until smooth. (The texture should resemble runny applesauce; you may need more water to reach this consistency.) Transfer to a bowl and serve, or cover well and keep refrigerated for up to 2 days.

Fresh Mint Chutney
PODINA CHATNI

Fresh mint chutney, like coriander chutney, is refreshingly sharp and bracing. Long recognized for its digestive properties, it is a very popular accompaniment to fried savories and highly spiced dishes. The overall character of the chutney depends on the type of mint you use, be it from the supermarket or freshly harvested from your herb garden. I have tested the recipe with numerous species and come up with different results. For example, the dappled cream and pale green leaves of pineapple mint (*Mentha suaveolens variegata*) has a fruity flavor, while the rounded downy leaves of Egyptian mint (*M. suaveolens*) has fresh apple overtones. For best all-around use, I prefer Bowles mint (*M. x villosa*), with its fresh scent and mild flavor. No matter what your source, if the mint is pungent, with a coarse flavor, temper it with coconut, nuts or dried fruits.

Preparation time (after assembling ingredients): 10 minutes
Makes: about 1 cup (240 ml)

2 tablespoons (30 ml) each fresh lime juice and orange juice
2 tablespoons (30 ml) finely chopped dried papaya or honey
3 tablespoons (45 ml) water
1¾ cups (420 ml) trimmed fresh mint, packed
1–2 hot green chilies, seeded and chopped
¼ cup (25 g) fresh or dried coconut, lightly packed
1 teaspoon (5 ml) salt

Combine all of the ingredients in a food processor fitted with the metal blade, or a blender, and process until smooth. (The texture should resemble runny applesauce; you may need more water to reach this consistency.) Transfer to a bowl and serve or cover well and keep refrigerated for up to 2 days.

Creamy Cashew Chutney
KAJU CHATNI

This creamy chutney from Kerala, made from raw cashews, is versatile, wholesome and irresistible. It not only serves as a perfect accompaniment to traditional South Indian savories, but extends itself to accommodate a bowl of crunchy vegetable crudités or, thinned down, becomes an elegant salad dressing. Fresh cashews make the dish outstanding, for they are plump, white and sweet (stale nuts are gray and shriveled). Cashews are softer than most nuts, composed of about 47 percent oil, 22 percent carbohydrates and 21 percent protein, and provide excellent food value. This chutney is quickly assembled, keeps well and is easy to use. I have folded the last two tablespoons into a pan of stir-fried green beans, with smashing results.

Preparation time (after assembling ingredients): 10 minutes
Makes: about 1¼ cups (300 ml)

1 cup (140 g) raw cashews, bits or halves
¼ teaspoon (1 ml) lemon juice
1 teaspoon (5 ml) salt
½-inch (1.5 ml) piece of peeled fresh ginger root, sliced
1–2 hot green chilies, seeded and chopped
up to ⅓ cup (80 ml) water
2 tablespoons (30 ml) chopped fresh coriander

Combine the cashews, lemon juice, salt, ginger and chilies with ¼ cup (60 ml) of the water in a food processor fitted with the metal blade, or a blender, and process until smooth, adding more water as necessary to produce a loose purée. Transfer to a bowl, add the fresh coriander, and serve, or cover well and keep refrigerated for up to 3 days.

Note: This chutney thickens as it sits. Thin it with water to the desired consistency.

Shredded Mango and Coconut Chutney
AAM NARIYAL CHATNI

Green mango makes delicious raw or cooked chutney. In this much loved South Indian varia-tion, the rock-hard type is preferred. On the other hand, in the North fruit just short of ripe is favored. Use whatever is to your liking and convenient. The peppery orange–lime dressing beauti-fully sets off the near tart mango and sweet coconut–dried fruit mixture. This textured, nearly raw chutney has a character similar to *kachamber* and makes a pleasant contrast for soups, *dals* or stews. It is best assembled at least ½ hour before serving.

Preparation and marinating time (after assembling ingredients): 1–3 hours
Makes: 1½ cups (360 ml)

2 medium-sized firm unripe mangoes (about 2 pounds/1 kg)
¼ cup (25 g) dried or fresh coconut ribbons
1 tablespoon (15 ml) diced dried fruit, such as papaya or apricot
1 tablespoon (15 ml) each orange and lime juice
½ teaspoon (2 ml) salt
⅛ teaspoon (0.5 ml) cayenne pepper or paprika
1–2 hot green chilies, halved, seeded and slivered
2 tablespoons (30 ml) sesame or coconut oil
1 teaspoon (5 ml) black mustard seeds
2 tablespoons (30 ml) finely chopped fresh coriander

1. Peel the mangoes with a vegetable peeler or paring knife. Coarsely shred the fruit and discard the seed. Combine the mangoes with the coconut, dried fruit, juices, salt, cayenne or paprika and green chilies in a serving bowl, gently toss, cover, and marinate for ½ hour. It can be refrigerated for up to 6 hours before serving.

2. Heat the oil in a small pan over moderate heat until hot but not smoking. Drop in the black mustard seeds and fry until they turn gray and sputter (keep a lid handy to catch flying seeds). Pour the *chaunk* into the salad, add the fresh coriander, toss to mix, and serve.

COOKED CHUTNEYS

Simple Tomato Chutney
TAMATAR CHATNI

I was first introduced to one of Srila Prabhupada's famous tomato chutneys in 1966, and it still remains one of my favorites today. In my early days as his cook, I recall few feasts, banquets or journeys that did not include some variation or another. I have taken the liberty of approximating measurements, as Srila Prabhupada cooked without measuring tools. Try this chutney with any rice or dal, or vegetables that are compatible with tomatoes.

Preparation and cooking time (after assembling ingredients): about 25 minutes
Makes: about 1 cup (240 ml)

2 tablespoons (30 ml) *ghee*
1–2 whole dried red chilies
1 teaspoon (5 ml) cumin seeds
1-inch (2.5 cm) piece of cinnamon stick
1⅔ cups (about 1¼ pounds/570 g) coarsely chopped ripe tomatoes
3 tablespoons (45 ml) maple sugar, date sugar or *jaggery*
½ teaspoon (2 ml) salt

Heat the *ghee* in a large frying pan over moderate heat. When it is hot but not smoking, add the chilies, cumin seeds and cinnamon stick, and fry until the cumin seeds turn brown. Carefully add the tomatoes, sweetener and salt, and stir the sizzling ingredients for 10–15 minutes until the chutney is fairly dry. Serve warm, at room temperature or chilled. It can be kept, tightly covered and refrigerated, for 2–3 days.

Note: If you make this dish in quantity, cook it over moderately low heat, not moderate. The cooking time increases considerably because of the increased juice in the larger quantity of tomatoes.

Sweet Tomato Chutney with Fennel

MEETHA TAMATAR CHATNI

This dish, from a banquet at Calcutta's famous Radha Govinda Temple on Mahatma Gandhi Road, was served near the end of the meal. Depending on the number of courses, every regional cuisine has an order of serving, and sweet chutneys—often served with plain rice or toasted *pappadum*—are considered palate cleansers after other spicy dishes. This is a versatile chutney that complements many types of cuisine.

Preparation and cooking time (after assembling ingredients): about 30 minutes
Makes: about 1 cup (240 ml)

3 tablespoons (45 ml) *ghee* or mustard oil
½ teaspoon (2 ml) fennel seeds
¼ teaspoon (1 ml) nigella *kalonji*
¼ teaspoon (1 ml) cumin seeds
¼ teaspoon (1 ml) black mustard seeds
½ cassia or bay leaf
1–2 whole dried red chilies
1⅔ cups (570 g) firm ripe tomatoes,
    peeled and coarsely chopped
⅓ cup (50 g) maple sugar or *jaggery*
⅓ cup (50 g) golden raisins
¼ teaspoon (1 ml) turmeric
½ teaspoon (2 ml) salt

1. Heat the *ghee* or oil in a large heavy frying pan over moderate heat. (If you use mustard oil, bring it to the smoking point for about 5 seconds to make the pungent oil docile.) When it is hot but not smoking, add the fennel seeds, nigella, cumin seeds and black mustard seeds. When the fennel seeds darken one or two shades or the mustard seeds begin to pop, drop in the cassia or bay leaf and red chilies. Within 5 seconds, carefully add the chopped tomatoes and their liquid. Stir to mix, and cook over moderately low heat for 10 minutes.

2. Add the remaining ingredients and continue to cook for about 20 minutes or until the chutney is glazed and fairly thick. You should have about 1 cup (240 ml). Serve at room temperature, or cover and refrigerate for up to 4 days.

Fresh Pineapple and Raisin Chutney
ANANAS KISMISH CHATNI

Within India's districts, even towns and villages have their own distinct cuisines. Mayapur, in West Bengal, is associated with foods loved by Shree Chaitanya Mahaprabhu, the founder of Gaudiya Vaishnavism, and on his birthday, called *Gour Purnima*, thousands of dishes are made in his honor. On Srila Prabhupada's first *Gour Purnima* in America, he taught his students to make a handful of dishes loved by Lord Chaitanya, including *laphra*, *charchari*, *payasa*, *bhaji* and this chutney. Its character is outstanding, and although over the years many imitations have come to my attention, none match the original. It makes even a humble meal an event.

Preparation and cooking time: about 1 hour
Makes: about 2 cups (480 ml)

3 tablespoons (45 ml) *ghee*
1–2 whole dried red chilies
½ tablespoon (7 ml) cumin seeds
½ tablespoon (7 ml) coriander seeds
1 large ripe pineapple (about 2½ pounds/1.5 kg)
    peeled, quartered, cored, and cut into pieces
    ¾ x ¼ x ¼ inch (2 cm x 6 mm x 6 mm);
    reserve the juice
½ teaspoon (2 ml) cardamom seeds, slightly crushed
½ teaspoon (2 ml) *garam masala* or ¼ teaspoon (1 ml)
    each ground cloves and cinnamon
⅔ cup (100 g) maple sugar, brown sugar or *jaggery*
⅓ cup (50 g) raisins or currants

1. Heat the *ghee* in a 2-quart/liter heavy-bottomed pan (preferably nonstick) over moderate heat until it is hot but not smoking. Add the red chilies, cumin seeds and coriander seeds and fry until they darken a few shades. Carefully add the pineapple and its juice (they tend to splatter), cardamom seeds and *garam masala*. Stirring now and then, gently boil over moderate to moderately low heat until the fruit is tender and the juice has cooked off. Toward the end, stir constantly to keep the fruit from scorching in the nearly dry pan.

2. Add the sweetener and raisins or currants, reduce the heat slightly and cook, stirring frequently, until the chutney is glazed and thick. Serve at room temperature, or cover and refrigerate for 3–4 days. Bring to room temperature before serving.

Cranberry Chutney
TOPOKUL CHATNI

Topokul is not a cranberry but a sour berry that makes a chutney similar to whole-berry American cranberry sauce. There are two main types of cranberries: small wild European berries and the larger red cultivated American berries. India *topokul* is like a cross between the two. Because fresh berries freeze well, this selection can be made on short notice, especially in the fall.

Preparation and cooking time (after assembling ingredients): about 45 minutes
Makes: about 3 cups (710 ml)

3-inch (7.5 cm) piece of cinnamon stick
3–4 whole green cardamom pods, crushed open
1 teaspoon (5 ml) whole cloves
1–2 hot green chilies, seeded
3-inch (7.5 cm) piece of orange zest
1½ cups (360 ml) white grape juice or water
¾ cup (120 g) raw sugar or maple syrup (180 ml)
½ cup (80 g) pitted dates, sliced
1 pound (455 g) cranberries

1. Tie the cinnamon, cardamom pods, cloves, green chilies and orange zest in a small piece of cheesecloth. Combine the juice or water, sweetener, dates and spice bag in a heavy-bottomed, 2-quart/liter saucepan over moderate heat, and cook, stirring, until the sugar dissolves. Reduce the heat to low and simmer for ½ hour.

2. Remove the spice bag, pressing it to extract the flavor. Stir in the cranberries and cook for 7–10 minutes or until the mixture thickens and the berries pop. Serve at room temperature, or cover and refrigerate for up to a week.

Pear Chutney with Dates and Pecans
NASHPATI CHATNI

While residing in the vale of Evesham, I had the opportunity to sample some of England's best produce. Every day for weeks on end I took on the challenge of coming up with a different cooked chutney, and in due course this recipe emerged from the test kitchen as everyone's favorite.

Preparation and cooking time (after assembling ingredients): about 1 hour
Makes: about 1½ cups (360 ml)

¼–½ teaspoon (1–2 ml) crushed dried red chilies
1 tablespoon (15 ml) scraped, finely shredded or minced fresh ginger root
½ tablespoon (7 ml) grated orange zest
¼ teaspoon (1 ml) crushed cardamom seeds
2-inch (5 cm) piece of cinnamon stick
2 tablespoons (30 ml) *ghee* or unsalted butter
½ cup (120 ml) fresh orange juice
¼ cup (40 g) maple sugar or brown sugar, packed
6–7 medium-sized Bosc pears (about 2½ pounds/1.5 kg), peeled, quartered,
    cored and cut crosswise into ⅓-inch (1 cm) slices
½ cup (95 g) pitted soft dates, snipped into ⅓-inch (1 cm) pieces
⅓ cup (40 g) chopped toasted pecans

1. Combine the red chilies, ginger, orange zest, cardamom seeds and cinnamon on a saucer. Place the *ghee* or butter in a 3-quart/liter saucepan over low heat. Before the *ghee* is hot or the butter froths, add the combined spices. Fry for 1–2 minutes to release flavors. Add the orange juice and sugar, and stir until the sugar dissolves. Stir in the pears, bring to a gentle boil, and cook until syrupy and thick, about 30 minutes. Stir often during the last 5 minutes to prevent scorching.

2. Remove the pan from the heat, stir in the dates and pecans, and cool to room temperature. Serve, or cover and refrigerate for 3–4 days.

Golden Papaya Chip Chutney
KACHA PAPITA CHATNI

I was introduced to this dish at a lavish Bengali feast in the suburban Calcutta estate of Mr. Tarun Kunti Ghosh, the publisher of *Amrita Patrika Bazaar*, Calcutta's largest newspaper. The memorable *prasadam* repast contained some of the finest Bengali cuisine I have ever tasted, made with great care in a newly constructed kitchen equipped with freshly made clay stoves, by a fleet of Brahman cooks decked out in new clothes, and using mountains of fresh produce, grains and milk products. The end result of this kitchen army included 108 exquisite preparations served to the 100-plus guests dining village style: seated on an open veranda behind newly picked throw-away banana leaf plates and clay cups. Before I stopped counting, more than forty servers had brought in relay after relay of indescribably delicious *prasadam*—and this chutney, made from unripened papaya, caught my attention at the first bite. Inquiring after the recipe in the kitchen, I was laughingly told in halting pidgin English that I was eating Tarun Baba's famous "plastic chutney": when shavings of green fruit are simmered in an acidulated syrup, they become transparent, and to the Bengali cooks, resembled chips of plastic.

Unripened, green papaya has very hard, white flesh and is frequently used in Bengali and Oriyan chutneys, *dals* and vegetables. It is available at Indian, Chinese and Latin greengrocers. Because most supermarket papaya is picked quite green, to ripen in transit and in the stores, half-ripe fruit is more than acceptable. The thin papaya slices rest in a glistening golden sauce. Try it as a relish with a formal full-course meal or as a jam.

Preparation time (after assembling ingredients): 15 minutes
Cooking time: 30 minutes
Makes: 1½ cups (360 ml)

2 pounds (1 kg) unripe green papaya (about
    2½ cups/600 ml of thinly sliced fruit)
1¼ cups (265 g) sugar
⅓ cup (80 ml) water
¼ cup (60 ml) strained lime juice
¼ teaspoon (1 ml) salt
1 hot green or dried red chili (or as desired)

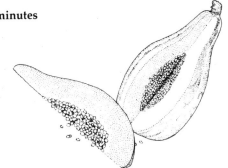

1. Quarter the papaya lengthwise, peel with a paring knife, and scoop out the center seeds and fibers. Cut each quarter in half lengthwise, then slice the papaya wedges crosswise into thin wafers.

2. Combine the sugar and water in a 2-quart/liter saucepan. Place over moderately low heat and stir until the sugar is dissolved; then add the papaya, raise the heat slightly, and gently boil until the fruit is soft.

3. Remove the papaya slices with a slotted spoon and set aside. Continue to boil the sugar–water mixture for about 20 minutes or until it is reduced to a one-thread consistency. When it is thick, add the papaya, lemon juice, salt and whole chili. Cook until the papaya is translucent and the texture jam-like.

Gooseberry Chutney
AMLA CHATNI

I have been told that gooseberries are not popular in America because they are not a good commercial crop. Evidently, they are susceptible to pests and nasty American gooseberry mildew. They are, nonetheless, available in the wilds—in damp woods, valleys and mountain regions from Maine to Oregon, as well as at roadside stalls and co-ops in season. In India they are widely used, both ripe and unripe, in jams, chutneys and sweet syrups. This chutney resembles a preserve in texture but is characteristically Bengali in seasoning.

Preparation and cooking time: 10 minutes
Makes: about 2½ cups (600 ml)

4 cups (1 liter) gooseberries, stemmed and washed
½ cup (120 ml) water
2–3 cups (425–635 g) sugar
¼ teaspoon (1 ml) cayenne pepper
½ cassia or bay leaf
½-inch (1.5 cm) piece of peeled fresh ginger root
¼ teaspoon (1 ml) *panch puran* (optional)
¼ teaspoon (1 ml) salt

1. Place the gooseberries in a 3-quart/liter heavy saucepan, add the water and bring to a boil over high heat. Add the remaining ingredients, reduce the heat, and simmer until the berries are clear and the juice is thick, about 15–20 minutes.

2. Remove the pan from the heat and lift out the cassia or bay leaf and ginger with fork tongs. Cool to room temperature and serve as a sweet chutney, even as a jam, or cover well and refrigerate for 2–3 days.

Currant and Date Chutney

KISHMISH KHAJUR CHATNI

Like gooseberries and cranberries, fresh currants are highly acidic, and therefore quite tart and sour. Though they can be eaten raw, most people prefer them transformed into sugar-sweetened cooked jams, chutneys, fruit syrups or desserts. Red and white currants are less well known than black—famous in England as a vitamin C–rich, delicious beverage called Ribena. I prefer red currants for this chutney.

Preparation and cooking time: about 30 minutes
Makes: about 2¼ cups (530 ml)

2 cups (245 g) fresh red currants,
    washed and stemmed
½ cup (120 g) *jaggery* or maple sugar
¾ cup (120 g) chopped soft dates
¼ cup (40 g) monukka or muscat raisins
¼ cup (60 ml) white grape juice
¼ teaspoon (1 ml) cayenne pepper
¼ teaspoon (1 ml) each ginger,
    nutmeg, cloves and cinnamon
½ teaspoon (2 ml) salt

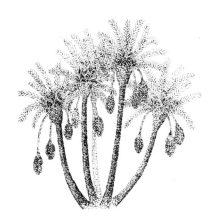

Combine all of the ingredients in a 3-quart/liter heavy stainless steel or enamel saucepan, place over moderate heat, and, stirring occasionally, bring to a gentle boil. Reduce the heat to moderately low and cook for about 20 minutes or until the liquid is thick. (It should reach 215°F/101°C on a thermometer.) Serve at room temperature, or refrigerate, covered, for 3–4 days.

Apricot Chutney with Currants
KHUMANI CHATNI

This is an outstanding chutney, especially when the apricots are tree-ripened, sweet and fragrant. For those of us resorting to fruits sold at supermarkets or corner grocers, look for barely ripened fruit with a fragrant smell. If they are absolutely without smell, use dried apricots which require an overnight soaking in lime juice and water and a slight increase in cooking time. American dried apricots little resemble their shriveled Indian counterpart, *aloo bookhara*, but they are almost as tasty as the fresh fruit.

Preparation and cooking time for fresh apricots: 30 minutes
Preparation, soaking and cooking time for dried apricots: overnight
Makes: 1½ cups (360 ml)

½ pound (230 g) dried apricot halves,
    quartered and soaked overnight in 3
    tablespoons (45 ml) lime juice and
    2 cups (480 ml) hot water; or
2 pounds (1 kg) fresh apricots, seeded
    and sliced, plus 3 tablespoons (45 ml)
    lime juice and ½ cup (120 ml) water
2 tablespoons (30 ml) *ghee* or butter
3-inch (7.5 cm) piece of cinnamon stick
½ teaspoon (1 ml) *kalonji* or black sesame seeds
½ tablespoon (7 ml) scraped fresh ginger root, minced
⅔ cup (85 g) dark raisins or currants
½ cup (75 g) maple sugar or brown sugar, packed
¼ teaspoon (1 ml) salt
⅛–¼ teaspoon (0.5–1 ml) cayenne pepper

1. If you are using dried apricots, drain the soaked fruit in a strainer and collect the liquid.

2. Heat the *ghee* or butter over moderate heat in a 3-quart/liter stainless steel or enamel saucepan. When it melts, add the cinnamon, *kalonji* or black sesame seeds and ginger, and fry for about ½ minute. Stir in the remaining ingredients, raise the heat slightly, and bring to a boil. Reduce the heat to moderately low and simmer, stirring now and then, especially in the last 10 minutes, until the chutney is thick and glazed, about 30 minutes for fresh apricots and 45 minutes for dried. Serve at room temperature, or refrigerate, covered, for 2–3 days.

Zesty Green Tomato Chutney

KACHA TAMATAR CHATNI

Bengalis love green tomato chutney—either sweet or sweet 'n' sour—for although it is made from a plebeian ingredient, it has a wonderfully delicate flavor. In this century-old recipe from Bir Nagar, saffron and lime juice beautifully set off a green tomato–papaya combination. Bengalis are fond of both unripened mango and papaya, and many cooks might toss in a handful of diced fruit about halfway through the cooking. A relative newcomer to greengrocers' shelves and roadside stalls, yellow tomatoes make a fine golden variation in summer.

Preparation time (after assembling ingredients): about 30 minutes
Makes: about 1 cup (240 ml)

4 medium-sized green or yellow tomatoes (about 1¼ pounds/570g)
3 tablespoons (45 ml) *ghee*, or corn or mustard oil
1 tablespoon (15 ml) minced yellow banana chilies,
    or 1–2 seeded and minced hot serrano chilies
½ teaspoon (2 ml) black mustard seeds
8–10 curry leaves, preferably fresh
⅛ teaspoon (0.5 ml) saffron threads
2 tablespoons (30 ml) each finely chopped candied ginger
½ cup (120 ml) peeled and diced green papaya or mango
    and papaya or other slightly underripe fruit
½ teaspoon (2 ml) salt
2 tablespoons (30 ml) coarsely chopped fresh coriander

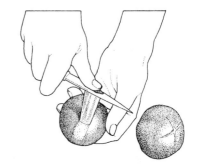

1. Plunge the tomatoes into a pan of boiling water for 30 seconds. Drain immediately and peel the tomatoes. Cut each in half crosswise and squeeze out most of the seeds. Dice the tomatoes.

2. Heat the *ghee* or oil in a heavy frying pan over moderate heat until it is hot but not smoking. (If you use mustard oil, bring it to the smoking point for about 5 seconds to make the pungent oil docile.) Drop in the black mustard seeds and fry until they turn gray and sputter. Add the curry leaves, and in seconds carefully add the tomatoes and saffron. Stir and cook for about 15 minutes over moderately low heat.

3. Add the candied fruit, diced green fruit and salt. Stirring often toward the end, cook for about 15 minutes or until fairly thick. Remove the pan from the heat, stir in the fresh coriander, and let cool. Serve at room temperature, or cover and refrigerate for up to 2 days.

Light Meals
and
Savories

Pakoras, deep fried fritters, are the simplest of India's classic light meal selections. Like the other recipes for *uppma* grain pilaf, they can be served any time of the day or night. Just as easily, they can be a side dish at a holiday feast or special luncheon. From noon to midnight, they are perfect snacks with a zesty chutney.

PAKORAS: VEGETABLE FRITTERS

In India, *pakoras* are almost a national passion. Anywhere people congregate—from bustling city street corners to remote village railway stations—it is a common sight to see a small crowd encircling a hand-pushed *pakora* cart. In snack houses, they are favorites with little more than soup or a beverage. And in the home, from late breakfast to late supper, they are simple, inexpensive, easy-to-make finger foods for drop-in company or a relaxing family break.

Whether you make the fried fritters with vegetables, *panir* cheese or even fruits, there are two methods to choose from: batter-dipped or spoon-fried. The vegetables or other ingredients can simply be cut into rounds, sticks, fan shapes or slices, dipped in seasoned chickpea flour batter and deep-fried, or they can be coarsely chopped or shredded, mixed into a thick batter and spooned into hot oil. Either way, *pakoras* are served piping hot.

There is a choice of batter consistency as well, though the basic principle is to make a texture thick enough to envelop the foods in a thorough coating. A thin batter is used to put a crisp, delicate coating on irregularly-shaped items such as spinach leaves, watercress or Swiss chard leaves. A thick batter is recommended for coating moist foods such as tomatoes or *panir* cheese. A medium-consistency batter will do for such items as eggplant, bell peppers, zucchini, potatoes, blanched cauliflower flowerets and countless more. If you prefer a noticeably crisp outside crust, a little *ghee* or oil is added to the batter and the *pakoras* are fried at a temperature slightly lower than usual, sometimes even double-fried.

To make *pakoras* that are soft and cake-like on the outside, a little baking powder in the batter will suffice. Like Japanese tempura, one batter will do for almost any vegetable, but to show a sample of regional variations, I have suggested eight different seasoned batters. Whether you mix your batter in a food processor or blender or by hand, do not add all of the liquid to the flour at once. Add only two-thirds to three-quarters of the liquid and blend until smooth, then slowly add the remaining liquid until the batter is thinned to the desired consistency.

Unlike crumb-coated ice cream, cheese or butter or delicate phyllo pastry—which is deep-fried at high temperatures and only long enough to toast the coating—*pakoras* are fried at lower temperatures to both cook the vegetables and brown the batter. Healthy deep-frying depends on the quantity of oil in relation to frying items and temperature control. Foods that are correctly fried are neither greasy nor soggy, but crispy outside and sufficiently cooked on the inside. *Ghee* begins to smoke at a relatively low temperature—365°–370°F (185°–187°C), while light vegetable oils begin much higher—440°F (226°C) for peanut oil and 465°F (240°C) for soybean oil. Since most *pakoras* are fried at 345°–355°F (173°–180°C), most nut and vegetable oils can be used without the risk of smoking. Recently a new light olive oil has reached the market which can be used for deep frying. Darker, fruity virgin oils smoke at low temperatures and are best reserved for salads.

Avoid crowding the frying pan with too many *pakoras*: the temperature will drop, foods may stick together, and, most of all, they will absorb unwanted excess oil. Many temple kitchens, even white tablecloth restaurants, will not use a frying oil a second time, encouraging chefs to fry carefully with attention to the quantity of oil in relation to frying demands. If you choose to deep-fry in *ghee*, cost efficiency and waste should be a natural concern. Frugal homecooks will likely re-use oil a second, even third time. No matter what your choice, it is best to strain still warm *ghee* or oil through a fine sieve before storage, and refrigerate when cool. With the exception of mustard oil, if the oil has been allowed to reach its smoking point, it begins to chemically decompose and darken and must soon be discarded.

A Batter for All *Pakoras*

Mixed vegetable *pakoras* are one of the most popular of all finger-food snacks. At home, they are not only a late-afternoon favorite at tiffin time, but are also frequently served on entertainment menus, from holidays to wedding buffets. If you are frying several types of vegetables with one batter, here is a good choice. Made with chickpea flour, ground spices and ice water, the batter puts a crisp crust on fried foods. If you prefer a cake-like, light crust, add baking powder. You need a medium consistency batter that will thoroughly coat moist foods like *panir* cheese or tomatoes, but will not be too thick for delicate foods such as spinach or Swiss chard.

One flour absorbs water differently than another, and one cook's measurement of flour varies from another's. For 1⅓ cups (135 g) of sifted chickpea flour (3½ ounces/135 g), 8 tablespoons (120 ml) of ice water yields a thickish batter; 10 tablespoons (150 ml) a thinnish one. Add water in small amounts toward the end of mixing to achieve the desired results.

Try any of the following *pakora* suggestions, allowing 25–35 cut pieces for this amount of batter. Depending on the accompanying dishes, allow 4–5 *pakoras* per person.

Preparation time (after assembling ingredients): 10 minutes
Resting time: 10–15 minutes
Cooking time: about 30 minutes
Serves: 6

1⅓ cups (135 g) sifted chickpea flour (sifted before measuring)
2 teaspoons (10 ml) melted *ghee* or vegetable oil
1 tablespoon (15 ml) lemon juice
¼ teaspoon (1 ml) cayenne pepper
½ teaspoon (2 ml) turmeric
1 teaspoon (5 ml) *garam masala* or ¼ teaspoon (1 ml)
    each ground cardamom, cumin, cinnamon and cloves
2 teaspoons (10 ml) ground coriander
1–1½ teaspoons (5–7 ml) salt
9 tablespoons (135 ml) cold water, or as needed
⅓ teaspoon (1.5 ml) baking powder (optional)

Pakora Suggestions:

underripe banana, cut into rounds ⅓ inch (1 cm) thick
cauliflower flowerets, 1½ inches (4 cm) long
    and ½ inch (1.5 cm) square, half-cooked
eggplant, cut into rounds ¼ inch (6 mm) thick
potato or yam, peeled and cut into rounds ⅛ inch (3 mm) thick
lotus root, washed, peeled, steamed for ½ hour, cut
    on the diagonal ¼ inch (6 mm) thick, and patted dry
pumpkin, cut into 2-inch (5 cm) squares ¼ inch (6 mm) thick,
spinach, medium-sized leaves, stemmed, washed and dried
bell peppers (red, yellow or green), sliced crosswise
    ¼ inch (6 mm) thick, seeded and ribbed
green tomatoes, cut into rounds ⅓ inch
    (1 cm) thick and thoroughly patted dry
zucchini, cut on the diagonal ¼ inch (6 mm) thick
asparagus tips, blanched and dried

1. Combine the flour, melted *ghee* or oil, lemon juice, spices and salt in a bowl and mix well. Add 5 tablespoons (75 ml) of water slowly, beating with an electric beater or wire whisk until the batter is smooth and free of lumps. Slowly add 3 tablespoons (45 ml) more water, continuing to beat until well mixed. Check the consistency, and if necessary, slowly add the remaining water until the batter resembles the consistency of heavy cream and easily coats a wooden spoon.

Alternately, place the batter ingredients in a food processor fitted with the metal blade, or a blender, process until smooth, then transfer to a bowl. Cover the batter and set aside for 10–15 minutes.

2. Again beat with an electric beater, wire whisk or your hand for 2–3 minutes to further lighten the batter. (Check the batter consistency: if it is too thin, moist foods will spatter as they fry; if it is too thick, they will not cook properly. Add flour or water as necessary.) Stir in the baking powder at this time if you prefer a cake-like crust. Set all of the items to be fried next to the stove. They should be patted dry and at room temperature.

3. Heat 2½–3 inches (6.5–7.5 cm) of fresh *ghee* or vegetable oil in a *karai,* wok or deep-frying pan until the temperature reaches 355°F (180°C). Dip 5 or 6 of your selected ingredients in the batter and, one at a time, carefully slip them into the hot oil. The temperature will fall but should then be maintained at between 345°–355°F (173°–180°C) throughout the frying. Fry until the *pakoras* are golden brown, turning to brown evenly. Leafy greens may take as little as 1 or 2 minutes per side, while potatoes may take up to 5 minutes per side. Remove with a slotted spoon and drain on paper towels. Serve immediately, or keep warm, uncovered, in a preheated 250°F (120°C) oven until all the *pakoras* are fried, for up to ½ hour.

Note: It is convenient to keep a bowl of water and a tea towel near the frying area. After batter-dipping the items to be fried, rinse and dry your hands before continuing your frying.

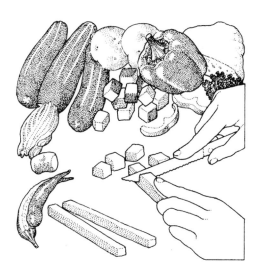

Zucchini *Pakora* with Crushed Peanuts
LOUKI PAKORA

Any type of summer squash can be substituted for green zucchini: yellow crookneck, patty-pan, yellow zucchini or Indian bottle gourd (*louki*). Cut them into rounds ¼ inch (6 mm) thick straight across or on the diagonal. The batter should be thick enough to completely coat the slices and keep the peanut bits from sliding off. Stir the batter before dipping each batch of zucchini.

Preparation time (after assembling ingredients): 10 minutes
Resting time: 10–15 minutes
Cooking time: about 30 minutes
Serves: 6 as a snack or 8 at a meal

1⅓ cups (135 g) sifted chickpea flour (sifted before measuring)
1½ teaspoons (7 ml) melted *ghee* or vegetable oil
1 tablespoon (15 ml) lemon juice
1 teaspoon (5 ml) crushed cumin seeds
1–2 hot green chilies, seeded and minced
1 teaspoon (5 ml) salt
up to 9 tablespoons (135 ml) cold water or enough
     to make a medium-consistency batter
¼ teaspoon (1 ml) baking powder
3 tablespoons (45 ml) finely chopped peanuts
2 medium-sized zucchini (about ½ pound/230 g),
     cut into 30–35 slices ¼ inch (6 mm) thick
ghee or vegetable oil for deep frying

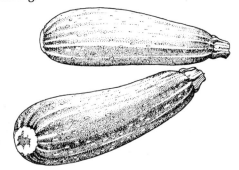

1. Combine the flour, melted *ghee* or oil, lemon juice, cumin seeds, chilies and salt in a bowl and mix well. Add 8 tablespoons (120 ml) of water slowly, beating with an electric beater or wire whisk until the batter is smooth and free of lumps. Slowly add the remaining water until the batter consistency is similar to cream and easily coats a wooden spoon. Alternately, place the batter ingredients in a food processor fitted with the metal blade, or a blender, process until smooth, then transfer to a bowl. Cover the batter and set aside for 10–15 minutes.

2. Again beat with an electric beater, wire whisk or your hand for 2–3 minutes to further lighten the batter. (Check the batter consistency: if it is too thin, moist foods will spatter as they fry; if it is too thick, they will not cook properly. Add flour or water as necessary.) Stir in the baking powder and peanuts. Set the zucchini, a bowl of water, tea towels and paper towels for draining near the stove.

3. Heat 2½–3 inches (6.5–7.5 cm) of fresh *ghee* or vegetable oil in a *karai*, wok or deep-frying pan until the temperature reaches 355°F (180°C). Dip 6–8 pieces of zucchini in the batter and carefully slip them into the hot oil. Avoid crowding the pan, which would make the temperature of the oil drop. Fry the zucchini *pakoras* 3–4 minutes per side or until golden brown. Remove with a slotted spoon and drain on paper towels. Serve immediately, or keep warm, uncovered, in a preheated 250°F (120°C) oven until all of the *pakoras* are fried, up to ½ hour.

Note: After batter-dipping each batch of squash rounds, rinse your hands and dry them on a tea towel before you continue frying.

Potato *Pakora* with Dried Pomegranate Seeds
ALOO PAKORA

Pomegranate seeds, used predominantly in North Indian cooking, are dried from wild pomegranate or *daru* that grow in the Himalayan foothills. The pleasantly sour flavor of the seeds are best for complementing potatoes and other starchy vegetables. Potato slices are handsomely jacketed in a medium-consistency batter that puts a crunchy crust on the soft potatoes. The food processor crushes the seeds while whisking the batter until it is light and airy. This is one *pakora* that lends itself to double-frying: the first frying may be done several hours before serving time, the second one warms the thin fritters and gives them their final crunch.

Preparation time (after assembling ingredients): 10 minutes
Resting time: 10–15 minutes
Cooking time: 30 minutes
Serves: 6 as a snack or 8 at a meal

1⅓ cups (135 g) sifted chickpea flour (sifted before measuring)
2 teaspoons (10 ml) melted *ghee* or vegetable oil
½ tablespoon (7 ml) dried pomegranate seeds
¼ teaspoon (1 ml) cayenne pepper or paprika
¼ teaspoon (1 ml) turmeric
1½ teaspoons (7 ml) salt
up to 9 tablespoons (135 ml) cold water, or enough
    to make a medium-consistency batter
1 large baking potato (about ½ pound/230 g), peeled, cut into a rectangle
    and sliced ⅛ inch (3 mm) thick (cut just before frying)
ghee or vegetable oil for deep-frying

1. Place the flour, melted *ghee* or oil, pomegranate seeds, cayenne or paprika, turmeric and salt in a blender or a food processor fitted with the metal blade. Pulse on and off 3 or 4 times. With the machine running, slowly pour in ½ cup (120 ml) of water and process for 2–3 minutes until smooth and airy. In 1 teaspoon (5 ml) amounts, add water until the batter consistency is similar to heavy cream. Transfer to a bowl, cover and set for 10–15 minutes. (Check the batter consistency: if it is too thin, moist foods will spatter as they fry; if it is too thick, they will not cook properly. Add flour or water as necessary.)

2. Place the sliced potatoes (about 30–35 pieces), a bowl of water, tea towels and paper towels for draining near the stove. Heat the *ghee* or vegetable oil in a *karai*, wok or deep-frying pan until the temperature reaches 355°F (180°C). Fry 6–7 potato *pakoras* at a time, maintaining the temperature at 345°–355°F (173°–180°C), for about 2 minutes per side if you will be serving them later, or 4–5 minutes per side until golden brown if you are frying them for serving now. Remove with a slotted spoon and drain on paper towels. If not serving immediately, fry a second time for about 2 minutes or until hot, crispy and golden brown. Serve hot.

Note: After batter-dipping each batch of the potato rounds, rinse your hands and dry with a tea towel before you continue frying.

Bell Pepper *Pakora* with Nigella Seeds
SIMLA MIRCH PAKORA

Nigella seeds, or *kalonji*, have a peppery lemon flavor and are widely used in Bengali cooking, on their own or as part of the five-seed spice blend known as *panch puran*. Unfortunately, they are sometimes called "onion seeds" in Indian grocery stores, even though they have nothing to do with onions. The nigella seeds should be left whole, so if you make the batter in a blender or food processor, stir them in after you transfer the batter to a bowl. Yellow, red or green bell peppers can be used with this *pakora* batter.

Preparation time (after assembling ingredients): 10 minutes
Resting time: 10–15 minutes
Cooking time: about 30 minutes
Serves: 6 as a snack or 8 at a meal

1⅓ cups (135 g) sifted chickpea flour
    (sifted before measuring)
½ tablespoon (7 ml) salt
2 teaspoons (10 ml) melted *ghee* or vegetable oil
1–2 hot green chilies, seeded and minced
½ tablespoon (7 ml) nigella seeds (*kalonji*)
½ teaspoon (2 ml) turmeric
9 tablespoons (135 ml) cold water, or enough
    to make a medium-consistency batter
⅛ teaspoon (0.5 ml) baking powder (optional)
25–35 long strips or rounds of seeded
    bell pepper (3 medium-sized peppers)
ghee or vegetable oil for deep-frying

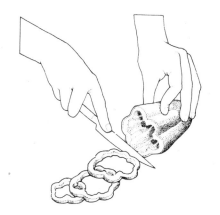

1. Combine the flour, salt, melted *ghee* or vegetable oil, green chilies, nigella seeds and turmeric in a bowl and mix well. Add ½ cup (120 ml) of water slowly, beating with an electric beater or wire whisk until the batter is smooth and free of lumps. Slowly add the remaining water until the batter consistency is similar to cream and easily coats a wooden spoon. Alternately, place the above ingredients in a food processor fitted with the metal blade, or a blender, adding the nigella seeds after the mixture is transferred to a bowl. Cover the batter and set aside for 10–15 minutes.

2. Again beat with an electric beater, wire whisk or your hand for 2–3 minutes to further lighten the batter. (Check the batter consistency: if it is too thin, moist foods will spatter as they fry; if it is too thick, they will not cook properly. Add more flour or water as necessary.) Stir in the baking powder at this time if you prefer a cake-like crust. Set the bell peppers to be fried next to the stove. They should be patted dry and at room temperature.

3. Heat 2½–3 inches (6.5–7.5 cm) of fresh *ghee* or vegetable oil in a *karai*, wok or deep-frying pan until the temperature reaches 355°F (180°C). Dip 5 or 6 bell pepper rings in the batter and, one at a time, carefully slip them into the hot oil. The temperature will fall but should be maintained at 345°–355°F (173°–180°C) throughout the frying. Fry for 3–4 minutes on each side until the *pakoras* are golden brown. Remove with a slotted spoon and drain on paper towels. Serve immediately, or keep warm, uncovered, in a preheated 250°F (120°C) oven until all the *pakoras* are fried, for up to ½ hour.

Pumpkin *Pakora* with Crushed Coriander Seeds
KADDU PAKORA

Any type of winter squash—butternut, acorn, turban or Indian wax gourd (*petha*)—as well as yams or sweet potatoes may be substituted for pumpkin. This is a good batter to make in a food processor, for along with crushing whole coriander seeds, the processor makes the batter light and smooth. If you make the batter by hand, add freshly crushed coriander seeds.

Preparation time (after assembling ingredients): 10 minutes
Resting time: 10–15 minutes
Cooking time: about 30 minutes
Serves: 6 as a snack or 8 at a meal

1⅓ cups (135 g) sifted chickpea flour (sifted before measuring)
1½–2 teaspoons (7–10 ml) salt
2 teaspoons (10 ml) melted *ghee* or vegetable oil
½ teaspoon (2 ml) turmeric
¼ teaspoon (1 ml) yellow asafetida powder (*hing*)*
1 tablespoon (15 ml) crushed coriander seeds
2 tablespoons (30 ml) yogurt
½ cup (120 ml) cold water, or enough to make a batter of medium consistency
¼ teaspoon (1 ml) baking powder (optional)
25–35 pieces of trimmed, peeled ripe pumpkin, cut into
    2-inch (5 cm) squares ¼ inch (6 mm) thick
ghee or vegetable oil for deep-frying

*This amount applies only to yellow Cobra brand. Reduce any other asafetida by three-fourths.

1. Place the flour, salt, melted *ghee* or vegetable oil, turmeric, asafetida, crushed coriander seeds and yogurt in a bowl and mix well. Add ½ cup (120 ml) of water slowly, beating with an electric beater or wire whisk until the batter is smooth and easily coats a wooden spoon. Alternately, place the batter ingredients in a food processor fitted with the metal blade, or a blender, and process until the coriander seeds are crushed and the texture is smooth, then transfer to a bowl. Cover the batter and set aside for 10–15 minutes.

2. Again beat with an electric beater, wire whisk or your hand for 2–3 minutes to further lighten the batter. (Check the batter consistency: if it is too thin, moist foods will spatter as they fry; if it is too thick, they will not cook properly. Add water or flour as necessary.) Stir in the baking powder at this time if you prefer a cake-like crust. Set the pumpkin pieces to be fried next to the stove. They should be patted dry and at room temperature.

3. Heat 2½–3 inches (6.5–7.5 cm) of fresh *ghee* or vegetable oil in a *karai*, wok or deep-frying vessel until the temperature reaches 355°F (180°C). Dip 5–6 pieces of pumpkin in the batter and, one at a time, carefully slip them into the hot oil. The temperature will fall but should then be maintained at between 345°–355°F (173°–180°C) throughout the frying. Fry until the *pakoras* are golden brown, turning to brown evenly, 3–4 minutes per side. Remove with a slotted spoon and drain on paper towels. Serve immediately, or keep warm, uncovered, in a preheated 250°F (120°C) oven, until all of the *pakoras* are fried, for up to ½ hour.

Cauliflower *Pakora*

GOBHI PAKORA

North Indians frequently serve this luscious *pakora* selection at wedding feasts. It adds a festive touch to almost any occasion, from brunch to late-night supper. Unless the cauliflower flowerets are cut very small, parboil or half-steam them before deep-frying. Make certain that the pieces are thoroughly patted dry and at room temperature before batter-dipping. If you are making the batter by hand, rather than in a food processor or blender, use ground coriander or fenugreek instead of the whole seeds.

Preparation and resting time (after assembling ingredients): 40 minutes
Cooking time: about 30 minutes
Makes: 25–35 pieces

1⅓ cups (135 g) sifted chickpea flour (sifted before measuring)
1½ teaspoons (7 ml) salt
2 teaspoons (10 ml) melted *ghee* or vegetable oil
2–4 hot green chilies, seeded and minced
1 inch (2.5 cm) piece of scraped, finely shredded or
    minced fresh ginger root
1 teaspoon (5 ml) dry-roasted fenugreek seeds or
    1 tablespoon (15 ml) coriander seeds
2 tablespoons (30 ml) coarsely chopped
    fresh fenugreek or coriander
about 9 tablespoons (135 ml) cold water, or enough to make a
    medium-consistency batter
¼–½ teaspoon (1–2 ml) baking powder
ghee or vegetable oil for deep-frying
25–35 cauliflower flowerets, 1½ inches (4 cm) long and
    ½ inch (1.5 cm) thick, parboiled or half-steamed

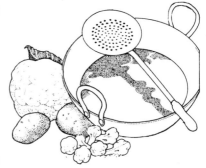

1. Combine the flour, salt, 2 teaspoons (10 ml) *ghee* or vegetable oil, chilies, ginger, fenugreek or coriander seeds, fresh herbs and 7 tablespoons (105 ml) of cold water in a blender or a food processor fitted with the metal blade. Cover and process until smooth. (If you mix the batter by hand, substitute ground spices for the seeds and work with a balloon whisk until smooth.) Gradually add the remaining water, or enough to make a batter the consistency of heavy cream. Cover and set aside for 10–15 minutes.

2. Again beat with an electric beater, wire whisk or your hand for 2–3 minutes to further lighten the batter. (Check the batter consistency: if it is too thin, moist foods will spatter as they fry; if it is too thick, they will not cook properly. Add flour or water as necessary.) Stir in the baking powder.

3. Heat 2½–3 inches (6.5–7.5 cm) of fresh *ghee* or vegetable oil in a *karai*, wok or deep-frying vessel until the temperature reaches 355°F (180°C). Dip 5 or 6 flowerets in the batter and, one at a time, carefully slip them into the hot oil. The temperature will fall but should then be maintained at between 345°–355°F (173°–180°C) throughout the frying. Fry until the *pakoras* are golden brown, turning to brown evenly. Remove with a slotted spoon and drain on paper towels. Serve immediately, or keep warm, uncovered, in a preheated 250°F (120°C) oven until all of the *pakoras* are fried, for up to ½ hour.

Spinach *Pakora* with *Ajwain* Seeds
PALAK PAKORA

This is a wafer-thin, crunchy *pakora*. Because the batter is assembled just before frying, with ground rice and ice water, the *pakoras* turn out crispy and delicate. The batter should be thin enough to allow the irregularly shaped leaves to get a good coating of flavor. The predominant seasoning is *ajwain* seeds. The seeds and flour are available at Indian grocery stores, and they lend a spicy, lemony twist to the otherwise plain batter. Try to use spinach leaves of similar size, and trim off all but 1 inch (2.5 cm) of the stem.

Preparation time (after assembling ingredients): 10 minutes
Resting time: 10–15 minutes
Cooking time: about 20 minutes
Serves: 6 as a snack or 8 at a meal

1 cup (100 g) sifted chickpea flour (sifted before measuring)
¼ cup (40 g) rice flour
1½ teaspoons (7 ml) *ajwain* seeds
scant ½ teaspoon (2 ml) cayenne pepper or paprika
1 teaspoon (5 ml) salt
¼ teaspoon (1 ml) baking powder
9–10 tablespoons (135–150 ml) ice cold water, or enough to
    make a thin batter similar in consistency to light cream
25–30 medium-sized fresh spinach leaves, trimmed,
    washed and patted dry (about ½ pound/230 g)
ghee or vegetable oil for deep-frying

1. Combine the flours, *ajwain* seeds, cayenne pepper or paprika, salt, baking powder and ½ cup (120 ml) of ice water in a bowl and work with a whisk until smooth. Slowly whisk in the remaining water or enough to make a crêpe-like batter, similar to cream.
2. Next to the stove, set out the spinach leaves, a bowl of hand rinsing water and drying towel, and paper towels for draining the finished fritters. Heat the *ghee* or vegetable oil in a *karai*, wok or deep-frying pan until the temperature reaches 350°F (175°C). Dip a spinach leaf in the batter so it is lightly coated, lift it and drain off the excess momentarily, then carefully slip it into the oil. Batter-coat only 4 or 5 leaves per batch, maintaining the oil at 350°F (175°C). Quickly rinse and dry your hands, then fry the leaves on both sides for 1–2 minutes or until crisp and pale gold. Remove with a slotted spoon and drain on paper towels. Serve immediately or keep warm, uncovered, in a preheated 200°F (120°C) oven until all the *pakoras* are fried, for up to 30 minutes.

Green Tomato *Pakora* with Cornmeal
TAMATAR PAKORA

If you have a tomato patch or even one plant on the patio, harvest 3 or 4 tomatoes when they are green and try this delicious dish. Alternately, you can purchase green or firm red tomatoes, but if they are soft and ripe, they will exude too much moisture when heated. Though cornmeal makes the most flavorful coating, a mixture of half semolina and half chickpea flour is also pleasant. Semolina flour is sold at Indian grocery stores, large health food stores and in supermarket gourmet aisles. If you wish, season the coating with 1 teaspoon (5 ml) of any dried herb, such as crushed summer savory, marjoram, oregano, chervil or basil.

Preparation and drying time: 15 minutes
Cooking time: 15 minutes
Serves: 4 to 6

4 medium-sized green tomatoes
⅔ cup (95 g) yellow or white cornmeal, preferably stone-ground,
    or ⅓ cup each semolina (70 g) and chickpea flour (30 g)
1½ teaspoons (7 ml) salt
½ teaspoon (2 ml) cracked black pepper
⅛ teaspoon (0.5 ml) cayenne pepper or paprika
2 teaspoons (10 ml) coarsely crushed cumin seeds
4 tablespoons (60 ml) *ghee* or a mixture of vegetable oil and unsalted butter

1. Slice the tomatoes, unpeeled, about ½ inch (1.5 cm) thick and save the ends for another use. Pat the slices dry with paper towels. Combine the cornmeal or semolina–chickpea flour mixture, salt, pepper, cayenne or paprika and crushed cumin seeds in a pie dish, and mix well. Press both sides of each tomato slice in the coating and set on a cake rack to air-dry for 5–10 minutes.

2. Place 2 tablespoons (30 ml) of the *ghee* or oil–butter mixture in a large heavy nonstick or cast-iron skillet over moderately high heat. When it is hot but not smoking, place in the pan as many coated slices as will easily fit. Fry until the bottoms are lightly browned, about 1½ minutes, then turn with tongs or a spatula and brown the second side. Remove and fry the remaining coated slices, adding *ghee* or the oil–butter mixture as necessary. Serve hot.

Herbed Cornmeal *Pakora*

MAKKAI PAKORA

With a texture similar to hush puppy or cornmeal muffin batter, these shallow-fried *pakoras* are made from stone-ground corn, either white or yellow.

Preparation time (after assembling ingredients): 5 minutes
Cooking time: 10 minutes
Serves: 4

½ cup (75 g) stone-ground cornmeal
½ cup (65 g) unbleached white flour,
    chapati, or whole wheat pastry flour
1¼ teaspoons (6 ml) baking powder
½ teaspoon (2 ml) salt
½ teaspoon (2 ml) sugar
a generous ¼ teaspoon (1 ml) of crushed red chilies
2 teaspoons (10 ml) chopped fresh dill or
    1½ teaspoons (7 ml) dried dill
½ cup (120 ml) milk
2 tablespoons (30 ml) melted *ghee* or vegetable oil
ghee or vegetable oil for shallow-frying

1. Blend the cornmeal, flour, baking powder, salt, sugar, crushed red chilies and dill in a mixing bowl. Whisk together the milk and *ghee* or oil in a small bowl, then pour into the cornmeal mixture and stir just until blended.

2. Heat ½ inch (1.5 cm) of *ghee* or oil in a large frying pan until it is hot but not smoking. Scoop up roughly 1 tablespoon (15 ml) amounts of the batter and carefully lower into the hot oil. Fry until golden brown on both sides (3–4 minutes per side), and serve immediately.

Batter-Coated Mashed Potato Balls
ALOO BONDA

This finger food is popular as the focal point of a late afternoon tiffin or as the savory part of a late night supper. The ginger-flavored mashed potatoes are dipped in an herbed chickpea flour batter and deep-fried into golden globes. One note of caution: be sure to thoroughly coat the balls with batter; exposed areas of mashed potatoes tend to splatter and disintegrate in the hot oil.

Preparation and frying time (after assembling ingredients): about ½ hour
Serves: 6

Potato Balls:

2 cups (480 ml) warm mashed potatoes
2 tablespoons (30 ml) finely chopped toasted almonds, peanuts or cashews
½ teaspoon (2 ml) *amchoor* or ½ tablespoon (7 ml) lemon juice
¼ teaspoon (1 ml) cayenne pepper or paprika
2 tablespoons (30 ml) scraped, finely shredded or minced fresh ginger root
½ teaspoon (2 ml) salt
2 tablespoons (30 ml) whole wheat flour

Batter:

1¼ cups (125 g) sifted chickpea flour (sifted before measuring)
1 tablespoon (15 ml) arrowroot
½ teaspoon (2 ml) each baking powder, salt, turmeric,
    garam masala and ground coriander
3 tablespoons (45 ml) finely chopped fresh coriander
9 tablespoons (135 ml) cold water or enough
    to make a medium-consistency batter
ghee or vegetable oil for deep-frying

1. Mix the mashed potatoes with the remaining potato-ball ingredients and roll into 16 balls.

2. Place the flour, arrowroot, baking powder, salt, turmeric, *garam masala*, ground coriander and fresh coriander in a mixing bowl. Working with a wire whisk, make a smooth batter, adding 7 tablespoons (105 ml) of water initially and then 2 more tablespoons (30 ml) or enough to make a smooth, slightly thick, crêpe-like batter.

3. Heat 2½–3 inches (6.5–7.5 cm) of *ghee* or vegetable oil in a *karai*, wok or deep-frying pan over moderately high heat until it reaches 350°F (180°C). Dip 5 or 6 balls in the batter and, one at a time, lift out with two fingers. Let the excess batter drip back into the bowl and, with a twist of the wrist, carefully slip the ball into the hot oil. Fry without crowding the balls (crowding makes them stick together and makes the oil temperature drop). Cook, turning gently after they float to the surface, until golden brown or for about 4–5 minutes. Remove and drain on paper towels. Keep warm in a 250°F (120°C) oven until all the *bondas* are fried, or serve immediately.

The Great Shallow-Fried Vine Leaf Rissole
ANGOOR PATTA PAKORA

Fresh vine leaves are a rarity, unless you have an arbor in your yard. Most likely you will purchase them preserved in water, salt and citric acid, in 6–8-ounce (170–230 g) jars or plastic pouches. They are available at most gourmet stores or Greek groceries. The leaves are blanched, drained, finely shredded and folded into a seasoned, herbed batter. The mixture is then poured into an 8 or 9-inch (20–22.5 cm) sauté pan and shallow-fried into a large round rissole that is golden brown and crunchy on the outside and soft on the inside. Cut the rissole into pie-shaped wedges for serving and accompany with a wedge of lemon or a seasoned sauce.

Preparation time (after assembling ingredients): 30 minutes
Cooking time: 10–15 minutes
Makes: 6 or 8 wedges

2 cups (205 g) sifted chickpea flour
    (sifted before measuring)
1½ teaspoons (7 ml) salt
1 cup (85 g) shredded fresh or dry
    unsweetened coconut, lightly packed
1 teaspoon (5 ml) paprika or a scant
    ½ teaspoon (2 ml) cayenne pepper
1 tablespoon (15 ml) cumin seeds
½ teaspoon (2 ml) yellow asafetida powder (*hing*)*
1 cup (240 ml) cold water
1 teaspoon (5 ml) baking powder
1 6–8-ounce (170–230 g) package of grapevine
    leaves, blanched for 5 minutes, rinsed,
    drained thoroughly and finely shredded
1 cup (240 ml) *ghee* or light vegetable oil
a few sprigs of fresh parsley for garnishing

*This amount applies only to yellow Cobra brand. Reduce any other asafetida by three-fourths.

    1. Blend the flour, salt, coconut, paprika or cayenne, cumin seeds and asafetida in a large bowl. Add the water and, working with a wire whisk, blend into a smooth, light batter. Add the baking powder and vine leaves, and stir with a few swift strokes, until mixed.
    2. Heat the *ghee* or vegetable oil in an 8–9-inch (20–22 cm) sauté pan over moderately low heat until it is hot but not smoking. Gently transfer the mixture into the hot oil, quickly spreading it evenly to the edges of the pan, into a flat cake. After 4–5 minutes, when one side is golden brown, lift the rissole with a wide spatula or two small spatulas and flip it over to brown the other side. When golden brown, transfer to paper towels to drain momentarily, then to a serving tray. Garnish with minced parsley and serve hot, cut into wedges. (Cut with a sharp serrated knife. If the vine leaves are not sufficiently blanched, they tend to tear when cut.)

Batter-Coated Stuffed Baby Tomatoes
TAMATAR BONDA

For entertaining, it is hard to top this hot-off-the-flame *pakora*—cherry tomato cups stuffed with fresh farmers cheese. They can be stuffed well ahead of serving time and fried just before they are required. It is important to fully cover the tomato with batter, especially the stuffing, as it sputters and tends to fall apart in the frying oil. They must be served piping-hot and crisp, for as they cool they soften from the moisture in the stuffing. If you make the dish in quantity, organize carefully and collect a few helping hands.

Hollowed-out tomato cups are ideal containers for a number of stuffings, and you may want to include low calorie variations along with the fried *pakora*. Try stuffing small tomato cups, 1½–2 inches (4–5 cm) in diameter, with yogurt, puréed vegetables, cracked wheat or rice salad. Pasta salad also makes a good stuffing, dressed with pesto: use very fine fedelini (vermicelli), soup stars or any small pasta shape you might use in a broth.

Preparation and cooking time (after assembling ingredients): 30–40 minutes
Serves: 6 as hors d'oeuvres or 8 as a side dish

24–28 cherry tomatoes (about ¾–1 pound/340–455 g)
freshly made cheese or farmer's cheese
    (about 5 ounces/140 g)
¼ teaspoon (1 ml) each freshly ground black pepper,
    yellow asafetida powder (*hing*)* and turmeric
2 tablespoons (30 ml) finely chopped fresh herbs, such as dill
    coriander, parsley, summer savory, basil or chervil
⅔ cup (60 g) sifted chickpea flour (sifted before measuring)
¼ teaspoon (1 ml) each cayenne pepper, salt and baking powder
about ¼ cup (60 ml) cold water
ghee or vegetable oil for deep-frying

*This amount applies only to yellow Cobra brand. Reduce any other asafetida by three-fourths.

    1. Slice the stem off each cherry tomato and carefully hollow out with a small melon baller. Drain upside down on paper towels or a rack.

    2. Bray and knead the cheese, spices and herbs until fairly smooth. Divide into 24–28 portions and stuff into the tomato cups.

    3. Combine the flour, cayenne, salt and baking powder in a bowl and mix well. Add 3 tablespoons (45 ml) of water slowly, beating with a wire whisk until the batter is smooth and free of lumps. If necessary, slowly add the remaining water until the consistency is similar to that of cream. It must be thick enough to seal in the cheese filling and thoroughly coat the tomatoes.

    4. Heat 2½–3 inches (6.5–7.5 cm) of *ghee* or oil in a *karai*, wok or sauté pan to 350°F (180°C). Place 4 or 5 tomatoes in the batter, lift them up one by one with a chocolate dipping fork, drain off excess batter momentarily, then slip into the hot oil. Fry until golden brown on all sides, turning gently once they rise to the surface, or for about 3 minutes. Remove with a slotted spoon and drain on paper towels. Serve immediately, or keep warm in a 250°F (120°C) oven until the remaining tomatoes are fried. Allow 4 each for hors d'oeuvres or 3 as a side-dish savory.

LIGHT MEAL FAVORITES

Cauliflower and Farina *Uppma* with Fenugreek Seeds
GOBHI SOOJI UPPMA

Farina is a granular meal made from hard, but not durum, wheat. Cream of Wheat brand sells three types: Instant, Quick-Cooking and Regular, while Malt-O-Meal and Farina brands are only sold in the Quick-Cooking form. Malt-O-Meal is a pre-roasted grain, so it saves you the roasting time necessary to bring out a nutty flavor in the grain and helps make the finished dish light and fluffy.

Preparation and cooking time (after assembling ingredients): ½ hour
Serves: 6

5 tablespoons (75 ml) *ghee* or a mixture of
    light sesame oil and unsalted butter
2 whole dried red chilies, halved and seeded
½ tablespoon (7 ml) minced fresh ginger root
½ tablespoon (7 ml) cumin seeds
½ teaspoon (2 ml) fenugreek seeds
2 tablespoons (30 ml) sesame seeds
10–12 curry leaves, preferably fresh
1 small cauliflower (¾–1 pound/340–455 g),
    trimmed, cored and cut into pieces roughly
        1 x ½ x ½ inch (2.5 x 1.5 x 1.5 cm)
scant ½ teaspoon (2 ml) turmeric
1 teaspoon (5 ml) ground coriander
1 cup (180 g) Malt-O-Meal brand farina
⅔ cup (160 ml) buttermilk mixed with
    1½ cups (360 ml) hot water
1¼ teaspoons (6 ml) salt
2 tablespoons (30 ml) finely chopped fresh fenugreek or coriander

1. Heat the *ghee* or oil-butter mixture in a 4–5-quart/liter casserole over moderately high heat. When it is hot but not smoking, add the chilies, ginger, cumin seeds and fenugreek seeds, and fry until the fenugreek seeds darken slightly. Add the sesame seeds and fry until the fenugreek turns reddish-brown. Drop in the curry leaves, and a few seconds later add the cauliflower. Stir-fry for 2–3 minutes, then reduce the heat to moderate, add the turmeric and ground coriander, and cook, stirring frequently, until the cauliflower is almost fork-tender.

2. Add the pre-roasted farina and gently stir to coat the vegetable. Pour in the buttermilk–water mixture and salt and, stirring, bring to a boil over high heat, then cook for 1 minute. Cover, remove the pan from the heat, and set aside for 4 minutes so the grains can expand and absorb the liquid. Fluff with a spoon and sprinkle with the fresh herbs before serving.

Herbed Cracked Wheat *Uppma* with Fried Vegetables
DALIA UPPMA

If you have the luxury of a kitchen herb garden, feel free to add your favorites. I enjoy summer savory, coriander, parsley, mint and marjoram. If you must resort to dried herbs, at least feature fresh parsley, a year-round staple even in supermarkets. Cracked wheat and bulgur can be used interchangeably and are available at supermarkets, specialty stores and many co-ops. Bulgur is a wheat that has been boiled, dried and cracked, with outstanding whole grain food value and a delicious, nutty taste. With a tossed green salad and a light soup, you have a complete lunch.

Preparation time and cooking time (after assembling ingredients): about ½ hour
Serves: 4 to 6

3 tablespoons (45 ml) *ghee* or vegetable oil
1 teaspoon (5 ml) split *urad dal*, if available
1½ teaspoons (7 ml) cumin seeds
½ teaspoon (2 ml) black mustard seeds
1–3 fresh green chilies, finely sliced
½ cup (120 ml) finely chopped cored and seeded red bell peppers
½ cup (120 ml) finely chopped celery stalks with tops
⅔ cup (160 ml) zucchini, cut into ¼-inch (6 mm) dice
1 cup (155 g) cracked wheat or bulgur
2 cups (480 ml) water
1 cup (240 ml) packed chopped spinach
½ cup (120 ml) chopped fresh herbs (coriander, parsley, basil, summer savory, mint, marjoram, as
    desired) or ⅓ cup (80 ml) chopped fresh parsley and ½ tablespoon (7 ml) mixed dried herbs
1½ teaspoons (7 ml) salt
tomato flower garnish (optional)

    1. Heat the *ghee* or oil over moderate heat in a heavy nonstick saucepan. When it is hot, add the *urad dal*, and in a few seconds follow with the cumin seeds, black mustard seeds and green chilies. Fry until the *dal* turns reddish-brown and the mustard seeds pop.

    2. Stir in the bell peppers, celery and zucchini and fry for 2–3 minutes. Pour in the cracked wheat or bulgur and stir-fry to toast it for another 2–3 minutes.

    3. Add the water, spinach, half of the fresh mixed herbs or parsley and all of the dried herbs, and the salt, cover, and reduce the heat to low. Simmer for about 15 minutes or until the liquid is absorbed into the grains and the dish is light and fluffy.

    4. Fold in the remaining herbs and serve garnished with optional tomato flowers.

Crispy Puffed Rice Snack with Fried Cashews and Green Peas

KAJU MOORI CHIDWA

In Indian bazaars, it is a familiar sight to see men puffing rice. A sand-filled *karai* is placed over glowing coals, and when the coarse sand is hot, rice is added. Using a long paddle, the sand is patiently stirred, until one by one, the rice grains pop into long pointed puffs. With nothing more than straining it through a fine sieve, hot puffed rice, called *moori*, is ready to be sold in recycled newspaper bags. Like everything in India, you have to search for quality and then haggle for it—and even if you pay dearly, much of the puffed rice tastes a little dusty. Homemade puffed rice is always more delectable. Par-boiled rice is stir-fried in a dry pan until very hot, and immediately dropped into hot oil where it expands into puffs. This is the basis of numerous munchy snacks, much like this one.

This dish can be made with any puffed grain—from *moori* sold at Indian grocery stores, to supermarket Quaker puffed rice or a health food store puffed brown rice. Serve for breakfast or a light snack.

Preparation and cooking time (after assembling ingredients): 30 minutes
Serves: 4 to 6

¼ cup (60 ml) *ghee* or a mixture of
    sunflower oil and unsalted butter
⅓ cup (50 g) split raw peanuts
⅓ cup (45 g) cashew pieces
½ tablespoon (7 ml) minced fresh ginger root
1–2 fresh green chilies, seeded and minced
½ teaspoon (2 ml) turmeric
1 teaspoon (5 ml) ground coriander
1 teaspoon (5 ml) ground cumin
¼ teaspoon (1 ml) yellow asafetida powder (*hing*)*
¾ cup (180 ml) steamed fresh peas or
    frozen baby peas, defrosted
2½ cups (45 g) puffed rice
½ teaspoon (2 ml) fine popcorn salt
1 teaspoon (5 ml) date or maple sugar (optional)

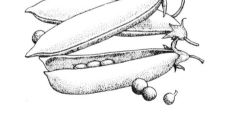

*This amount applies only to yellow Cobra brand. Reduce any other asafetida by three-fourths.

    1. Heat the *ghee* or oil-butter mixture in a heavy 5-quart/liter pan over moderate heat for about 1 minute. Add the peanuts and fry until they turn golden brown. Remove with a slotted spoon and drain on paper towels. Fry the cashew nuts until golden brown, then remove and set aside with the peanuts.

    2. Drop in the minced ginger, chilies, turmeric, coriander, cumin and asafetida, one after another in quick succession, and fry for no more than 3–4 seconds. Immediately add the peas, raise the heat to moderately high, and cook for 2 minutes.

    3. Add the puffed rice and, stirring constantly, cook until it is slightly crisp and well coated with powdered spices. Add the nuts, salt and sugar. Mix well. Serve hot and crisp.

Puffed Rice and Nut Snack with Raisins

MOORI KISHMISH CHIDWA

Though not widely available in India, sunflower and pumpkin seeds help to make this a nutritious snack. Recently, seven-grain puffed cereal packaged as Kashi has reached health food stores shelves. It is wonderfully crunchy and flavorful, an excellent alternative to puffed rice—and to popcorn.

Preparation and cooking time (after assembling ingredients): 20 minutes
Serves: 6

¼ teaspoon (1 ml) cayenne pepper
¼ teaspoon (1 ml) turmeric
¼ teaspoon (1 ml) freshly ground nutmeg
¼ teaspoon (1 ml) freshly ground black pepper
⅛ teaspoon (0.5 ml) each ground cloves and cinnamon
1¼ teaspoons (6 ml) salt or herb salt
2 tablespoons (30 ml) confectioner's sugar
¼ cup (60 ml) *ghee* or a mixture of vegetable oil and unsalted butter
⅓ cup (45 g) sunflower seeds
⅓ cup (45 g) pumpkin seeds
⅓ cup (50 g) raisins
2 tablespoons (30 ml) chopped fresh coriander or parsley
2½ cups (45 g) puffed rice or Kashi

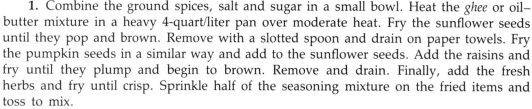

1. Combine the ground spices, salt and sugar in a small bowl. Heat the *ghee* or oil–butter mixture in a heavy 4-quart/liter pan over moderate heat. Fry the sunflower seeds until they pop and brown. Remove with a slotted spoon and drain on paper towels. Fry the pumpkin seeds in a similar way and add to the sunflower seeds. Add the raisins and fry until they plump and begin to brown. Remove and drain. Finally, add the fresh herbs and fry until crisp. Sprinkle half of the seasoning mixture on the fried items and toss to mix.

2. Add the remaining seasoning and puffed rice to the remaining oil and stir-fry until warm and a little crispy. Add the remaining seasonings and fried things and toss to mix. Serve hot.

Snacks
and
Nibblers

The Vedic culture places great importance on hospitality. Anyone, whether a casual visitor or an old friend, is immediately offered refreshment on entering even the most humble home. No gathering, whether of friends, acquaintances or business associates, is complete without offering and receiving food. It is socially imperative.

If you know beforehand that someone is coming over, you will usually have time to make one of the savory snacks described in the previous chapter that can be assembled just before serving and then served piping hot. The "nibbling" varieties in this chapter are the kind you might want to keep on hand for the unexpected guest. These between-meal foods, generally deep-fried and salty, have a diverse range of exquisite textures and flavors. They are either ready to eat at room temperature or easily warmed. Either way, they go well with a cool drink, fresh cut fruits or a sweet. They also make excellent traveling companions.

Nut Medley
BHONA BADAAM KAJU

Hot peanuts, cashews, pistachios, Brazil nuts, almonds and hazelnuts are mouth watering when properly fried. They require a controlled heat source and must be well drained before salting. If you are going to serve an assortment of fried nuts, contrast sizes and colors.

Preparation and cooking time: 25 minutes
Makes: 2 cups (480 ml)

sunflower or vegetable oil for frying
2 cups (275 g) of 3 or 4 of the following:
    whole peanuts, with skins;
    half peanuts, without skins;
    whole cashews;
    cashew halves;
    whole almonds, with skins;
    whole almonds, blanched;
    whole pistachios, with skins;
    whole Brazil nuts, with skins;
    whole hazelnuts, without skins
¼–½ teaspoon (1–2 ml) salt

Heat the oil to a depth of 1 inch (2.5 cm) in a heavy large frying pan or sauté pan over moderately low heat. When the temperature reaches 310°F (155°C), add the nuts. Fry at 300–310°F (150–155°F), stirring often, for 10–12 minutes or until golden brown. Remove with a slotted spoon and drain in a strainer resting over a cake pan, then transfer to several thicknesses of paper towels. Blot off the excess oil with more paper towels. While still warm, toss in the salt and mix.

Deep-Fried Batter-Coated Mixed Nuts

BHONA BADAAM

Use large plump nuts—cashews, almonds and Brazils—for ease in handling. The chickpea flour–rice flour batter puts a crisp crust on the nuts.

Preparation and cooking time: about 40 minutes
Makes: 1½ cups (360 ml)

3 tablespoons (45 ml) sifted chickpea flour
    (sifted before measuring)
1 tablespoon (15 ml) rice flour
¼ teaspoon (1 ml) turmeric
½ teaspoon (2 ml) ground cumin
¼ teaspoon (1 ml) cayenne pepper
⅛ teaspoon (0.5 ml) yellow asafetida powder (*hing*)*
⅛ teaspoon (0.5 ml) baking powder
¾ teaspoon (3.5 ml) salt
3 tablespoons (45 ml) water
1½ cups (210 g) mixed raw cashews, almonds and Brazil nuts
vegetable oil for deep-frying

*This amount applies only to yellow Cobra brand. Reduce any other asafetida by three-fourths.

    1. Combine the flours, spices, baking powder and salt in a bowl and blend well. Add the water and whisk with a fork until smooth. Stir in the nuts.

    2. Heat 2½ inches (6.5 cm) of oil in a *karai* or deep-frying pan over moderate heat. When the temperature reaches 340°F (170°C), one by one slip about 15 of the batter-coated nuts into the oil. Fry, stirring gently once the batter firms up, until they are crisp and golden brown. Remove and drain on paper towels. Fry the remaining nuts in the same way. Serve warm.

Spicy Nuts
MASALA BADAAM KAJU

These are best served warm and are a popular snack with drop-in guests. Serve with hot or cold beverages.

Preparation time (after assembling ingredients): a few minutes
Makes: 2 cups (480 ml)

2 cups (275 g) freshly fried *Nut Medley* (page 183)
½ teaspoon (2 ml) salt
1 teaspoon (5 ml) *garam masala*
¼ teaspoon (1 ml) cayenne pepper
½ teaspoon (2 ml) *amchoor* powder
1 tablespoon (15 ml) confectioners' sugar (optional)

Toss the nuts with the salt, spices and sugar, if desired. Keep warm in a 200°F (95°C) oven until serving. Can be kept for 2–3 weeks. To rewarm, place in a 250°F (120°C) oven for 7–8 minutes.

Nut and Raisin Nibbler
KAJU KISHMISH CHIDWA

You can vary the formula—cashews and currants, peanuts and golden raisins, almonds and raisins—in this nutritious snack. Srila Prabhupada recommended this combination on *Ekadasee* fasting days.

Preparation time (after assembling ingredients): a few minutes
Serves: 10

1 teaspoon (5 ml) fine salt
½ tablespoon (7 ml) ground coriander
2 teaspoons (10 ml) ground cumin
¼ teaspoon (1 ml) each freshly ground pepper or grated
    nutmeg, ground cardamom, ground cinnamon and cayenne pepper
⅛ teaspoon (0.5 ml) ground cloves
2 tablespoons (30 ml) finely crushed rock candy or date sugar
2 cups (275 g) freshly fried *Nut Medley* (page 183)
½ cup (65 g) currants or raisins

Combine the salt, spices and sweetener in a small dish and blend well. Sprinkle half of the seasoning on the hot nuts and half on the currants or raisins and toss separately. Mix together before serving.

Thin 'n' Crisp Chickpea Flour Noodles
MASALA SEV

Sev rivals peanuts as India's most popular munching snack. Anywhere people gather, a *sev* vendor is sure to appear with an assortment of freshly made fried noodles. Some noodles are spicy and spaghetti-thick, while others are very fine and unseasoned.

Sev noodles are shaped with a *seviya* machine, a unique brass utensil equipped with an assortment of interchangeable disks. A fine-holed disk is attached to the container and filled with dough, which is then pressed into hot oil where it fries into crisp crunchy noodles. This utensil has two *sev* disks—thick and thin—with additional disks for several other fried snacks. It is available at most Indian grocery stores. You can use a potato ricer as a substitute.

Preparation and frying time: 25 minutes
Serves: 10–12

2¼ cups (230 g) sifted chickpea flour
   (sifted before measuring)
½ tablespoon (7 ml) salt
½ teaspoon (2 ml) cayenne pepper
½ teaspoon (2 ml) turmeric
1 tablespoon (15 ml) vegetable oil
½ tablespoon (7 ml) lemon juice
¾ cup (180 ml) water
ghee or vegetable oil for deep-frying

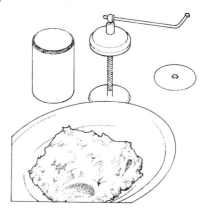

1. Blend the chickpea flour, salt, cayenne and turmeric in a mixing bowl. Add the oil and lemon juice to the water and pour into the flour. Mix into a thick paste, adding additional flour as necessary so that the mixture is not sticky. It should resemble the texture of mashed potatoes. Divide into three portions, then fill the *seviya* machine with one portion, or place that amount in a potato ricer.

2. Heat *ghee* or oil to a depth of 2½ inches (6.5 cm) in a *karai* or deep-frying pan over moderate heat until it reaches 345°F (175°C). Holding the utensil over the hot oil, force the mixture through the holes by turning the handle. As the noodles fall, slowly move the machine around in a circular motion so that they do not clump together. Fry for 1½ minutes per side or until crisp and lightly browned. Remove with a slotted spoon and drain on paper towels. Fry the remaining paste in the same way. Cool to room temperature, then break into uniform pieces. They can be kept in airtight containers for 2 weeks. To reheat, place in a 250°F (120°C) oven for 8 minutes.

Golden Pastry Chips
NIMKIN

In Bengal, this snack is sold everywhere, from shops and roadside hand-pushed carts to vendors carrying baskets on their heads and wandering from place to place. They are seasoned with one of three spice seeds: caraway, fennel or *kalonji*.

Preparation time (after assembling ingredients) 30 minutes
Serves: 8-10

1½ cups (175 g) unbleached white flour
½ teaspoon (2 ml) salt
⅛ teaspoon (0.5 ml) baking soda
1 teaspoon (5 ml) either caraway seeds, fennel seeds or *kalonji*
2½ tablespoons (37 ml) melted unsalted butter or *ghee*
4½–5½ tablespoons (67–82 ml) water
ghee or vegetable oil for deep–frying

1. Combine the flour, salt, baking soda and caraway seeds in a large bowl and mix well. Add the melted butter or *ghee* and rub between your palms to evenly distribute. Pour 4½ tablespoons (67 ml) of water over the flour and quickly mix into a rough, shaggy dough. If necessary, add the remaining water, a few drops at a time, until the mass can be kneaded into a stiff dough. Knead on a clean work surface for about 8 minutes or until the dough is firm but pliable. Cover with a damp towel or plastic wrap and allow it to rest for at least ½ hour.

Alternately, fit a food processor with the metal blade, add the flour, salt, baking soda and caraway seeds and pulse twice. Add the melted butter and pulse 8-10 times to mix. With the motor running, pour 4½ tablespoons (67 ml) of water through the feed tube and process until the mixture masses together. You may need to add up to 1 tablespoon (15 ml) more water to make a stiff dough. (The mixture should not form a ball in the bowl, but should easily form into a ball with your hands.) Gather the ingredients into a ball, cover with a damp towel or plastic wrap, and set aside for at least ½ hour.

2. Roll the dough into a log 14 inches (35 cm) long, cut into 12 pieces, and flatten each piece into a patty. Drape a damp towel over the patties.

3. Pour *ghee* or oil into a *karai* or deep-frying pan to a depth of 2½ (6.5 cm) inches and place over moderate heat. Roll a patty into a 5½-inch (14 cm) round on a lightly floured board. Cut with a sharp knife into strips ½ inch (1.5 cm) wide and again cut across into ½ inch (1.5 cm) strips, to yield squares. Brush off the excess flour with a pastry brush. When the temperature of the *ghee* or oil reaches 335°F (170°C), fry the squares, stirring constantly, until they turn almond brown and are crisp on all sides. Remove with a slotted spoon and drain on paper towels. Shape and fry the remaining patties in this way.

4. Cool to room temperature, then store in a container with a tight-fitting lid for up to 2 weeks.

Savory Butter Crackers with Lemon
NUN GAJA

In Bengal, there are two types of *gaja*: salty and sweet. Within these two types, several shapes and flavors are possible: poppy seed cubes, sesame seed oblongs, *kalonji* curls and this variation: lemon zest diamonds. These crackers are somewhat crumbly, with a faintly sour taste. They are a much-loved delicacy throughout Orissa and Bengal, popular at late afternoon tiffin with contrasting sweet *gaja* and tropical fresh fruits.

Preparation and resting time (after assembling ingredients): 45 minutes
Cooking time: 50 minutes
Makes: about 60 *gajas*

2 cups (235 g) unbleached white flour
1¼ teaspoons (6 ml) salt
⅛ teaspoon (0.5 ml) baking soda
½ teaspoon (2 ml) finely grated lemon zest
4½ tablespoons (67 ml) unsalted butter, chilled and cut into small pieces
2 tablespoons (30 ml) cold yogurt, stirred until smooth
1 tablespoon (15 ml) ice water
¼ cup (60 ml) strained fresh lemon juice
ghee or vegetable oil for deep-frying

1. Place the flour, salt, baking soda and lemon zest in a large bowl and mix well. Add the butter and rub between your palms until the texture resembles coarse bread crumbs. Blend the yogurt, ice water and lemon juice and pour slowly into the flour until the dough can be gathered into a shaggy mass. Knead for only 2–3 minutes.

Alternately, fit a food processor with the metal blade. Place the flour, salt, and baking soda in the processor bowl and pulse 6 times. Add the lemon zest and butter and process for one minute or until the mixture resembles fine breadcrumbs. Blend the yogurt with the water, and while the machine is running, slowly pour in the liquid and process until the consistency is the size of peas. Do not allow a ball of dough to form. Gather the dough into a ball by hand and cover it with a damp towel or plastic wrap. Set aside for at least ½ hour.

2. Divide the dough into 5 balls. Cover 4 balls with a damp towel and roll the remaining one out on a lightly floured work surface into a 7-inch (17.5 cm) round. With a sharp knife, cut into diamond shapes—cutting across from east to west into 1-inch (2.5 cm) strips, then on the diagonal, from northeast to southwest, in 2-inch (5 cm) strips. This will form diamonds about 1 inch (2.5 cm) wide and 2 inches (5 cm) long. Prick the diamonds with a fork at 1-inch (2.5 cm) intervals and remove any small scraps of dough. Roll the scraps into a final ball of dough.

3. Pour *ghee* or oil to a depth of 2 inches (5 cm) into a *karai* or deep-frying pan and place it over moderate heat. When the temperature reaches 320°F (160°C), slip in all of the crackers. Fry, maintaining the heat at between 310–320°F (155–160°C), for about 5 minutes on each side or until they are pale gold (not brown) and crispy. Remove with a slotted spoon and drain on paper towels. Roll out, cut and fry the remaining dough in the same way. Can be kept, well sealed, for 2–3 weeks.

Munchy Chickpea Flour Spirals with Sesame Seeds
CHAKLI

This snack could easily become as popular as pretzels. It is a crunchy spiral, made from roasted chickpea flour and rice flour, shaped by forcing soft dough through a star-shaped nozzle or disk. A *seviya* machine is used to shape this and several other fried snacks in this chapter. It is available at Indian grocery stores. Because any star shape will do, you can also use a pastry bag fitted with a 5-star nozzle or a continuous-flow cookie gun, like the *sawa*, available through the William Sonoma mail order catalogue.

Preparation time (after assembling ingredients): 20 minutes
Frying time: 15 minutes
Makes: about 24 *chaklis*

1½ cups (145 g) sifted chickpea flour
    (sifted before measuring)
½ cup (80 g) coarse rice flour or ground rice
1¼ teaspoons (6 ml) salt
1¼ teaspoons (6 ml) cayenne pepper
¼ teaspoon (1 ml) yellow asafetida powder (*hing*)*
⅛ teaspoon (0.5 ml) baking soda
¼ cup (40 g) sesame seeds
3 tablespoons (45 ml) grated fresh coconut
    or dry coconut, unsweetened
1 tablespoon (15 ml) vegetable oil
¾ cup (180 ml) water
ghee or vegetable oil for deep-frying

*This amount applies only to yellow Cobra brand. Reduce any other asafetida by three-fourths.

    1. Place the chickpea flour in a heavy pan over moderate heat and dry-roast, stirring constantly, for 3–4 minutes or until the color darkens one or two shades.
    2. Transfer to a large bowl, add the rice flour, salt, cayenne, asafetida, baking soda, sesame seeds and coconut, and stir to mix. Pour in the oil and then rub between your palms until the mixture resembles coarse bread crumbs. Add the water and work into a soft dough (similar in texture to cold mashed potatoes) that can easily be forced through a star nozzle. If necessary, add sprinkles of flour or water. Divide the dough into 2 or 3 portions.
    3. Brush oil on the inside of one of the suggested utensils and add a portion of dough. Line a baking tray with aluminum foil and brush the foil with vegetable oil. Starting at the center and using steady pressure, force the dough out of the utensil in a continuous outward spiral until the diameter is 2 inches (5 cm). Shape all of the *chaklis* in this way.
    4. Heat 2½ inches (6.5 cm) of *ghee* or oil in a *karai* or deep-frying pan over moderate heat until the temperature reaches 335°F (170°C). Using a spatula, transfer 8–10 *chakli* spirals to the hot oil, or as many as will float on the surface without crowding. Fry for 3–4 minutes on each side or until crispy and golden brown. Remove with a slotted spatula and drain on paper towels. Fry the remaining pieces in this way. Serve at room temperature. Can be stored in an air-tight container for 2–3 weeks.

Spicy Matchstick Potatoes

MASALA ALOO LATCHE

Potatoes are a good vegetable for deep-frying and can be cut a number of ways for dramatic effects: shavings, spirals, waffles, chips and fine sticks. For this recipe you need a fine matchstick cut, with a maximum width of ⅛ inch (3 mm). You can produce fine strips by hand cutting them into slices ⅛ inch (3 mm) thick and then cutting them again lengthwise into strips about ⅛ inch (3 mm) wide. Save considerable time by using the fine julienne slicing blade of a mandoline or food processor. My late friend and mentor Pishima, a great Bengali Vaishnava cook, often combined carrots and potatoes in this spicy nibbler.

Preparation and soaking time (after assembling ingredients): up to 1½ hours
Frying time: 10–15 minutes
Serves: 6

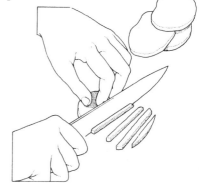

2 large baking potatoes (about 1 pound/455 g)
ghee or nut or vegetable oil for deep-frying
½–1 teaspoon (2–5 ml) fine salt
¼ teaspoon (1 ml) cayenne pepper
1 teaspoon (5 ml) ground coriander
½ teaspoon (2 ml) ground cumin
½ teaspoon (2 ml) *amchoor* powder or *chat masala*

1. Peel the potatoes and cut into fine matchsticks. Soak in cold water for at least 1 hour, changing the water twice. Drain and pat dry with paper towels.

2. Pour *ghee* or oil to a depth of 2½–3 inches (6.5–7.5 cm) into a *karai* or deep-frying pan and place over moderate heat. (Do not fill the pan more than half-full.) When the temperature reaches 375°F (190°C), add a handful of potatoes and stir to prevent them from sticking together. Fry until golden brown, then remove with a slotted spoon and drain on paper towels. Fry the remaining batches in the same way. Place the salt and spices in a bowl, mix together, and sprinkle on the hot potatoes. These nibblers can be kept in airtight containers for up to a week.

Sweets

India is a nation with a penchant for sweets. This is not a new phenomenon but one which dates back to Vedic times. The living art of preparing sumptuous sweets, puddings and desserts has been preserved largely by successive generations of temple cooks and professional sweetmakers, know as *halwais*. Today, as in centuries past, presenting sweets conveys gratitude, affection, respect, joy or reward. Even an unexpected visitor is welcomed with a sweet beverage, fruit or confection.

This chapter is divided into a few sections: easy-to make confections, candies, cookies and *halvas*. The recipes conclude with delectable fruit desserts.

The type of sweetener used in a recipe will greatly affect its finished taste and appearance. The word sugar is derived from the Sanskirt word *sarkar*. Since Vedic times, sugar cane has been cultivated in India's western regions, and various date palm trees have flourished along the eastern coast. Both sugar cane and date palm trees were treasured for their sweet sap which was cooked down and concentrated to make fudge-like brown sugars known as *jaggery* and *gur*. India's epic tale *Mahabharata* describes that these solid sweeteners were used in sophisticated and artful toffees, fudges, confections and boiled-sugar candies at the time of Lord Krishna's appearance 5,000 years ago.

Of less importance were liquid sweeteners made from grains. In the arid farming regions of Central and Northwest India where sorghum (a tall grass of the millet family), corn and barley have been cultivated since Vedic times times, sweet syrups were made to provide an alternative to solid sugars. Today these sweeteners, along with *jaggery* syrup, are not available commercially in India and often never leave the areas where they are produced. However, several grades of maple syrup, barley, wheat, corn, sorghum and rice syrup are sold in most Western health food stores. Sweetening power, flavor and consistency vary in these liquid sugars: dark, strong-flavored syrups can be used with grains; light, mild-flavored ones should be used in milk-based sweets.

Though much of the ancient world is supposed to have used honey as a sweetener, India tapped other sources for cooking. *Ayur Veda*, the science of herbal medicine, warns against letting honey boil, as it purportedly affects the flavor and develops toxicity. Therefore, honey is rarely if ever used in sweetmaking. Exceptions are using it as a binder in uncooked confections or in instances where temperatures are kept below the boiling point.

A few recipes specify a particular unrefined sugar—most often *jaggery* or *gur*—not only because they have origins dating back centuries and are traditional, but because they work well and taste better than the alternatives. Unfortunately, todays *gur* production is limited, making it rare outside of bengal and Orissa. Though labeled *gur* or *goodh* at Indian grocery stores, the aromatic sweetener you purchase is most likely *jaggery*. If purchased in lump form, coarsely grate or sliver it to facilitate accurate measuring and dissolving. Two equally delicious sugars to use in sweetmaking are maple sugar and date sugar, both sold at health food and specialty stores. Relative newcomers on the market, both of these sugars are expensive but contain a flavor worth showcasing. If circumstance dictates a substitution for these solid sugars, use light brown sugar.

Before the turn of the century, refined sugars were all but nonexistant in kitchens the world over; however, like elsewhere, they have become a part of contemporary Vedic cooking. Granulated white sugar, large preserving sugar crystals, powdered or confectioners'' sugar and rock candy sugar—made from either sugar cane or sugar beets—lend no flavor to a dish, only pure sweetness. The vitamin, mineral and iron content of refined and unrefined sugars are similar, though the sweetening power, consistency and flavor vary.

In comparison with the same dish made in India, the quantity of sugar in these recipes is greatly reduced. Indian sweet shops often use inordinate amounts of sugar because it costs a fraction of what the cost of other raw ingredients such as nuts and seeds. While the ration of sugar to powdered milk for a milk fudge might be 1 to 4 in Bombay, this book suggests a 1 to 5 or 6 ratio. Through a personal quest to create healthful variations of the classic dishes, I have sweetened some of the confections entirely with dried fruit purées, fruit concentrations or date sugar.

A well–stocked sweetmaking kitchen should contain a supply of flavoring agents such as green cardamom pods, whole nutmegs, cloves, good quality saffron, black peppercorns and pure camphor. Liquid essences such as rose, *khus*, *kewra* and sandalwood, though not essential, bring Bengali syrup sweets and confections to life. Fresh coconut, nuts, seeds and dried fruits are important for flavor, nutrition and texture. Most sweets are garnished in some way: either with a dusting of powdered nuts or sugar or royally topped with a small piece of paper–thin gold or silver foil, called *varak*. All of these ingredients are available at Indian grocery stores.

QUICK AND EASY SWEETS

Simply Wonderfuls
KHARA PERA

My spiritual master, Srila Prabhupada, called this mock milk fudge a "simply wonderful sweet." Some varieties include a dash of essence such as vanilla, almond, lemon or lime. This version resembles firm, uncooked fondant in texture and is so easy to assemble that kindergarten children can turn out a successful batch for grown-up treats.

I have made this sweet around the world, using different processed ingredients. Health-food-store non-instant skim milk powder yields the creamiest consistency; whole milk powder has a firm fudge-like consistency; and Milkman brand instant non-fat milk powder is somewhere in-between and slightly granular. If you use a granulated sugar—raw or white—process it in a blender until superfine. Because these ingredients are processed and stored under varied conditions, you may need to use more or less milk powder to achieve the desired texture.

Preparation time (after assembling ingredients): 10 minutes
Makes: 24 *Simply Wonderfuls*

½ cup (120 ml) unsalted butter, at room temperature
⅔ cup (60 g) confectioners' sugar
1¾ cups (220 g) dry milk powder, or as needed
1 teaspoon (5 ml) milk or cream, or as necessary
a few drops of flavoring essence (as suggested above), or
    2 tablespoons (30 ml) grated nuts or dried fruit purée

1. Cream the butter and sugar in a mixing bowl until light and fluffy. Using your hands, work in the milk powder and milk or cream, (adjusting proportions as necessary) to make a medium-soft fondant. Flavor with essence, nuts or fruit purée and continue to work until well blended.
2. Wash and dry your hands, then roll the fondant into smooth balls. (You can also roll the fondant around whole nuts or sandwich a pellet between nut halves.) Place the confections in paper candy cases and keep refrigerated in a well sealed container for up to 4 days. Serve chilled or at room temperature.

Coconut and Cream Cheese Simply Wonderfuls
KHARA NARIYAL PERA

This mock milk fudge takes only minutes to assemble. I find homemade yogurt cheese a pleasant alternative to cream cheese because it has fewer calories and adds its own distinctive flavor.

Preparation time (after assembling ingredients): 10 minutes
Makes: 24 *peras*

¼ cup (60 ml) unsalted butter, at room temperature
¼ cup (60 ml) neuchatel or cream cheese at room temperature,
 or fresh yogurt cheese (page 116)
¼ cup (60 ml) frozen apple concentrate, thawed
½ cup (45 g) toasted grated coconut
1⅓ cups (165 g) dry milk powder, or as needed
generous ¼ teaspoon (1 ml) freshly ground nutmeg

Cream the butter, cheese and apple concentrate in a mixing bowl until light and fluffy. Add the coconut and blend well. With your hands, work in powdered milk until it forms a medium-stiff dough. Wash and dry your hands, then roll the fondant into smooth balls and place them in paper candy cases. Sprinkle with ground nutmeg. Keep refrigerated, in a well sealed container, for up to 4 days.

Maple Cream Simply Wonderfuls
KHARA JAGGERY PERA

A friend introduced me to the wonder of maple sugar as a sweetener, and we never tire of exchanging new ways to showcase its delicate flavor. It is the closest counterpart to Bengal's exquisite *nalin gur*, an ingredient rarely found outside of West Bengal. The confection is equally delicious sweetened with date sugar or date purée, all of them available at health food stores or mail order suppliers.

Preparation time (after assembling ingredients): 10 minutes
Makes: 24 *peras*

½ cup (120 ml) unsalted butter, at room temperature
½ cup (75 g) sieved and lightly packed maple or date sugar,
    or ⅓ cup (80 g) seeded and puréed soft dates, or
     ½ cup (85 g) light brown sugar with 4 drops of maple extract
½ teaspoon (2 ml) coarsely crushed cardamom seeds
a pinch of freshly ground white pepper
1⅔ cups (205 g) non-fat skim milk powder, or as needed

Cream the butter and sweetener in a mixing bowl until light and fluffy. Add the cardamom seeds, pepper and milk powder and work into a medium-soft dough. Wash and dry your hands and roll the fondant into 24 round balls. Place the balls in paper candy cases and refrigerate, well sealed. They will keep for up to 4 days.

Quick and Easy Milk Fudge

KHARA BURFI

For centuries, Vedic cooks have been making milk fudge *burfi* from the same ingredients: milk reduced to a pasty-dough, and unrefined sugars—either cane *jaggery* or palm *gur*. *Burfi* has changed very little since its beginnings, but with the twentieth century came powdered milk and shortcut procedures. Rather than boiling milk to reduce it to a paste, modern cooks can stir powdered milk into a flavored syrup and cook it very briefly until thick. The hot mixture is spread out, garnished, and when it sets, cut into decorative shapes. Plain milk fudge is receptive to additions; for this recipe, try adding ⅓ cup (50 g) of chopped toasted hazelnuts, pecans, walnuts, almonds, dried figs, dried apricots or dried mangoes.

This quick milk fudge can be made with several sweeteners, but each will yield a different result. Granulated white sugar allows the flavor from supporting ingredients to shine through and lends no color or flavor of its own. Liquid sweeteners such as rice, barley, malt and maple syrup vary in sweetening power and color, making the finished texture chewy instead of creamy.

Preparation time (after assembling ingredients): 30 minutes
Makes: 24 pieces

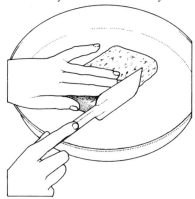

½ cup (110 g) white or brown sugar
    plus 1 cup (240 ml) water, or
    ¾ cup (180 ml) liquid sweetener
3 tablespoons (45 ml) *ghee* or unsalted butter
1⅔ cups (165 g) low-fat milk powder,
    or as necessary
⅓ cup (50 g) chopped nuts or dried fruits
dried fruit pieces for garnishing

1. Combine the sugar and water, or liquid sweetener, in a heavy-bottomed 3-quart/ liter nonstick saucepan and place over moderately low heat. Stir until the sugar dissolves, then raise the heat slightly and gently boil for 8 minutes. Remove the pan from the heat and let the syrup cool for 10 minutes or until the temperature reaches 110°F (45°C).

2. Add 1 tablespoon (15 ml) of *ghee* or butter and, stirring constantly, pour in the milk powder. When the mixture is smooth, place the pan over moderate heat and cook, constantly stirring and scraping the sides and bottom of the pan with a wooden spatula, for up to 4 minutes. When the mixture is reduced to a thick paste that draws away from the sides of the pan, remove the pan from the heat and stir in the remaining 2 tablespoons (30 ml) *ghee* or butter and the ⅓ cup (50 g) chopped nuts or dried fruit.

3. Using a rubber spatula, scrape the sticky paste onto a buttered cookie sheet. Spread out, pat and mold the hot mixture into a smooth square cake about ¾ inch (2 cm) thick. Depending on the finished shape of the fudge pieces, press nut halves or dried fruit pieces into the surface at regular intervals. When the fudge is thoroughly cool, cut it into 24 pieces with a knife dipped into hot water and dried before each cut. This fudge is best used within 4 days. Keep refrigerated in an airtight container and bring to room temperature before serving.

Pistachio Milk Fudge
KHARA PISTA BURFI

Plain milk fudge marries well with chopped pistachios and rose water. The mixture can be left just marbled with nuts or tinted a pistachio green color. For a classic look, garnish with a piece of edible silver foil (*varak*) and slivered pistachios.

Preparation time (after assembling ingredients): 30 minutes
Makes: 24 pieces

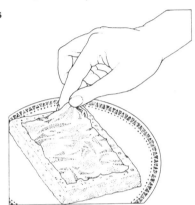

½ cup (110 g) sugar
1 cup (240 ml) water
3 tablespoons (45 ml) *ghee* or unsalted butter
¼ teaspoon (1 ml) powdered cardamom seeds
½ cup (75 g) raw pistachio nuts,
    blanched and finely chopped
1⅔ cups (165 g) low-fat or whole milk powder
1 teaspoon (5 ml) rose water or a few drops rose essence
2 drops green plus 1 drop yellow food coloring (optional)
one 4-inch (10 cm) piece of edible silver foil (*varak*)
    for garnishing, if available
3 tablespoons (45 ml) blanched pistachios, slivered

1. Combine the sugar and water in a heavy-bottomed 3-quart/liter nonstick saucepan and place over moderately low heat. Stir until the sugar dissolves, then raise the heat and gently boil for 8 minutes. Remove the pan from the heat and allow the syrup to cool for 10 minutes or until it reaches 110°F (45°C).

2. Add 1 tablespoon (15 ml) *ghee* or butter and the cardamom seeds and pistachio nuts, and, stirring constantly, mix in the milk powder. When the mixture is smooth, place the pan over moderate heat and cook, stirring constantly and scraping the sides and bottom of the pan with a wooden spatula, for up to 4 minutes. When the mixture is reduced to a thick paste that draws away from the sides of the pan, remove the pan from the heat, add the remaining 2 tablespoons (30 ml) *ghee* or butter and the rose water or essence and optional food coloring and stir until thoroughly incorporated.

3. Using a rubber spatula, scrape the sticky paste onto a buttered cookie sheet. Spread out and pat the hot mixture into a smooth-surfaced square cake about ¾ inch (2 cm) thick. When thoroughly cool, press the silver foil on the surface, cover with waxed paper and gently secure with a rolling pin. Cut with a hot knife into 24 squares and press slivered pistachios into each square. This quick fudge is best used within 4 days. Refrigerate in an airtight container. Bring to room temperature before serving.

Coconut Milk Fudge Log
KHARA NARIYAL BURFI

This uncooked confection is quick to assemble and power-packed with nutrition.

Preparation time (after assembling ingredients): 15 minutes
Makes: 24 pieces

½ cup (120 g) honey, rice or maple syrup
½ cup (120 g) almond, cashew or peanut butter
½ cup (80 g) finely chopped dates
⅔ cup (85 g) low-fat or whole milk powder
1½ cups (130 g) grated fresh coconut, lightly packed
    or 1½ cup (215 g) frozen coconut, defrosted
½ tablespoon (7 ml) rose water or *kewra* water

1. Combine the sweetener, nut butter, dates and milk powder in a bowl, and, using your hands, work into a soft, non-sticky dough. (You may have to add additional milk powder or a sprinkle of water.) Wash and dry your hands and roll the dough into a log about 20 inches (50 cm) long.

2. Place the coconut on a large square of waxed paper, sprinkle with the rose or *kewra* water and toss to mix. Cut the log in half and roll each half in the coconut to cover well. Slice each log into 10 pieces and place them in candy cases, if desired. This confection keeps well for up to 7 days. Keep refrigerated, well covered in an airtight container. Bring to room temperature before serving.

Cardamom Shortbread Cookies
ELAICHE GAJA

This buttery cookie bears some resemblance to Scottish shortbread. To the basic recipe, try one of the following additions: ¼ cup (25 g) ground pecans, cashews, almonds, pistachios or walnuts; or 3 tablespoons (45 ml) purée of dried mango, apples, cherries or papaya.

Preparation time (after assembling ingredients): 15 minutes
Baking time : 1 hour
Makes: 2 dozen small bars

1 cup (240 ml) unsalted butter, at room temperature
1 teaspoon (5 ml) crushed cardamom seeds or
    2 teaspoons (10 ml) fresh ginger paste
½ cup (110 g) superfine sugar or jaggery
2½ cups (300 g) unbleached white flour
½ cup (85 g) fine semolina (pasta flour)
¼ teaspoon (1 ml) salt
¼ teaspoon (1 ml) baking powder

1.   Preheat the oven to 250°F (120°C). Cream the butter and cardamom or ginger in a mixing bowl, then gradually add the sugar and beat until light and fluffy. (If you are using a dried fruit puree, work it into the sugar–butter mixture.) Combine the flour, semolina, salt and baking powder on a sheet of waxed paper and mix well. (If you are using nuts, add them to the dry ingredients.) Add the dry mixture to the butter and work with your hands until thoroughly blended into a dough. Alternatively, place all of the ingredients in an electric mixer, and with a dough hook, mix on low speed until thoroughly blended.

2.   Press into an 8 x 10–inch (20–25 cm) rectangle on an ungreased baking tray. Score the surface to make 24 cookies, and prick the surface with fork tines at 1–inch (2.5 cm) intervals. Bake for about 1 hour or until pale gold but not brown. Cool for 10 minutes in the pan. Carefully cut again over the scored markings. (If you want to sprinkle the surface with sugar, do it as soon as it comes out of the oven.)

Sesame–Nut Nibbler

GAJJAK

I learned how to make several kinds of boiled-sugar candies from a sweetmaker in Vrindavan, India. Every afternoon for a fortnight, I sat, notebook and thermometer in hand, and scribbled down the B. K. Sharma family secrets. His leather-like hands seemed heat-resistant as he toasted sesame seeds or patted out soft-crack syrups without tools. Though he used peanuts in this sweet, I retested the recipe using hazelnuts, pecans and walnuts with equal success.

Preparation and cooking time (after assembling ingredients): 30 minutes
Makes: about 1¼ pounds (570 g)

1 cup (160 g) sesame seeds
1 cup (about 4 ounces/115 g) coarsely chopped peanuts or
    mixed nuts
1½ cups (360 ml) maple syrup
1 tablespoon (15 ml) strained fresh lemon juice

1. Place the sesame seeds and nuts in a heavy frying pan over moderate heat and, stirring constantly, cook for about 10 minutes or until toasted.

2. Lightly oil the inside of a heavy-bottomed 3-quart/liter saucepan. Combine the sesame–nut mixture, maple syrup and lemon juice in the pan, place over moderate heat and bring to a boil. Stirring constantly with a wooden spoon, boil until the temperature reaches 280°F (140°C).

3. Immediately pour the mixture onto an oiled marble slab or into a jelly roll pan. Place a piece of buttered parchment or waxed paper over the candy and, using a rolling pin, roll the mixture into a layer about ¼ inch (6 mm) thick. While the candy is still warm, remove the paper and, using a sharp knife, cut into 2 x 4-inch (5 x 10 cm) bars. When cool, separate the pieces, wrap individually, and store in airtight containers.

Melt-in-Your-Mouth Chickpea Flour Confection
BESAN LADOO

This is the most popular flour-based confection in North India, where several versions are sold in sweet shops. You could use any type of solid or liquid sweetener, bearing in mind that each varies in sweetening power and that adjustments in cooking time will be necessary. This version, served at the home of the late Prime Minister of India, Indira Gandhi, is one of my favorites.

Cooking and preparation time (after assembling ingredients): about 20 minutes
Makes: 2 dozen balls

¾ cup (180 ml) *ghee* or unsalted butter
2 cups (205 g) sifted chickpea flour
   (sifted before measuring)
2 tablespoons (30 ml) grated dried coconut
2 tablespoons (30 ml) chopped pecans or walnuts
¼ teaspoon (1 ml) freshly ground nutmeg
¾ cup (110 g) brown sugar or maple sugar, packed

   1. Melt the *ghee* or butter in a heavy-bottomed frying pan over moderately low heat. Add the chickpea flour, coconut, nuts and nutmeg and cook, stirring constantly with a wooden spoon, for about 5 minutes. Add the sweetener and continue to cook for 10–15 minutes or until the mixture is thick and deep golden brown.

   2. Scrape it onto a marble surface or countertop, and, while hot, spread it into an even slab with a buttered spatula. When cool enough to handle, roll into 24 balls, or cool until set and cut into squares.

HALVA PUDDINGS

To many Westerners, *halva* means a chewy Middle Eastern candy made with crushed sesame seeds bound with honey. Though these recipes bear the same name, they differ considerably. More like fluffy puddings, these *halvas* are made with grains, vegetables, fruits, seeds or legumes. The most popular *halva* is little more than a fusion of toasted semolina and flavored sugar syrup with nuts and dried fruits added for texture.

In the most enduring vegetable *halvas*—carrot, winter melon, yam or *louki* summer squash—shredded vegetables are cooked in cream and reduced to a paste-like fudge. In North India, these dense *halvas* are served as desserts, snacks and even late morning brunches. Fruit *halvas*—more cooked fruit purées than puddings—are the sweetest of all, served in small quantity with fried biscuits or breads.

Srila Praphupada's maxim, "Good *halva* means good *ghee*," underscores the importance of the one ingredient used in all types of *halva*. Connoisseurs insist on it, perhaps adding a flavor dimension with clove- or ginger-flavored *ghee*. However, I feel that the recipes work best using unsalted butter. For many, it will be much more convenient. By varying sweeteners, the flavor cornucopia increases.

Semolina *Halva* with Golden Raisins
SOOJI HALVA

A popular item on a wedding or banquet menu, I have seen this *halva* made in enormous bowl-shaped iron pans with two or three pairs of hands steadily stirring the semolina while it plumps to tenderness. With stoves and pans large enough for the job, this dessert can be made from start to finish in one hour—for 300 people. It is best served hot, or at least warm; as the butter cools to room temperature, the consistency firms up and loses its fluffy texture. Served as a dessert, it can be dressed up with a dollop of whipped cream or even a spoonful of custard.

Preparation and cooking time (after assembling ingredients): about 25 minutes
Serves: 6 to 8

2 cups (480 ml) water
¾ cup (160 g) sugar
¼ teaspoon (1 ml) each ground
   cloves, nutmeg and cinnamon
1 teaspoon (5 ml) crushed cardamom seeds
¼ teaspoon (1 ml) saffron threads
3 x ½-inch (7.5 x 1.5 cm) strip of orange zest
⅓ cup (50 g) golden raisins
½ cup (120 ml) *ghee* or unsalted butter
1 cup (185 g) fine-grained semolina (pasta flour)
¼ cup (40 g) sliced almonds or chopped Brazil nuts
1 cup (240 ml) whipped cream (optional)

1.   Combine the water, sugar, ground spices, cardamom seeds, saffron and orange zest in a heavy 2–quart/liter saucepan over low heat and, while stirring, dissolve the sugar. Raise the heat and bring the mixture to a boil. Gently boil for a few minutes, then add the raisins. Strain through a sieve and set aside, covered.

2.   Heat the *ghee* or butter in a large nonstick saucepan over moderately low heat. When it is hot, add the semolina and rhythmically stir–fry until the grains swell and darken to a warm golden color, about 10 minutes. (To make white *halva*, reduce the heat to a very low setting and cook for about 1/2 hour, stirring now and then until the grains expand, invisibly toast, and slightly color.)

3.   Stirring steadily, gradually pour syrup into the semolina. At first the grains may sputter, but will quickly cease as the liquid is absorbed. Place the pan over very low heat and, stirring steadily, cook uncovered until the grains absorb the liquid and the texture is fluffy, up to 10 minutes. Serve in dessert cups or stemmed glasses, garnished if desired. If necessary, reheat slowly in a double boiler, mashing and stirring to lighten the texture.

Nutty Farina *Halva* with Sliced Carrots
SOOJI GAJAR HALVA

Supermarket farina replaces semolina in this *halva*. This enriched wheat cereal is available in most supermarkets in three types: instant, quick–cooking, and regular. For convenience, you can use one of two types: pre–toasted Malt–O–Meal farina or Cream–of–Wheat brand quick–cooking farina. For additional fiber, nutrition, texture and flavor, a mélange of nuts, seeds, dried fruits, bran and wheat germ can be added. If you do not have all these items, replace the missing ones with substitutes. For example, you could use granola instead of bran or wheat germ. This dish is a power-packed way to warm up an icy winter morning, or celebrate a fire-side evening.

Preparation and cooking time (after assembling ingredients): 15–20 minutes
Serves: 8

1 cup (240 ml) maple, barley or rice syrup
1½ cups (360 ml) water
2–inch (5 cm) piece of cinnamon stick
4–5 cloves
2 medium–sized carrots, scraped and thinly sliced
½ cup (120 ml) unsalted butter or *ghee*
1 cup (185 g) Malt–O–Meal brand pre–toasted farina or
    quick–cooking farina, dry–roasted over low heat for 10 minutes
2 tablespoons (30 ml) each chopped walnuts, cashews and almonds
2 tablespoons (30 ml) each sesame seeds and sunflower seeds
3 tablespoons (45 ml) each bran flakes and wheat germ
2 tablespoons (30 ml) each currants, golden raisins and grated coconut

1. Place the sweetener, water, cinnamon, cloves and carrots in a heavy saucepan over moderate heat. Stirring occasionally, bring to a boil. Gently boil for about 5 minutes, or until the carrots are just tender. Remove from the heat and set aside, covered.

2. Place the butter or *ghee* in a large saucepan over moderate heat. When it is hot but no smoking, stir in farina, nuts, seeds, bran and wheat germ. Stir–fry for a few minutes, then remove the pan from the heat. Stirring constantly, pour the carrots and syrup into the hot grains. At first the grains may sputter but will quickly cease as the liquid is absorbed. Place the pan over low heat and simmer, stirring often, for about 2 minutes. Stir in the dried fruits and coconut. Turn off the heat, cover and let the pan rest undisturbed for 2–3 minutes. Uncover and fluff with a spoon. (If the *halva* is dry, add water. If it is still liquid, place over heat and cook until thickened.) Serve hot.

Semolina and Chickpea Flour *Halva* with Almonds and Saffron
SOOJI BESAN HALVA

In Bengal this *halva* is called *mohan bhog*, "captivating dish," and is a personal favorite. Flavored with warm aromatics—saffron, black pepper, fennel seeds and cassia leaves—it is rib-sticking fare for a cold winter day.

Preparation and cooking time (after assembling ingredients): about 30 minutes
Serves: 6 to 8

2¼ cups (540 ml) milk or a mixture of 1 cup
    (240 ml) milk and 1¼ cups (300 ml) water
1 cup (210 g) sugar
¼ teaspoon (1 ml) good-quality saffron threads
¼ cup (35 g) currants
½ cup (120 ml) *ghee* or unsalted butter
1 cassia or allspice leaf, or ½ bay leaf
½ teaspoon (2 ml) fennel seeds
½ cup (50 g) sifted chickpea flour
    (sifted before measuring)
¾ cup (125 g) fine-grained semolina (pasta flour)
½ cup (55 g) sliced or slivered almonds
⅛ teaspoon (0.5 ml) freshly ground black pepper
¼ teaspoon (1 ml) freshly ground nutmeg

   1. Combine the milk or milk–water mixture and sugar in a heavy saucepan and, stirring constantly, bring to a boil over moderately high heat. Reduce the heat to the lowest setting, add the saffron and currants, and cover.
   2. Place the *ghee* or butter in a heavy pan over moderate heat. When it is hot, add the cassia, allspice or bay leaf and fennel seeds, and fry for several seconds. Stir in the chickpea flour, semolina or farina and almonds. Reduce the heat to moderately low and, stirring constantly, toast the ingredients for 10–12 minutes. It is ready when the chickpea flour and semolina darken a few shades to a warm golden color; they should not be allowed to brown.
   3. Remove the pan from the heat. Stirring constantly, slowly pour in the sweet liquid into the grains. At first the grains may sputter but will quickly cease as the liquid is absorbed. Place the pan over low heat and, while stirring, simmer until all of the liquid is absorbed and the grains are swollen, from 5–8 minutes. Garnish each serving with a sprinkle of black pepper and nutmeg.

FRESH FRUIT DESSERTS

A simple dessert in England might be fruit and cream. In France, it might be fruit and cheese. In India, it would be several types of fruits cut in their prime of ripeness, served plain or with a sprinkle of lime juice, salt, pepper, or a spice blend called *chat masala*. This would not be the finale to the menu, however, for in India all desserts, sweets and fruits are served along with the entire meal—acting as "palate cleansers" or cool contrasts to hot foods.

From the cook's point of view, nothing could be easier to serve than fruits. I remember one sunny day when Srila Prabhupada was cooking lunch in his kitchen. My sister came in with an unexpected gift: a large bowl of fresh whipped cream. Srila Prabhupada graciously accepted the offering, and into the cream he adroitly folded some powdered spices, sweetener, raisins, buttered rice and lots of fresh pineapple. This ambrosial dessert won instant praise, and we began making it and serving it regularly during the open-house feasts we held each Sunday.

With the revived popularity of fresh fruits and vegetables, the opportunity to serve special produce is becoming a reality even in large cities. There are, for example, exotic imported fruits available from gourmet green grocers. I have found Indian alphonso mangos—hand-picked just before they are ripe and carefully packed in straw—air-shipped to England with exquisite taste intact.

Fresh Fruit Plate
PHAL CHAT

There are no separate courses in a Vedic meal, though for a full-scale feast menu—more than 30 dishes—there is an order of serving. Fruits may be served at any time in the meal, from beginning to sweet conclusion. For breakfast, cut fruits often make up the entire meal. As a snack, a combination of three or four fruits is infinitely satisfying. Fruit combinations are endless, limited only by availability and imagination. Try specialty fruits such as cherimoyas, guavas, kiwis, carambolas, persimmons and fresh figs.

Chat plates require no preparation except the peeling and cutting of the fruits. Fruits are served in large pieces with a lime wedge and an optional sprinkle of either *chat masala* or black salt. To enhance the flavor of the fruits, I have suggested two fruit dressings: *Crème Fraîche–Cardamom* and *Fruit Juice*. The following recipes make about 1 cup (240 ml) of dressing. Simply combine all of the ingredients in a bowl and whisk until blended.

Fruit Combinations:

tangerines, blueberries and cherimoyas
orange and papaya slices with pineapple cubes
avocado slices,* grapefruit segments and stuffed fresh dates
sweet cherries, bananas* and yellow peaches*
sliced pears,* seedless green grapes and prickly pears
guava cubes, kiwi slices and persimmons
apple slices,* raspberries and fresh figs
cucumber slices, strawberries and blue plum slices
passion fruit, lychees and cape gooseberries
carambolas, tangelos and pomegranates
casaba melon, cantaloupe and crenshaw melon

Dip in lemon, lime or pineapple juice to prevent discoloration.

For the Crème Fraîche–Cardamom Dressing:

1 cup (240 ml) *crème fraîche*, yogurt or sour cream
2 tablespoons (30 ml) honey
2 tablespoons (30 ml) strained fresh orange juice
1 teaspoon (5 ml) ground cardamom

For the Fruit Juice Dressing:

⅓ cup (80 ml) strained fresh lime juice
⅓ cup (80 ml) strained fresh orange juice
3 tablespoons (45 ml) honey
2 tablespoons (30 ml) olive oil
2 tablespoons (30 ml) finely chopped fresh mint

Sliced Oranges with Maple Cream

SANTARA MITHAI

If you can find candy-like lumps of *gur* in Indian grocery stores, buy it, for it is hard to come by. It is made in a similar fashion to maple candy—syrups are boiled down until a solid cake remains. Grated, shredded or powdered, their flavor is similar and elegant. Though expensive, equally delicious alternatives are maple sugar granules or date sugar, both available at health food stores and specialty shops.

Preparation time (after assembling ingredients): 15 minutes
Chilling time: 1 hour
Serves: 5 or 6

4 large navel or blood oranges
1 tablespoon (15 ml) rose or *kewra* water
2 tablespoons (30 ml) honey
¼ cup (60 ml) lime juice
1 cup (240 ml) whipping cream, chilled
¼ cup (40 g) of one of the above suggested sweeteners
8 orange segments for garnishing

1. With a sharp serrated knife, peel the oranges and cut them into ¼-inch (6 mm) slices. Remove any seeds with the tip of a knife. Reserve the juice in a small bowl.

2. Add the rose water or *kewra* water, honey and lime juice to the reserved orange juice. Decoratively arrange the orange slices in overlapping rows in a shallow round or rectangular serving dish, then sprinkle with the juice mixture. Chill for at least 1 hour.

3. Whip the cream and spread it over the surface of the oranges with an icing spatula. Just prior to serving, sprinkle the cream with maple sugar or *gur*. If desired, make a starburst of peeled orange segments in the center as a garnish.

Broiled Bananas with Toasted Almonds
KELA MITHAI

You can try this dish with a date sugar–citrus juice topping or with an apple juice–apricot purée. Both are excellent contrasts to the banana halves. This quick, natural dessert should be assembled just before serving, for it takes only a few minutes to prepare. To make the apricot purée, place 8 peeled apricot halves and 2 tablespoons (30 ml) apple juice in a blender and reduce to a purée.

Preparation and cooking time (after assembling ingredients): 15 minutes

Serves: 4

1 tablespoon (15 ml) fresh lime juice
¼ cup (60 ml) strained fresh orange juice
¼ teaspoon (1 ml) freshly ground nutmeg
¼ teaspoon (1 ml) ground cardamom
2 tablespoons (30 ml) melted *ghee* or butter
4 firm bananas
¼ cup (40 g) date sugar or maple sugar granules
2 tablespoons (30 ml) blanched sliced almonds

1. Combine the lime juice, orange juice, nutmeg and cardamom in a small dish. Preheat the grill. Brush a film of *ghee* or butter on a small cookie sheet. Peel the bananas, split them lengthwise in half, and lay them, cut side up, on the cookie sheet.

2. Spoon the juice over the banana halves, drizzle with the remaining *ghee* or butter, then evenly sprinkle with the sugar. Grill the bananas for 3–4 minutes or until the surface is bubbly and lightly browned. Remove from the grill, sprinkle the almonds evenly over the banana halves, and grill again until the almonds are toasted and golden brown. Serve piping hot.

Stuffed Dessert Grapes
BHARA ANGOOR MITHAI

Large black grapes and cheese are made for each other, both for taste and appearance. In this version, pepper and saffron bring warmth to the cheese. While living in South Cornwall with acres of garden and orchard at my disposal, I sweetened the cheese with fresh mashed figs, crushed and drained raspberries and wild dewberries. In New York, I love to use strawberry farmers cheese from Ben's Cheese Shop. As finger foods for entertaining, these stuffed grapes look wonderful set out on a bed of geranium leaves. On a dinner menu, arrange 2 or 3 grapes in a cluster and set them on a fresh vine leaf.

Preparation time (after assembling ingredients): 25 minutes
Chilling time: 3–4 hours
Serves: 3 or 4

freshly made cheese or farmers cheese (about 3 ounces/85 g)
2 tablespoons (30 ml) superfine sugar or
　　sugar-free apple butter
⅛ teaspoon (0.5 ml) freshly ground pepper
¼ teaspoon (1 ml) good quality saffron threads
4 ounces (115 g) large firm dessert grapes

1. Place the cheese on a smooth countertop or marble slab and, working with the heel of your hand, knead and bray the cheese until it is creamy smooth without a trace of graininess. Sprinkle in the sugar, black pepper and saffron, and knead until the ingredients are blended. Place in a bowl and chill until firm.

Alternately, fit a food processor with the metal cutting blade. Break the cheese into 1-inch (2.5 cm) pieces. Combine the cheese, sugar, pepper and saffron in the work bowl and process until light and creamy smooth. Scrape the mixture into a bowl and chill until firm.

2. Slice the grapes lengthwise about three-quarters through and remove the seeds with the tip of a knife. Stuff each grape with the cheese filling; smooth the edges and wipe the grapes clean. Chill before serving.

Creamy Pineapple and Rice Jubilee
ANANAS CHAVAL MITHAI

This dish goes well on a festive holiday menu but does not keep well. It should be made within a few hours of serving.

Preparation time (after assembling ingredients): 10 minutes
Chilling time: at least ½ hour
Serves: 6 to 8

2 cups (260 g) freshly cooked *basmati*
   or other long-grain white rice
1 tablespoon (15 ml) unsalted butter or *ghee*
¼ teaspoon (1 ml) ground cinnamon
½ teaspoon (2 ml) freshly ground nutmeg
½ teaspoon (2 ml) freshly ground cardamom seeds
⅛ teaspoon (0.5 ml) ground cloves
½ cup (65 g) currants
¼ cup (30 g) toasted sliced almonds
2 cups (480 ml) whipping cream, chilled
3 cups (710 ml) fresh pineapple, well drained and cut
   into 1 x ½ x ¼-inch (2.5 x 1.5 x 6 mm) pieces
⅓ cup (70 g) sugar
pineapple rings for garnishing (optional)

1. Spread the hot rice onto a baking tray, dot with butter or *ghee*, and add the spices, currants and 3 tablespoons (45 ml) of almonds. Cool to room temperature and transfer to a bowl.

2. Chill a mixing bowl and a whisk or beater in the freezer for 10 minutes. Whip the cream into soft peaks, add it to the rice along with the pineapple and sugar, and gently fold to mix. Chill for ½ hour. Mound on a flat serving dish, sprinkle with the remaining almonds, and, if desired, garnish with pineapple rings.

Melon Bowl Supreme with Honey–Lime Dressing

CARBOOJ MITHAI

This is a good dish for summer entertaining—a buffet showstopper, an appetizer at a party, or a fruit dessert for a garden party. Watermelons are best at the height of the summer season. Vine-ripened sweet melons have a glossy thick skin with juicy scarlet or yellow flesh. Honeydew, casaba, Ogden, *charentais* and cantaloupe are excellent choices. The fruit is served in a melon bowl—a hollowed-out watermelon with a zig zag or ruffed cut edge. A 3–4-pound (1.5–2 kg) round melon will form the basis of a serving bowl; a 10-pound (5 kg) oblong melon can hold up to 20 servings.

Preparation time (after assembling ingredients): 40 minutes
Chilling time: at least 1 hour
Serves: 4 to 6

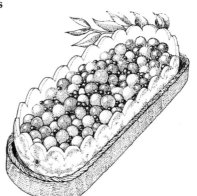

one 3–4-pound (1.5–2 kg) round watermelon
1 small cantaloupe or Ogden melon
1 small honeydew or *charentais* melon
⅓ cup (80 ml) honey
¼ cup (60 ml) lime juice
2 tablespoons (30 ml) orange juice
2 tablespoons (30 ml) lemon juice
¼ teaspoon (1 ml) ground ginger or ½ tablespoon (7 ml)
**   scraped, finely chopped fresh ginger root**
½ teaspoon (2 ml) cardamom seeds
2 tablespoons (30 ml) olive oil or almond oil
2 cups (480 ml) blueberries
a few sprigs of mint for garnishing

1. Using a large sharp knife, cut off the top third of the watermelon. Using a melon baller or a large spoon, scoop balls from the large section of the melon. Remove the seeds and refrigerate the balls. Spoon out the remaining melon flesh, leaving a melon shell. With a small sharp knife, cut a saw-toothed or scallop design around the top edge of the melon shell. Cut a thin slice of rind from the base of the shell so it will stand without tipping. Cover with plastic wrap and refrigerate until required.

2. Halve the other melons and scoop out the flesh with a melon baller. Combine these balls in a bowl, mix, cover and refrigerate.

Beverages

As elsewhere in the world, hospitality in India is expressed by offering a beverage to guests. This custom is mandatory etiquette in all Indian homes, and the beverage can be as simple as cool, clear water. In fact, from the Southern tropics to the Himalayan foothills, India is a nation of water connoisseurs. Ideally, drinking water is fetched twice daily and stored in unglazed earthenware jugs. These vessels cool water by evaporation, keeping the temperature at 48°–54°F (9°–12°C), ideal for Indian tastes. Some temples store water in silver or copper jugs, used traditionally in temple worship and known to destroy some forms of bacteria.

Going beyond the humble offering of water, there is a wonderful variety of non-alcoholic beverages to be had in India. Vaishnavas, devout worshippers of Lord Krishna, avoid caffeine, alcohol and other intoxicants completely. Historically, coffee was introduced by the Moguls and tea crops (as recently as the nineteenth century) by the British. To this day, followers of Vedic tradition abstain from these drinks, preferring a host of alternative liquid refreshments.

Fresh juices and flavored liquids can be extracted from raw ingredients in a number of ways—by squeezing, crushing, cooking, infusing and the use of centrifugal force. Before my first trip to India in 1970, I would never have considered hand-crushing fruits to extract juice, but in 115°F (45°C) temperatures, with no electricity, you become resourceful. Besides, it proved to be a more than adequate method for extracting the juice from soft fruits—all types of berries, grapes, currants or melons. These juices can be slowly strained through a jelly bag to obtain a clear juice or effectively squeezed through cheesecloth for fruit nectar. Undeniably, the quickest and easiest method for juicing hard vegetables and fruits like celery, carrots, beets and apples is a centrifugal juicer or a food processor with a juice attachment. In the absence of abundant fruit and fresh homemade juice, take advantage of the many organic unsweetened juices available at health food stores. Knudsen, Westbrae, and Lakewood are just a few high-quality products.

Still another means for extraction of a host of other dry ingredients is infusion. Coconut, nuts, grains, seeds, citrus zest, even sandalwood chips and flowers, can be infused in boiling water, sweetened, and strained to yield delicately flavored liquids. Citrus need only be squeezed against a reamer to release abundant juice. Some fibrous or firm-fleshed fruits require heat to release moisture and break down tissue. Rhubarb, cranberries and quinces need to be simmered before filtering for a clear juice. Finally, fruits with a low liquid content—bananas, guavas, papayas and mangoes—are best puréed in a food processor or blender before being strained for juice.

Chilled beverages frequently include milk products and some form of ice. They are blender or food processor drinks, puréed and aerated until frothy. Serve immediately in iced glasses or chilled fruit cups. A few garnishes lend visual appeal to cold drinks—citrus twists, mint sprigs, whole or cubed fruits on skewers or even sprinkles of freshly ground cardamom, coriander or nutmeg. The most popular chilled dairy drink in India is *lassi*. It is the equivalent of a smoothie and provides a low-calorie alternative to frothy milk shakes. *Lassis* can be as simple as sugar, yogurt and crushed ice; or fruit-sweetened using, for example, bananas instead of sugar.

The forerunner of punch is called *panchamrita*. While these are not exclusively dairy beverages, they generally contain the five ingredients milk, yogurt, honey, sugar and *ghee*. (The Sanskrit word *panch* means "five," and *amrita* means "nectar." More recently, "punch" has come to mean more or less any sweetened juice, served hot or cold.) There can be many variations on this theme, such as *thandai*—a luxurious amalgamation of nuts, raisins and fennel-flavored milk—which lends nutrition and imposing flavor to any light meal.

To make a delightful Vedic chilled punch, try any of the following combinations:

Punch Combinations:

Papaya nectar, pineapple juice, orange juice, guava nectar,
    yogurt, lime juice and crushed ice
Pineapple juice, coconut milk, apple juice, orange juice,
    ground cardamom and crushed ice
Passion fruit nectar, pineapple juice, orange juice,
    lemon and lime juice and crushed ice
Orange juice, apricot juice, powdered milk, crushed ice,
    a few drops of vanilla extract
Pineapple juice, pear nectar, coconut milk, orange juice,
    crushed ice and nutmeg
Buttermilk, banana, papaya concentrate
    and crushed ice
Apple juice with a little fresh ginger purée,
    fresh mint leaves and crushed ice
Banana, yogurt, minced dates, orange juice
    and lime juice
White grape juice, diced papaya, coconut milk,
    tangelo juice and crushed ice

Combine all of the ingredients in a blender or food processor and process until smooth and airy. Raisins or dried fruits need plumping and softening in hot water before use. Whole fruits should be chopped. Bananas and apples need a sprinkle of lemon juice to prevent discoloration. Proportions of the ingredients will determine the punch's flavor.

Warm drinks need little more than fresh or dried fruits, nuts, herbs and spices. The warming drinks in this chapter are variations on hot milk. In addition to these, try the following fruit juice and dried fruit combinations for wonderful warm punch pick-me-ups:

White grape juice offset with whole allspice,
    white peppercorns and Key lime zest
White grape juice offset with chopped dates,
    cardamom seeds and lemon zest
Red grape juice offset with chopped figs, cinnamon stick,
    apple slices and orange zest
White grape juice and water with fresh ginger root,
    cinnamon stick, honey and a pinch of cayenne

Apple juice offset with cloves, orange slices,
    fresh ginger root and cardamom pods
Red currant juice with raisins, cloves
    and orange zest
White grape juice with fennel seeds,
    cinnamon stick and lemon juice
Blackberry juice, grape juice and apple juice with
    allspice, lemon zest and cinnamon stick

When juices are simmered, their flavors intensify. If you prefer a more delicate beverage, heat the liquid to simmering and keep it there—a process generally called mulling. As a rule of thumb, allow the beverage 10–25 minutes over heat, then 5 minutes, covered, off the heat. Unprocessed juices should not come in contact with copper, iron or almunum utensils because they cause discoloration and impair flavor.

FRUIT JUICES AND SYRUPS

Zesty Grape Juice Cooler

ANGOOR SHARBAT

Homemade juices are more pure and fresh in flavor than their store-bought counterparts. Concord, Emperor and Cardinal red-purple grapes yield outstanding juice. Even if you do not have a juicer, it is relatively easy to pass the fruit through the fine disk of a food mill or simply purée it and press it through a fine sieve. Both methods produce a juice purée that takes well to the addition of sparkling water.

Preparation time (after assembling ingredients): 20 minutes
Makes: 2 quarts/liters

½ x 3-inch (1.5 x 7.5 cm) piece of orange zest
¼ teaspoon (1 ml) cardamom seeds
4 whole cloves
6 cups (1.5 liters) grape juice
¼ cup (60 ml) honey or maple syrup (optional)
3-inch (7.5 cm) piece of cinnamon stick
2 cups (480 ml) sparkling water

1. Tie the zest, cardamom seeds and cloves in a small piece of cheesecloth. Place the juice and optional honey or maple syrup in a large enamel or stainless steel pan and bring to near the boiling point over moderate heat.

2. Remove the pan from the heat, add the spice bag and cinnamon stick, cover, and set aside until the juice has cooled to tepid. Remove the spice bag and cinnamon stick and chill. Add the sparkling water before serving.

Lime Ginger Ale
ADRAK SHARBAT

I first served this beverage to Srila Prabhupada in Vrindavan, India, where the well water is distinguished by a slightly salty taste. He commented that his mother had made this summer thirst quencher with effervescent quinine water. It is pleasant with most carbonated mineral waters—from the gentle fizz of San Pellegrino to the brisk fizz of Perrier.

Double-boiling the ginger stretches the flavor of fresh ginger root. India's *nimbu* is a cross between Key limes and lemons, though any type of lime will do. You may or may not want to use peppercorns. I find that a blend of allspice and white, green and Malabar peppercorns lends pleasant spunk to the beverage.

Preparation time (after assembling ingredients): 15–20 minutes
Makes: 2 quarts/liters

1 x 2-inch (2.5 x 5 cm) piece of peeled fresh
    ginger root (about 1 ounce/30 g)
8 cups (2 liters) still water, or 4 cups (1 liter)
    still water and 4 cups (1 liter) carbonated water
1 teaspoon (5 ml) whole peppercorns (optional)
2⅓ cups (495 g) sugar or equivalent sweetener
12 limes, juiced and strained

1. Grind the ginger to a paste in a food processor or with an Oriental ginger grater or mortar and pestle. Mix with 2 cups (480 ml) of still water and the optional peppercorns. Bring the water to a boil over moderately high heat, then reduce the heat and simmer for 4–5 minutes. Strain the mixture through muslin and again place it in the saucepan. Add 2 more cups (480 ml) of water and repeat the process. After straining the liquid again, add the sweetener and stir until dissolved. Finally, mix in the lime juice. Chill well.

2. Before serving, top off with the remaining 4 cups (1 liter) still water or the 4 cups (1 liter) carbonated water. Serve over ice cubes.

Dainty Rose Water Drink
RUH GULAB SHARBAT

Homemade rose syrup, lemon or lime juice and fresh pomegranate juice make this pale pink beverage elegant and exotic. In India, a container made from freshly tinned metal is recommended for soaking the petals because the metal preserves their color. Be sure your garden roses are free of insecticides.

Infusion and chilling time: 8 hours or overnight
Makes: about 3 pints (1.5 liters)

1½ cups (360 ml) freshly picked rose petals, lightly packed
¾ cup (180 ml) boiling water
¼ teaspoon (1 ml) cardamom seeds
¾ cup (160 g) sugar or ¾ cup (180 ml) honey
¼ cup (60 ml) strained fresh lemon or lime juice
⅔ cup (160 ml) pomegranate juice
5 cups (1.25 liters) cold water

1. Crush the rose petals with a mortar and pestle and place them in a large bowl. Add the boiling water, then pour the mixture into a metal container and add the cardamom seeds. Set aside 8 hours or overnight to infuse.

2. Pour the rose–cardamom water through a muslin-lined strainer set over a bowl. Add the sweetener, and float the bowl in a hot-water-filled sink until the sugar dissolves. Remove from the hot water and filter once again. Cool to room temperature.

3. Combine all of the ingredients in a pitcher and stir well. Serve in goblets half-filled with crushed ice.

Perfumed Sandalwood Crush

VRINDAVAN GOSWAMI SHARBAT

Before Srila Prabhupada left India for America in 1965, he lived in Vrindavan, Lord Krishna's birthplace. When he visited the S. K. Joshi family in their Vrindavan home, Mrs. Joshi frequently served him this beverage in the late afternoon. She explained that this recipe originated from the famous Radha Ramana Temple of Gopal Bhatta Goswami in Vrindavan and was centuries old. This exotic beverage, known for its cooling effect on a scorching afternoon, can be served on its own or with cut seasonal fruits.

Pure sandalwood is sold in small bars—about 1½ inches (4 cm) diameter and 3–4 inches (7.5–10 cm) long. You will have to saw or chip off slices to make an infusion. Alternately, use sweetened sandalwood syrup, but eliminate the sweetener entirely or reduce it as desired. Both sandalwood and its syrup are available at Indian grocery stores. Camomile is a pleasant alternative.

Preparation time (after assembling ingredients): about 30 minutes
Infusion time: 6–8 hours or overnight
Chilling time: several hours
Makes: about 2½ pints (1.5 liters)

12 green cardamom pods
3 quarter-sized slices of pure sandalwood or
    ½ cup (120 ml) sandalwood syrup
6 cups (1.5 liters) spring or well water
2½ x 1-inch (6.5 x 2.5 cm) strip of orange zest
1½ x 1-inch (4 x 2.5 cm) strip of lime zest
⅔–¾ cup (140–165 g) sugar candy, crushed,
    or *gur* (100–115 g)
3 tablespoons (45 ml) dried *malati* or camomile flowers

1. Combine the cardamom pods, sandalwood slices, if using them, and water in a saucepan and bring to a boil. Reduce the heat to the lowest possible setting, cover, and let it steep, without simmering, for 25 minutes. Remove the pan from the heat, cover with a tea towel, and set aside in a cool place to infuse flavors for 6–8 hours or overnight.

2. Strain into a clean pan. Bring to a near boil, turn off the heat and add the remaining ingredients. Cover and steep for 5 minutes. Strain and cool to room temperature. If you are using sandalwood syrup, stir it in. Chill well. Serve in goblets over crushed ice.

CHILLED DAIRY DRINKS

Frosty Mango Milk Shake

AAM LASSI

India is a paradise for mango lovers. During the growing season, dozens of varieties reach the marketplace—some fruits as large as footballs. One of the most loved and outstanding varieties, Alphonso, is nearly fiber-free, rose-pineapple-perfumed and a brilliant orange-red in color. It is an excellent choice for any fruit dessert or beverage that stands on its own. Though this shake is traditionally made with rich milk, it is equally delicious with yogurt or buttermilk. If fresh mangoes are not available or are of poor quality, you can purchase good Alphonso mango pulp at Indian groceries. Because it is usually sweetened, omit or cut down on the sweetener.

Preparation and chilling time: 30 minutes
Serves: 4

1 cup (240 ml) diced fresh mango (about 1 pound/455 g)
       or ¾ cup (180 ml) mango pulp
½ cup (120 ml) chilled orange juice
3–4 tablespoons (45–60 ml) clear honey or vanilla sugar
2 cups (480 ml) rich milk, chilled in the freezer for 15 minutes
a few garden rose petals for garnishing (optional)

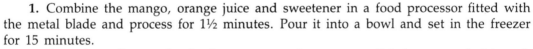

1. Combine the mango, orange juice and sweetener in a food processor fitted with the metal blade and process for 1½ minutes. Pour it into a bowl and set in the freezer for 15 minutes.

2. Pour the milk into the food processor and process until it has expanded in volume and become frothy. Add the mango purée and process for about a minute, then pour into chilled glasses. Garnish with rose petals, if desired, and serve immediately. (Made with milk, this drink is light and airy, but it will thin down within a few minutes. Assemble just before serving.)

Minty Yogurt Shake
KARA PODINA LASSI

In India, mint follows coriander and *neem* leaves as the most widely used herb. It is an important flavoring in soups, savories, vegetables, rice, *dals* and beverages. American seedsmen offer herb gardeners a good selection of scented hybrids, from apple mint to cinnamon mint, each type with a different flavor. My favorite mint *lassi* combines homemade vanilla yogurt with licorice mint and coarsely powdered fennel seeds. These hinted sweet ingredients are offset with a splash of rose water for a very refreshing summer thirst quencher.

Preparation time (after assembling ingredients): 10 minutes
Serves: 4

2 cups (480 ml) homemade or Brown Cow vanilla yogurt or
    Dannon low-fat vanilla yogurt
3 tablespoons (45 ml) sour cream, cream, or half-and-half
¼ cup (60 ml) trimmed fresh mint, loosely packed
1 teaspoon (5 ml) dry-roasted fennel seeds, coarsely powdered
½ cup (110 g) superfine sugar or equivalent sweetener
½ tablespoon (7 ml) rose water
¼ cup (60 ml) ice water
8–10 ice cubes, cracked
4 sprigs fresh mint or rose petals for garnishing

Combine all of the ingredients, except the ice cubes and garnish, in a blender or food processor fitted with the metal blade, cover, and process for 2 minutes. Add the ice and process for another minute. Pour into frosted glasses and garnish with fresh mint or rose petals.

Banana Yogurt Shake
KELA LASSI

This is a perfect low-calorie alternative to rich banana milk shakes made with heavy cream. Bananas lend both body and natural fructose sweetener to yogurt drinks and complement almost any other fruit. In India, banana *lassi* is little more than banana, lime juice, yogurt and ice, but in the West I have made scores of exciting variations. For natural sweeteners, try blending in a few soaked raisins, currants, dates or figs. The beverage can also be made with apple, pineapple, coconut or peach juice. Since bananas are available year-round, this is a good all-season *lassi*.

Preparation time (after assembling ingredients): 10 minutes
Serves: 4

2 ripe bananas, peeled and sliced
2 tablespoons (30 ml) fresh lime or lemon juice
½ cup (120 ml) ice-cold white grape juice or water
3 tablespoons (45 ml) clear honey or maple syrup, optional
1 cup (240 ml) plain yogurt or buttermilk
6–8 ice cubes, cracked
¼ teaspoon (1 ml) ground cardamom
½ tablespoon (7 ml) *kewra* water or a few drops of *kewra* essence
⅛ teaspoon (0.5 ml) freshly ground nutmeg
grated lime zest for garnishing

Place the bananas, lime or lemon juice, grape juice or water, optional sweetener and yogurt or buttermilk in a blender or food processor fitted with the metal blade. Process for about 2 minutes, then add the ice, cardamom and *kewra* and process for another minute. (The ice does not need to be fully crushed.) Pour into glasses, sprinkle with nutmeg and lime zest, and serve.

Scented Almond Milk Cooler
BADAAM DHOOD

Phool Bhag, the palace compound of Pratapkumar, Crown Prince of Alwar, is an example of spiritual management and nature's perfect arrangements. Situated in Rajasthan's northeastern arid desert, the complex encompasses acres of flower-spangled gardens and lakes and offers sanctuary to numerous bird and animal species—elephants, camels, cows, buffaloes, deer, horses, peacocks, sheep, rabbits, goats, lions and tigers. Pratapkumar attributes his wealth and success in life to his dedicated daily worship in the Sri Janaki-Vallabha Temple. This statement reflects his personal lifestyle and philosophy: "In India, the temple is the center of activity in the royal palace. Worship of the Lord must personally be performed by the king before he can accept worship in the palace." The Janaki-Vallabha Temple kitchens engage nearly 20 expert cooks in the service of the Deities. Though they excel in local Rajasthani cuisine, they are proficient in numerous others. This is one of the cooling beverages served during the hot summer months.

Preparation and nut soaking time : about 1 hour
Serves: 4

⅔ cup (100 g) blanched almonds
½ teaspoon (2 ml) cardamom seeds
4 whole peppercorns
2 cups (480 ml) boiling water
¼ cup (60 ml) honey
2 cups (480 ml) white grape juice
½ tablespoon (7 ml) rose water
2 cups (480 ml) still water or sparkling water

1. Place the almonds, cardamom seeds and peppercorns in a bowl and add 1¼ cups (300 ml) boiling water. Set aside for 1 hour. Pour into a blender, cover, and reduce the nuts to a fine paste. Add the remaining ¾ cup (180 ml) boiling water and the honey and blend for ½ minute.

2. Line a sieve with three thicknesses of cheesecloth. Pour the nut milk through the sieve, then extract as much liquid as possible. (The nut pulp can be saved for cutlets or salad dressing.) Add a little grape juice to the blender and process briefly to release any almonds sticking to the sides of the jar. Add to the sieved nut milk.

3. Pour the remaining grape juice, rose water and water into the nut milk and blend well. Chill before serving.

ABOUT HIS DIVINE GRACE
A.C. BHAKTIVEDANTA SWAMI PRABHUPADA

His Divine Grace A.C. Bhaktivedanta Swami (1896–1977), known to his disciples as Srila Prabhupada, arrived in America in 1965 at the age of seventy. The following year, he founded the International Society for Krishna Consciousness and subsequently established more than 100 temples for the study of Vaishnava spirituality and culture. In his lifetime, he traveled the globe fourteen times, wrote more than sixty books and initiated some 8,000 disciples, introducing them to India's meditational practice known as *Bhakti-yoga* ("union with God through devotion").

Prabhupada was born Abhay Charan De on September 1, 1896, in Calcutta, India. His father, Gour Mohan De, was a well-respected Vaishnava who infused the devotional worship of Lord Krishna into the lives of his family. By the time he was six years old, Abhay had his own Deity of Lord Krishna and performed worship—chanting, playing instruments and observing Vaishnava festivals—that he would carry on throughout his life.

In 1922, in his fourth year at Scottish Churches' College, he met his spiritual master, Srila Bhaktisiddhanta Saraswati Goswami. A prominent religious scholar in Calcutta, Srila Bhaktisiddhanta was the founder of the Gaudiya Matha, a *Bhakti-yoga* society with sixty-four teaching institutes around India. At their first meeting, Bhaktisiddhanta liked the educated young man and convinced him of the importance of spreading the philosophy of *Bhakti-yoga* throughout the world and, more specifically, through the use of the English language.

In the years that followed, Srila Prabhupada wrote a commentary on the *Bhagavad Gita*, assisted the Gaudiya Matha in its work, and, in 1944, started *Back to Godhead*, an English fortnightly magazine, distributed by his disciples to this day in more than thirty languages.

Recognizing Abhay's learning and devotion, the Gaudiya Vaishnava Society honored him in 1947 with the title "Bhaktivedanta," meaning "one who has realized the import of the *Vedas* through devotion to God." In 1950, at the age of fifty-four, he retired from business and family life in order to devote his full time to studies and writing. Traveling to the holy city of Vrindavan, he resided in humble circumstances in the medieval temple of Radha Damodar. There he engaged in deep study for several years, single handedly writing, publishing and distributing his *Back to Godhead* magazines. He became known as Bhaktivedanta Swami when he accepted the renounced order of life (*sannyasa*) in 1959.

At Radha Damodar temple, he also began work on his life's masterpiece: a multi-volume translation of and commentary on the eighteen-thousand-verse *Srimad Bhagavatam*, India's epic historical narrative. After publishing three volumes of the *Srimad Bhagavatam* in India, he traveled to America in 1965 to fulfill the request of his spiritual master. Arriving in New York City practically penniless, after almost a year of great difficulty he established his Society in July, 1966.

By his demise in November, 1977, A.C. Bhaktivedanta Swami Prabhupada had accomplished the mission given him half a century before by his spiritual master. He had brought the message of *Bhagavad Gita* to Western shores and impressed upon the hearts of many the spirit of its teachings: that life's glory lies in our ability to rise above the ignorance of matter through a life of devotion to God.

His Divine Grace

A.C. Bhaktivedanta Swami Prabhupada

GLOSSARY

AJWAIN SEED: Also known as *ajowan* or bishop's weed. A celery-sized spice seed (*Carum ajowan*) closely related to caraway and cumin. The assertive flavor resembles thyme, with pepper and oregano overtones. Popular in North Indian vegetable cooking, especially with root vegetables such as potatoes, parsnips and radishes. Also used in fried snacks and nibblers. Available at Middle Eastern and Indian grocery stores.

AMCHOOR: A tan-colored powder made from sun-dried, tart, unripe mango slices. Seen in several regional cuisines, primarily in the North, *amchoor* is used, like pomegranate seeds, tamarind or lemon juice, to bring pungency to a dish. Available at Indian grocery stores.

ANARDANA: The sun-dried kernels of wild pomegranate fruit, called *daru*. The trees flourish in the Himalayan foothills and, though the fruits are not edible, the dried seeds are an important souring agent in Vedic cooking. Used either whole or ground, *daru* lends piquancy to vegetables, *karhis* and *dals* and is especially popular in Northwestern cuisines. Available at Indian grocery stores.

ANCHO CHILI: The sun-dried pod of ripe poblano chili. With relatively mild heat and a rich flavor, it is a good selection for *chaunks* (fried spice seasonings). The dried pods, 3-5 inches (7-12 cm) long, are chocolate-brown colored, but, once soaked in water, they turn brick-red. This soaking procedure tempers the heat somewhat and is a common practice in *Rajasthani* regional cuisine. Available at supermarkets and specialty stores.

ASAFETIDA: Known as *hing*. Obtained from several species of *Ferula* (fennel-related plants). I have tested all of the recipes in this book with mild, yellow-colored Cobra Brand asafetida compound, and I strongly recommend it. If you use any other form, reduce the quantities substantially, to one-half or three-quarters of the suggested amount. Often said to resemble the flavor of shallot or garlic, asafetida is almost unknown to American and European cooks, though it was popular in Roman times and is used extensively in all of the regional cuisines of India. Available at Indian and Middle Eastern grocery stores.

AVATARA: An incarnation of the Lord.

AYUR VEDA: A system of medicine based on the Vedas.

BHAGAVAD-GITA: The paramount scripture of the Vedic tradition.

BHAKTIYOGA: The science of devotion to God.

BLACK CUMIN SEED or ROYAL CUMIN: Known as *shahi* or *siyah jeera*, it is the spice seed of a wild annual plant (*Cuminum nigrum*) which grows profusely in North India's mountainous regions. The seed is blackish in color and slightly thinner than its close relative, cumin seed (*Cuminum cyminum*), known as *safed jeera* or *jeera*. While cumin seed is extensively used in all regional cuisines, black or royal cumin remains almost unknown outside of Kashmir, Punjab and Uttar Pradesh.

BLACK SALT or *KALA NAMAK*: It is not actually black but reddish-gray, due to the presence of small quantities of trace minerals and iron. Like pure sodium chloride, black salt is available either in lump form or ground, and is best stored, well sealed, in a cool dry place. It is not used interchangeably with sea salt or table salt because it has a distinct flavor—some say like hard-boiled egg yolks. It is a major ingredient in the spice blend called *chat masala*, a popular blend usually sprinkled on snack foods, from cut fruits to fried nuts.

TO BLANCH: To loosen the outer coverings of foods such as tomatoes, peaches, almonds or pistachios by scalding them briefly in boiling water. They may be cooled in cold water before draining and removing the skins.

To blanch almonds and pistachios, pour boiling water over the shelled nuts and let them sit for up to 1 minute. Drain them, cool them slightly, and slip off the skins individually. Alternately, place the blanched nuts on one end of a tea towel. Fold the towel over the nuts and rub your hands lightly back and forth over the towel so that the nuts roll inside it. (Most of the skins will loosen within a minute or two). Place the skinned nuts on a cookie sheet and dry them out in a 250+°F (120+°C) oven for 20 minutes.

BRAHMANA: A person qualified to instruct others on spiritual life.

BUCKWHEAT and BUCKWHEAT FLOUR: Known as *kutu* or *phaphra*, it is the triangular-shaped seed from any plant of *Genus fagopyrum*. Native to Siberia, China and Nepal, there are two prominent species: *esculentum (faafar)* and *tataricum* *(kutu)*. As a member of the *polyganaceae* family-like rhubarb, sorrel and dock-buckwheat has nothing to do with wheat and is not a true grain, though it is treated as such. As defined in George Usher's *Dictionary of Plants Used by Man*, it is botanically a "whole hulled fruit" but practically a "notched-seed." Sterdivant's *Edible Plants of the World* states that in summer, wild *tataricum* has been spotted in rocky crevices as high as 11,000 feet in the Himalayas. The cold-climate plant, with branching heart-shaped leaves and fragrant white or pink flowers, little resembles the reedy grasses that produce most grains. Of grain-type foods, the nutrient value of buckwheat is only surpassed by a similar seed called *quinoa*.

Even many Vedic cooks I questioned about buckwheat sustained the notion that it was a grain. Unfortunately, even good publications mistakenly call it a grain or cereal. To dispel this misnomer, I launched into extensive research. For those readers interested in my information sources, I am listing them, and encourage you to contact them if you are still in question: The National Buckwheat Institute in New York; the British Museum Reference Library, Botanical Section; the Horticultural Society of Philadelphia; and the Academy of Natural Sciences in Philadelphia.

CAMPHOR: Pure edible camphor, called *kacha karpoor*, is a crystalline compound that looks like coarse salt. It is obtained by steam distillation of the aromatic leaves and wood of the evergreen tree *Cinnamomum camphora* that grows in India and China. Unlike inedible synthetic camphor, which is used in everything from insect repellents to explosives, raw camphor is used in minute quantity as a flavoring agent in milk puddings and confections, especially in Bengal and Orissa. Like bitter *neem* leaves, it is almost impossible to ferret out in America and is best forwarded by friends in India.

CARDAMOM, Large Black Pods: Large oval-shaped black pods about 1 inch (2.5 cm) long, from a plant in the ginger family. The pods are rarely, if ever, used in sweets. The whole pods are slightly crushed and added to rice pilafs to release a warm, aromatic flavor with eucalyptus overtones. Available at Indian grocery stores.

CASSIA LEAVES: Known as *tejpatta*, the leaves of the tree *Cinnamomum cassia*, native to South India and Sri Lanka. Dried, the leaves are tan with an olive green tinge and are 7-8 inches (17-20 cm) long. In most cases, the leaves are fried briefly before cooking, releasing a strong, woodsy flavor. They are used extensively in Eastern regional cuisines, particularly in Bengal and Orissa. Available at Indian and Middle Eastern grocery stores.

CENTRAL CUISINES: The cooks in India's Central Provinces, including Madhya Pradesh and Bihar, have made the most of whatever the land produced, most notably grains and *dals*. Spanning a distance of nearly 500 miles (900 kilometers), the region presents an eclectic diversity in everything from its topography, culture, dress and dialects to its variegated cuisines. Bhopal, the capital of Madhya Pradesh, exemplifies culinary diversity through its acceptance of dishes from bordering states into its own cuisine—Gujarati chutneys and Rajasthani *dals* are popular examples.

CHAITANYA CHARITAMRITA: The biography of Shri Chaitanya Mahaprabhu.

CHAITANYA MAHAPRABHU: The *avatara* of Lord Krishna for the present age.

CHAUNK: Also known as *baghar* and *tadka*, a key seasoning technique used throughout India whereby selected seasonings are fried in *ghee* or oil and added to a dish to lend a distinctive flavoring. Typical seasonings include whole spice seeds, fresh ginger root, fresh green chilies or dried red chilies, *chana dal* or *urad dal*, cassia leaves, cinnamon or cloves. The *chaunk* may be made at the beginning or end of a dish, and, along with the endless possible combinations of ingredients, the cooking oils you choose also play a prominent role.

CHICKPEA FLOUR: Known as *besan* or gram flour and often sold under these names in Indian grocery stores. It is a finely milled, almost pale yellow flour made from roasted *chana dal (Cicer arietinum)* and is used extensively in batters for vegetable fritters (*pakoras*) and savories. Often, the chickpea flour sold in health food stores has not been roasted prior to milling and therefore has a raw taste. A light pan roasting will improve its flavor.

CORIANDER LEAVES, Fresh: Until recently, when California's chefs began using fresh coriander in restaurants, it was only available for the shopper as *cilentro* in Mexican or Latin grocery stores and as Chinese parsley in Oriental grocery stores. Today, it is found in ethnic and greengrocer stores nationwide, and even in some supermarkets. Coriander stores well for up to two weeks with the root ends in a glass of water and the leaves covered with a plastic bag. Use only the leaves from the coriander, never the stems.

CURRY LEAF: Known as *meetha neem* or *kadhi patta*, the powerfully fragrant small leafs of the plant *Murraya koenigii*. These look like miniature lemon leaves. In India, the plants have grown wild since Vedic times in almost all forest regions, from the Himalayas to Kanniya Kumari.

DATE SUGAR: This natural sweetener is not really a sugar but rather coarse brown crystals obtained from dehydrated dates. Pitted and sliced dates are dried until rock hard and ground into a "sugar" that looks and tastes much like raw brown sugar. It is delicious sprinkled on desserts, yogurt or bland fruits, but is not ideal for creamy consistency foods or when cooking temperatures are high. This is because it does not dissolve easily and burns quickly. Look for date sugar in health food stores or order by mail. Store, well sealed, on a cool dry shelf, or refrigerate.

EASTERN CUISINES: In the East, Bengali and Orissan cuisines are characterized by vivid lively seasonings, a few special ingredients, and outstanding sweet delicacies. From Calcutta to Gopalpur-on-Sea, coconut palms overhang the Bay of

Bengal's sandy beaches, while inland there seems to be an endless expanse of green or yellow fields from rice or yellow mustard plants. As a rule, Eastern cuisines are hot and spicy, typically seasoned with freshly ground wet spice *masalas* containing ginger root, hot red chilies, fresh coconut, and perhaps, white poppy seeds—a "digestive" balance of ingredients long considered helpful in combating the effects of the intense tropical heat.

EKADASEE: The twice-monthly fast day observed by Vaishnavas. Literally, the eleventh day of the waning and waxing moon, *Ekadasee* is honored by minimizing physical activity and increasing devotional activity. The fast requires that no grains or beans be eaten.

FENUGREEK SEED: Known as *methi*, this is actually a small legume (*Trigonella foenumgracum*) widely used as a spice seed. Brownish-yellow and rectangular, the seed is used both whole and ground. To develop its best flavor, it must be dry-roasted or fried, but only until lightly roasted. It should not be allowed to turn to reddish-brown shades because, at this point, the taste becomes intensely bitter. In some regions cooks allow the seeds to turn nearly black, as blackened seeds turn docile, with almost no pungency, and give off a pleasant charred flavor. Whole, the seeds are used in *dals* and pickles and play an important part in the Bengali five spice mixture called *panch puran*. Both whole and ground fenugreek are available in Indian and Middle Eastern grocery stores.

GARAM MASALA: An aromatic blend of several dry-roasted and ground "warm" spices. The ancient Sanskrit medical work *Ayur Veda* suggests that "warm" spices generate internal body heat, whereas "cool" spices help remove internal heat. Originating in the colder climates of North India, *garam masala* routinely combines such "warm" spices as cinnamon, cloves, coriander, cumin, black pepper, dried chilies, cardamom or mace. Most households have a few favorite recipes, some only using three ingredients, others using twelve or more. Unless otherwise specified, *garam masala* is added toward the end of cooking, a concluding garnish of flavor like paprika or seasoned pepper. It is available at an Indian grocery store, purchase the type sold in vacuum-packed tins and, once opened, use for no more than 4-5 months; when stale, it loses its impact.

GINGER ROOT, Fresh: The underground creeping rhizome of the tropical plant *Zingiber officinale* is native to most of Asia. Relished for its invigorating sharp taste, digestive properties and cleaning effect on the body, it is used extensively in every region, not only as a flavoring but as a food, much as shallots are used in the West.

Many recipes in the book call for puréed, finely shredded or minced fresh ginger root. Once prepared for cooking, it can be kept refrigerated for several days use: mix up to 1 cup (240 ml) of puréed ginger with a small spoon of oil, store in a tightly sealed container, and refrigerate.

HORSERADISH ROOT: The gnarled roots must be scrubbed and the skin peeled off before use. Large roots have a woody inner core which is not used at all; only the outer portion contains the volatile oils which give horseradish its pungency. Further, the desired pungency in fresh horseradish fades within a few hours of grating or when exposed to heat for any length of time. Fresh roots are finding their way on to more and more supermarket produce shelves and, once purchased, can be kept at least for two or three weeks.

JAGGERY and GUR: *Jaggery*, made from the juice crushed out of sugar cane stalks (*Saccharum officinarum*), accounts for over 50 percent of the sugar currently eaten in India. *Gur*—made from the sap drained from various palm trees, such as date, coconut or palmyra—is used primarily in the cuisines of the East and South.

JALAPEÑO CHILI: The medium-hot fresh green chili named after the capitol of Veracruz in Mexico, Jalapa. They average about 2 inches (5 cm) in length and are about 1 inch (2.5 cm) in diameter at the base. Good chilies are firm, with a waxy dark green skin and a blunt tip. Jalapeño chilies were used for all of the recipe testing in this book, not only because they are medium-hot, but because they are easily seeded. They are widely available at supermarkets and greengrocers.

KALONJI: Known as *nigella* or black onion seed. *Nigella sativa* has enough names in print to confuse even the most committed reader. While Middle Eastern grocery stores often sell the seeds under the label "black seeds" or "*siyah daneh*," many Indian grocers incorrectly sell the spice as black onion seed. *Kalonji* has no connection to the onion plant, but because the seeds resemble onion seeds, the name has found its way onto packages. Vedic vegetarians, who do not eat onions, need not be misled by the labeling.

KRISHNA: The name for God given in the Sanskrit Vedic texts of India. Historically, Krishna appeared in the village of Vrindavan 5,000 years ago. Revered in the *Vedas* as the original form of the Godhead, Krishna is the speaker of India's paramount spiritual text *Bhagavad-gita*.

MARAWADI: A Southwestern Indian cuisine.

MUSTARD SEED, Black: Known as *rai*, the tiny round brownish-black or purplish-brown seed obtained from the annual Indian mustard plant *Brassica juncea*. Available at Indian or Middle Eastern grocery stores.

NORTHERN CUISINES: The varied cuisines of the North are full-bodied and nourishing, noticeably influenced by climate, land cultivation and cow protection. The temperature extremes—from the subfreezing winters of the Himalayan foothills to the furnace-like heat of the Rajasthani deserts—have greatly influenced crop selections. Since ancient times, farmers have been cultivating wheat, barley, mung and *urad dals* in the fertile plains along the Ganges and Yamuna Rivers, while millet is the primary crop in the arid Rajasthani desert. In the colder but still temperate area of the Northeast Indus Valley, corn, oats, rye, *basmati* and similar rice crops, chickpeas and buckwheat flourish. North India is undoubtably the country's granary.

POMEGRANATE SEED, Dried: Known as *anardhana*, the dried seed of a variety of wild pomegranate (*Punica granatum*). Native to the Himalayan foothills of Kashmir and Jammu, *daru* or wild pomegranate, has a distinct sour, rather than sweet taste. When fresh, the sun-dried seeds are somewhat sticky to the touch, with a blackish-wine color; when old or stale, the seeds are dry and shriveled. Available at Indian grocery stores.

POPPY SEED, White: Known as *khas khas* and *posta* in Bengal, the ripe seeds of the poppy plant (*Papaver somniferum*). The creamy-white seeds used in India are much smaller than the blue-gray seeds sprinkled on cakes and breads in Europe and America, though the flavor is similar.

PRABHUPADA, SRILA: His Divine Grace A.C. Bhaktivedanta Swami (Page 231).

PRASADAM: A newcomer in India will likely hear three words used in relation to food: *prasadam, bhoga* and *bhojana*. For the most part, food which as been offered to God before being eaten is called *prasadam* or "God's mercy," whether in an established temple with formal worship or at home with a simple prayer. Depending on the name of the Deity it is being offered to, *prasadam* is prefixed by names such as Govinda, Damodar, Banabehari or any one of thousands of other names. Temples become well known for their special *prasadams*. For example, Vrindavan's temple of Radha Ramana is famous for a sweet called *kuliya*. *Bhoga* is a collective term meaning almost any food ingredient that is to be used for offering to God. *Bhojana* simply means either cooked or uncooked food.

SANKIRTAN: Congregational chanting of the Lord's names.

SOUTHERN CUISINES: Many outstanding regional cuisines make up the larger tapestry of the South. If there is one similarity between all of the regional cuisines, it is in their prodigious use of rice and *dal* making it the best high-fiber, high-carbohydrate diet in the nation. One ingredient usually plays counterpoint to the other: bland against spicy, sour against sweet, etc. When rice and dals are combined together, amazing things happen. They are simmered, wet-ground, steamed, fried, fermented, and more. Further, "dry" dishes, such as *iddlis, dosas* and *badas*, are invariably offset with moist or liquid ones like coconut chutneys, consommes and vegetable soups.

The *brahmanas*, or priests who oversee the Deity worship in ancient South Indian temples, are called *pancha-daksinatya-brahmanas* and come from the old areas known as Andhra, Karnata, Gujara, Dravida and Maharastra. The temples are famous for their chefs and massive *prasadam* distributions. Yearly, hundreds of thousands of pilgrims battle the elements for just one taste of these special sanctified foods. Many South Indian Temples kindly revealed their recipes for this book, while others served as inspirations. Special thanks to: Sree Krishna Matha in Udupi; Sree Balaji Mandir in Tirupati, B.V. Puri Maharaj's Ashram Temple in Visakhapatnam, and Sree Simhachalam Temple.

SRIMAD BHAGAVATAM: 18,000 verse history of Lord Krishna and his incarnations.

VAISHNAVA: Devotee of Lord Vishnu/Krishna.

VARAK: Also called *vark*, this is no doubt the most opulent garnish used in the world; exceptionally thin sheets of edible pure silver or gold. Apply *varak* in a windless place, as a breeze can cause the delicate foils to be swept away. Remove the top sheet of paper, holding the foil on the bottom sheet in an open palm. Invert your hand and gently press the foil onto the food.

VEDAS: Four ancient revealed scriptures.

VEDIC: Based on the *Vedas*.

VRINDAVAN: Village where Lord Krishna appeared.

WESTERN CUISINES: In the Western provinces of India, contemporary Marawadi and Maharastran cuisines are regarded as superior, largely due to their creative artistry. Almost everywhere in India, formal dinners are served on *thalis*, but here particular attention is paid to the placement and order of the dishes. The meal must be pleasing to the eye first, then the nose, and finally the palate. Temperature, taste, texture and appearance are meant to counterpoint: hot dishes are taken after chilled, spicy offsets mild, crunchy contrasts creamy, and sour enhances sweet.

The present State of Gujarat houses the largest concentration of vegetarians in India. Ahmedabad, Surat and Dwaraka are all cities respected for vegetarian specialties, dishes once hidden in private homes are now eaten around the world. Many light meal dishes are characterized by the addition of the seasoning combination of curry leaves, green chilies, lime juice and a little sugar. A typical fried *chaunk* would likely be made in *ghee* and contain black mustard seeds, cumin seeds, asafetida, and coriander leaves.

ZEST: 1) The oily outer portion of citrus peel. 2) To cut off citrus strips or shavings or grate citrus zest with a knife or zester tool. 3) To infuse a preparation such as *sandesh* with citrus strips to release their essential oil, and then remove them.

INDEX